FEMINIST AESTHETICS AND

THE POLITICS OF MODERNISM

FEMINIST AESTHETICS AND

THE POLITICS OF MODERNISM

Ewa Płonowska Ziarek

Columbia University Press   New York

Columbia University Press
Publishers Since 1893
New York   Chichester, West Sussex
cup.columbia.edu

Library of Congress Cataloging-in-Publication Data
Ziarek, Ewa Plonowska, 1961–
Feminist aesthetics and the politics of modernism /
Ewa Plonowska Ziarek.
p.   cm.
Includes bibliographical references and index.
ISBN 978-0-231-16148-0 (cloth: alk. paper)—ISBN
978-0-231-16149-7 (pbk. : alk. paper)—ISBN
978-0-231-53090-3 (e-book)
1. Feminist criticism.   2. Aesthetics.   3. Modernism (Aesthetics)   4. Feminist theory.   I. Title

HQ1190.Z556 2012   2012006808
305.4201—dc23

For Halina Płonowska and Łukasz Ziarek

Contents

Acknowledgments

It is my pleasure to acknowledge many colleagues and friends who read or discussed various parts of my book. I am indebted to Kalliopi Nikolopoulou, Devonya N. Havis, Alison Ross, Andrew Benjamin, Barbara Green, Kelly Oliver, Elizabeth Presa, and Krzysztof Ziarek for their helpful comments, suggestions, and support. I am especially grateful to Penelope Deutscher and Graham Hammill, who read the manuscript in its entirety and offered invaluable suggestions for revisions. I would like to thank the anonymous reviewers of Columbia University Press for their thoughtful engagement with my work and Wendy Lochner for her patience and support of this project. I am especially grateful to James Kurt for his expert help in the final preparation of the manuscript for production.

My mother Halina Płonowska's help and support was invaluable in the last stages of the manuscript preparation. Conversations with my son, Łukasz, about his dissertation was a source of loving companionship and inspiration for my own work. Krzysztof's patience, support, and intellectual insights made it a better book.

Earlier versions of several sections of this book have already appeared in print and I am grateful for permissions to use these materials in their revised form:

An earlier version of section 1 of chapter 1 appeared as "Right to Vote or Right to Revolt? Arendt and the British Suffrage Militancy," *differences* 19 (Fall 2008): 1–27, revised by permission. Section 4 of chapter 2 appeared as "Towards a Feminist Aesthetics of Melancholia: Kristeva, Adorno, and Modern Women Writers," *Critical Horizons: A Journal of Philosophy and Social Theory* 11, no. 3 (April 2011): 443–462, copyright 2010 Equinox Publishing Ltd. Section 2 of chapter 3 was published as "Woolf' Feminist Aesthetics: On the Political and Artistic Practice in *A Room of One's Own,*" *Parallax* 57 (December 2010): 70–83, used by permission of the publisher, Taylor and Francis, Ltd. An earlier version of section 1 of chapter 4 was published as "'Women on the Market': On Sex, Race, and Commodification" in *Re-Writing Difference: Luce Irigaray and "the Greeks"* (Albany: SUNY Press, 2010), all rights reserved, revised by permission; section 3 was published as "Bare Life on Strike: Notes of the Biopolitics of Race and Gender," *SAQ* (Winter 2008): 89–105, revised by permission. Section 3 of chapter 6 appeared as "Nella Larsen's Feminist Aesthetics: On Curse, Law, and Laughter" in Oren Ben-Dor, ed., *Law and Art* (London: Routledge, 2011), revised and expanded by the permission of the publisher, Taylor and Francis, Ltd.

Abbreviations

A   G. W. F. Hegel, *Aesthetics: Lectures of Fine Art*, vol. 1, trans. T. M. Knox (Oxford: Oxford University Press, 1975).

AI   Paul de Man, *Aesthetic Ideology* (Minneapolis: University of Minnesota Press, 1996).

AT   Theodor W. Adorno, *Aesthetic Theory*, trans. Robert Hullot-Kentor (Minneapolis: University of Minnesota Press, 1997).

BS   Julia Kristeva, *Black Sun: Depression and Melancholia*, trans. Leon S. Roudiez (New York: Columbia University Press, 1989).

C   Theodor W. Adorno, "Commitment," trans. Francis McDonagh, in *Aesthetics and Politics: The Key Texts of the Classic Debate within German Marxism*, ed. Ronald Taylor (London: Verso, 1977).

CA   Karl Marx, *Capital*, vol. 1, trans. Ben Fowkes (London: Penguin Classics, 1992).

CF   Virginia Woolf, "Character in Fiction" in *The Essays of Virginia Woolf*, vol. 3: *1919–1924*, ed. Andrew McNeillie (New York: Harcourt, 1992).

CNA   W. E. B. Du Bois, "Criteria of Negro Art," *Crisis* 32 (October 1926): 290–297, reprinted in Sondra Kathryn Wilson, ed., *The Crisis Reader: Stories, Poetry, and Essays from the N.A.A.C.P.'s "Crisis Magazine"* (New York: Modern Library, 1999).

EI   Sigmund Freud, *The Ego and the Id* in *The Standard Edition of the Complete Psychological Works of Sigmund Freud*, trans. Joan Riviere (New York: Norton, 1960).

H   Theodor W. Adorno, *Hegel: Three Studies*, trans. Shierry Weber Nicholsen (Cambridge: MIT Press, 1993).

HS   Giorgio Agamben *Homo Sacer: Sovereign Power and Bare Life*, trans. Daniel Heller-Roazen (Stanford: Stanford University Press, 1998).

ILA   G. W. F. Hegel, *Introductory Lectures on Aesthetics*, trans. Bernard Bosanquet (London: Penguin, 1993).

ILTY   Luce Irigaray, *I Love to You: Sketch of a Possible Felicity in History*, trans. Alison Martin (New York: Routledge, 1996).

ITB   Fred Moten, *In the Break: The Aesthetics of the Black Radical Tradition* (Minneapolis: University of Minnesota Press, 2003).

JTRU   Sigmund Freud, *Jokes and Their Relation to the Unconscious* in *The Standard Edition of the Complete Psychological Works of Sigmund Freud,* trans. James Strachey (New York: Norton, 1989).

LCJ   Nella Larsen, "Letter to Charles S. Johnson," reprinted in *Passing*, ed. Carla Kaplan (New York: Norton, 2007).

MBMB   Virginia Woolf, "Mr. Bennett and Mrs. Brown" in *The Essays of Virginia Woolf,* vol. 3: *1919–1924*, ed. Andrew McNeillie (New York: Harcourt, 1992).

MBPM   Hortense J. Spillers, "Mama's Baby, Papa's Maybe: An American Grammar Book," *Diacritics* 17, no. 2 (1987): 65-81.

MER   Karl Marx, *The Marx-Engels Reader*, ed. Robert C. Tucker (New York: Norton, 1978).

MF   Virginia Woolf, "Modern Fiction" in *The Gender of Modernism: A Critical Anthology*, ed. Bonnie Kime Scott (Bloomington: Indiana University Press, 1990).

MM   Sigmund Freud, "Mourning and Melancholia," in *Collected Papers,* vol. 4, ed. James Strachey, trans. Joan Riviere (New York: Basic Books, 1959), 152-170.

MN   Virginia Woolf, "Modern Novels" in *The Essays of Virginia Woolf,* vol. 3: *1919–1924*, ed. Andrew McNeillie (New York: Harcourt, 1992).

NT   Theodor W. Adorno, *Notes to Literature*, trans. Shierry Weber Nicholsen (New York: Columbia University Press, 1991).

O   Virginia Woolf, *Orlando: A Biography* (New York: Harcourt, 2006).

OR   Hannah Arendt, *On Revolution* (London: Penguin, 1990).

P   Nella Larsen, *Passing* in *"Quicksand" and "Passing,"* ed. Deborah E. McDowell (New Brunswick, NJ: Rutgers University Press, 1986).

PCE   Giorgio Agamben, *Potentialities: Collected Essays in Philosophy,* trans. Daniel Heller-Roazen (Stanford: Stanford University Press, 2000).

PM   Étienne Balibar, *The Philosophy of Marx,* trans. Chris Turner (London: Verso, 1995).

Q   Nella Larsen, *Quicksand* in *"Quicksand" and "Passing,"* ed. Deborah E. McDowell (New Brunswick: Rutgers University Press, 1986).

RO   Virginia Wolf, *A Room of One's Own* (New York: Harcourt, 1981).

SP   Jane Marcus, ed., *Suffrage and the Pankhursts* (London: Routledge, 1987).

SSD   Orlando Patterson, *Slavery and Social Death: A Comparative Study* (Cambridge: Harvard University Press, 1982).

TBG   Teresa Billington-Greig, *The Non-Violent Militant: Selected Writings of Teresa Billington-Greig,* ed. Carol McPhee and Ann Fitzgerald (London: Routledge, 1987).

TR   Giorgio Agamben, *The Time That Remains: A Commentary on the Letter to the Romans,* trans. Patricia Daily (Stanford: Stanford University Press, 2005).

TS   Luce Irigaray, *This Sex Which Is Not One,* trans. Catherine Porter (Ithaca: Cornell University Press, 1985).

TTL   Virginia Wolf, *To the Lighthouse* (New York: Harcourt, 1981).

WM   Nella Larsen, "The Wrong Man" in *An Intimation of Things Distant: The Collected Fiction of Nella Larsen,* ed. Charles R. Larson (New York: Anchor, 1992).

FEMINIST AESTHETICS AND

THE POLITICS OF MODERNISM

Introduction On Loss, Invention, and the Dilemmas of Feminist Aesthetics

I.

It is always surprising to see the final shape a book has taken. This experience has been more pronounced with this project than with my previous books because here I approached feminist aesthetics without any presuppositions about main concepts, themes, or even a theoretical approach. Given the paucity of studies on feminist aesthetics, I cast my net widely, without limiting myself to a particular philosophical tradition or theoretical orientation. I followed only two guiding threads. The first one was that my reflections on the possibility of feminist aesthetics would have to be based on my field of expertise in literary modernism and modern women writers, in particular, Virginia Woolf and Nella Larsen. Second, I wanted to move beyond the necessary critiques of the historical/institutional conditions of women's literary production and the gendered and racialized lexicons of aesthetics. Although these two levels of critique—of the political conditions of literature and of the political implications of seemingly gender-neutral concepts of aesthetics—are crucial starting points of any theory of feminist aesthetics, critique by itself is insufficient. The political critique of art's complicity with power often fails to account for the aesthetic specificity of art or to propose alternative feminist approaches to aesthetics and women's literature. In other words, my question was how to conceptualize feminist aesthetics beyond feminist critiques of philosophical aesthetics. Once we move beyond the critique of the material conditions and the philosophical conceptual apparatus of aesthetics—for instance, taste, genius, production, aesthetic judgment, aesthetic autonomy—how can we proceed? On what basis can one formulate a feminist approach to aesthetics without presuppositions of female experience, identity, or a uniquely feminine style of writing—the presuppositions so eloquently criticized by numerous feminist critics?

My initial response to these questions originated in reading Virginia Woolf's *A Room of One's Own* and Nella Larsen's novels. In different ways, both these writers explore the tenuous possibility of women's aesthetic innovation in relation to unbearable historical losses and damages inflicted by racist and sexist violence:

> One goes into the room—but the resources of the English language would be much put to the stretch, and the whole flights of words would need to wing their way illegitimately into existence before a woman could say what happens when she goes into a room.[1]

> Nothing remains of it all. All has vanished . . . the pressure of dumbness, the accumulation of unrecorded life.
>
> (*RO*, 89)

> Never could she recall the shames and often the absolute horrors of the black man's existence in America without the quickening of her heart's beating and a sensation of disturbing nausea. . . . The sense of dread of it was almost a tangible thing in her throat.[2]

> Even her tongue was like a heavy dying thing.
>
> (*P*, 233)

The problem these passages raise is how the destructive muteness and the erasure of the feminine, this "pressure of dumbness" of unrecorded women's lives and their destroyed bodies, can be transformed into a process of writing, into a possibility of inventing new ways of speaking, community, and acting. How, despite the weight of "dumb" muteness or "dying tongue," can new ways of speaking be "illegitimately" brought into existence? Nella Larsen makes these questions even more haunting and pressing since she investigates the impact of the exclusion of black women from literary and political practice in the context of the suffocating horror of racist violence. And yet she too posits a daring counterfactual possibility of aesthetic invention: if a black woman writer were free, "anything could happen. . . . Anything" (P, 236).

My investigations of the possibilities and impossibilities of a feminist aesthetics revolved around the gravitational pull of the unresolved tension between "dumb" muteness and literary innovation, between women's transformative practice in politics and literature and the devastating impact of sexist and racist violence on women's lives and bodies. As the project progressed, my thinking crystallized around two interrelated configurations: first, the contradiction between unbearable loss and "illegitimate" invention led me to examine the relation between women's literary practice and politics in modernism in the context of the entrenched opposition between revolt and melancholia. What the oscillation between revolution and melancholia reveals is the coexistence of particular struggles for freedom and multiple forms of domination—what feminist theory has theorized as the intersection of race, gender, class, and sexuality. Given this contradiction, the exclusive focus on melancholia, as Hannah Arendt argues in her book *On Revolution*, is a historical symptom of the forgetting of the revolutionary tradition in modernity. By contrast, the insistence on revolution and subversive literature disregards loss and domination, which persist despite multiple struggles and the gain of freedom by subjugated groups. Consequently, instead of choosing the melancholic or the revolutionary narrative of modernism, I reformulate this opposition in terms of a feminine aesthetics of potentiality.

However, to articulate the aesthetic possibilities emerging from destruction and muteness I had to address another opposition, namely, the opposition between material injuries and experimental literary forms. That women's experience of melancholic muteness is intertwined with violence inflicted on women's bodies, language, and nature is not difficult to accept. Conversely, a feminist creation of new possibilities of action, meaning, and community in politics and literature would have to entail a resignification and the invention of new experimental forms. What is far less evident, however, is the way material damages are related to the seemingly apolitical question of experimental literary forms. To answer this question, I replace the aesthetic form/political content opposition that structures most debates about aesthetics and politics with a more complex relationship between aesthetic form, materiality, and political violence.

Given these two configurations, the book is divided into two parts. In the first part I examine the unresolved and endlessly replicated contradiction between "revolutionary" and melancholic politics and art in Western modernity. What are the implications of this contradiction for the status of women's literary practice vis-à-vis gender and race politics? Since the oscillation between revolutionary and melancholic narratives of modernisms reflects the unresolved contradiction between freedom and racist, gender, and economic domination, it renders most discussion of feminist aesthetics and politics in modernism inadequate. On the one hand, the often impatient desire to politicize art, to integrate it into a larger social context, disregards the persisting unfreedom, loss, and domination in the political. On the other hand, the defense of the autonomy of art, understood either as art's transcendence of its material conditions or as the critical negation of these conditions, forgets transformative struggles in the political. Of course, the urgency of the struggle for freedom might make aesthetics seem unimportant, while the autonomy of art might disregard the transformative dimension of political praxis. Nonetheless, I contest *both* the anti-aesthetic subordination of modern literature to political ends *and* the aesthetic focus on the emancipatory potential of art alone at the expense of such potential in feminist, antiracist political struggles.

I begin this study by developing the political theory of revolution and female subjectivity produced by the British suffrage militancy in the context of Hannah Arendt's theory of revolution and Theodor Adorno's aesthetic theory. In so doing I raise a new question that has not yet been addressed by feminist critics of modernity, namely, the question of the political and aesthetic implications of the suffragettes' redefinition of the right to vote as the right to revolt. What is at stake in my analysis is the conflicting relation between women's political and literary discourses of revolution and their relevance for feminist aesthetics. In the second chapter I juxtapose the political and aesthetic notions of revolt with the widespread discussions of mourning and melancholia that span theories of modernism and aesthetics (Adorno, Horowitz, Marriott)[3] and racial and gender politics (Butler, Chen, Gilroy),[4] not to mention psychoanalysis (Freud and Kristeva)[5] and the theory of the novel (Ian Baucom).[6] My interpretation of melancholia examines not only psychic crisis but also the loss of the significance of art and the degradation of political praxis. I

argue that in aesthetics melancholia is a symptom of the struggle between excluded women's experimental writings and the hegemonic conception of modernism based on such exclusion. In politics it is the
struggle between multiple gendered and racialized forms of political
emancipatory movements—such as British militant suffrage and the
Harlem Renaissance—and the construction of the universal agent of
liberation that excludes these movements. Writing melancholia in wom-
en's texts is, therefore, an antagonistic practice, a struggle against both
political gender and racist exclusions and against the psychic struggle
raging within melancholic subjects.

The contradiction between transformative action and melancholic impasse raises a fundamental question for feminist aesthetics—the question
central to this book—namely, how the haunting history of destruction and
the ongoing exclusion of women from politics and literary production
can be transformed into inaugural possibilities of writing and action.
This question is crucial for my interpretation of a feminist aesthetics of
potentiality. Focusing on Woolf's essays and novels, I situate the transformative capacity of literature—its ability to contest gender domination,
imperialism, and the gendered division of labor—in relation to women's
political aspirations to freedom. And, conversely, I argue class, gender,
and racist domination threaten the very possibility of art even before its
inception: In fact, Woolf's imaginary history of women's literary production begins with the utter destruction of women's art and their bodies—a
destruction internalized as madness, melancholia, and resentment. It is
only by bearing witness to both the destruction of women's artistic capacities and women's revolutionary aspirations for political and economic
freedom that feminist aesthetics can inaugurate new possibilities of writing and passionate relations between women.

In the second part of the book I examine the political and aesthetic
problematic of materiality, violence, and form, which is already implied
in the first part, since the history of the destruction and exclusion of
women is inscribed in bodies and in the damaged materials of the work
of art. At first glance, this heterogeneous constellation of form, violence,
and materiality brings together seemingly apolitical gender-neutral aesthetic debates about experimental forms in modernism with the gender/
race politics of the body. I argue, however, that form cannot be limited to
aesthetics alone but has to be diagnosed within the political itself, which
also involves reproduction, contestation, and the creation of new forms of
collective life.

In chapter 4 I provide such a feminist diagnosis of form and political violence by juxtaposing the commodification of female bodies with the biopolitics of race and gender. In so doing I compare the operations of form in the two seemingly different domains—in civil society (the relations of production and exchange) and in the state (in particular, sovereign violence determining inclusion and exclusion from the political). What this confrontation of biopolitics with commodified sexed and racialized bodies shows is the mutual implication of political violence and the abstraction of social forms, in particular, the commodity form and that of citizenship. I examine diverse material effects of such violence— ranging from Agamben's bare life and the hunger striking suffragettes; Orlando Patterson's notion of social death and Hortense Spillers's hieroglyphics of black flesh; Irigaray's commodified bodies and Adorno's *membra disjecta*; to the destroyed bodies of the potential black female writers in Larsen's novels.

By juxtaposing the seemingly apolitical, gender-neutral aesthetic debates about experimental forms with the analysis of violence, materiality, and the abstraction of collective forms of life, my approach gives a new meaning and substance to formal experimentation in women's modernism. I argue that the frequently acknowledged sensibility of aesthetic form not only contests the violence of abstract political forms but also enables a resignification of damaged bodies and objects previously expelled from the realm of meaning. Since such resignification implies a dynamic model of interrelation between literary form and material elements of the work of art, women's experimental literature offers an alternative both to modern citizenship, separated from bare life, and to the commodity form, abstracted from the concreteness of time, labor, and the particularity of the object.

The the third part of this book is devoted to Nella Larsen's aesthetics of the black female re-naissance. By rejecting black propaganda for the sake of experimental female art, Larsen transforms the degraded language of commodification and racist violence, signified in her novel by the racist curse of slavery, into new modes of writing and being in common. Although opposed to the more explicit political dimension of propaganda, Larsen's choice of experimental art transforms the petrification of bodies and language into the possibility of writing, freedom, and nonoedipal female desires. Haunted by the spectrality of social death, signified in the novel by the figure of "walking on my grave,"[7] such a transformation reaches a liminal experience of language before it solidifies into the racist and gendered opposition between inclusion and exclusion, male-diction and bene-diction.

Ultimately, the most important contribution of this book to feminist theories of modernism and aesthetics is the argument that loss and violence could be aesthetically transformed into new, multiple possibilities of what literature and femininity might mean and might become. Moving beyond critique, the theory of feminist aesthetics and modernism I present does not rely on a futile attempt to recover or posit the occluded feminine essence in art, understood either as the expression of female subjectivity and bodies or as the invention of a uniquely feminine style of writing. On the contrary, this theory is counterfactual: it traces what has been violently erased from history and asks how this ongoing exclusion of women from political participation and literary production can be transformed into the inauguration of new possibilities of writing, sexuality, and being in common.

II.

One of the goals of this project is to recover and develop the political and philosophical complexities of early feminist debates about art and politics in modernism. Yet, when I discuss my theory of feminist aesthetics, the frequent response I receive is that it is a contradictory or impossible project. For feminist theory, such a project seems to betray the political commitments of feminism. For philosophical aesthetics, a feminist revision of aesthetics seems to depend on an unreflected sociologization, or even instrumentalization, of artistic production and aesthetic experience. Finally, in literary studies of modernism, where the feminist reflection and interpretation of specific literary works is most developed, the prospect of a feminist aesthetics, insofar as it belongs, partially at least, to feminist philosophy, carries paradoxically the threat of a betrayal of the specificity of literary works and their historical context. Yet the tension between the particularity of literary works and the generality of interpretive categories is at work in every literary interpretation and nowhere more pronounced than in the importation of new historicism into modernist studies; the novelty of my approach in this respect is that I analyze the way this contradiction inhabits not only interpretation but also the very structure of experimental literary works. Thus my approach to feminist debates about art and politics in modernism and in feminist theory today is at once more political and more philosophical in its orientation than historicism or gender or cultural studies.

These skeptical responses are a symptom of the belatedness and relative paucity of feminist theories of aesthetics, despite the presence of well-established feminist literary criticism, film theory, visual arts, and art history. In her 1995 *Art on My Mind: Visual Politics*, bell hooks deplores "the dearth of progressive critical writing by African-Americans on art and aesthetics" and the continuous subordination of art to either propaganda or documentary function.[8] In a different vein, in 2001 Sarah Worth suggests that as a philosophical project feminist aesthetics "is a relatively young discipline, dating from the early 1990s."[9] Ten years later, in the description of her forthcoming 2011 anthology *Feminist Aesthetics and Philosophy of Art: The Power of Critical Visions and Creative Engagement*, editor Lisa Ryan Musgrave repeats the same argument: "While much feminist philosophy is enjoying third- and fourth-wave developments and can build on its scholarly roots forged in the 1960's and 1970's, feminist contributions have taken what seems an exceptionally long time to break into the stubborn areas of aesthetics and philosophy of art . . . views on art practices or values have tended to seem less important than work in the sister area of feminist social and political theory."[10] If, as Hal Foster claims, "the adventures of the aesthetic make up one of the great narratives of modernity,"[11] then feminist theory has joined this adventure belatedly. This imbalance between the richness of the feminist theories of the political and the belatedness and still relative paucity of feminist philosophical aesthetics, despite the growing number of important studies from Julia Kristeva, bell hooks, Drucilla Cornell, and Elizabeth Grosz, is the main motivation for this project.

Since the very formulation "feminist aesthetics" reproduces the persisting division between the aesthetic and the political within feminism itself, it reopens the much debated methodological questions of aesthetics and politics in modernism. The dominant tenor of the discussion of aesthetics and politics in the last four decades has been the conflict between the political critique of aesthetic ideology and the growing number of critics who call for a critical return to "new aestheticism" or even to "new formalisms." Two of the most influential instances of the ideological critique imported into Anglo-American modernist studies are Bourdieu's claim that the categories of aesthetic autonomy, taste, and disinterestedness serve the interests of class distinctions and cultural capital and

Raymond Williams's characterization of aesthetics as "the main instrument" of ideological mystification and as an "absolute abstraction" from the larger socio-economical processes.[12] By rejecting the autonomy of aesthetics, Williams and his followers criticize art's complicity with class domination.[13]

Although numerous political critiques of aesthetics have been extremely important and influential, the critique of art's complicity with power often fails to account for the aesthetic specificity of art or consider its relative autonomy as a condition of critique. Critics as diverse as Drucilla Cornell, Hilde Hein, Paul Gilroy, Gregg M. Horowitz, or David Marriott argue that aesthetics is important because it enables complex negotiations between difference, otherness, and publicity, on the one hand, and between the traumatic memory of domination and utopian aspirations of freedom, on the other. When justifiable critiques of modernist ideologies of formalism are accompanied by the historical contextualization of art, they often collapse into the opposite reductive tendency, namely, the reenactment of the political "death of art."[14]

In opposition to "anti-aestheticism," more critics and philosophers, such as Thomas Docherty, Lydia Goehr, Jonathan Loesberg, Elaine Scarry, bell hooks, and Elizabeth Grosz, among others, call for a critical return to aesthetics or for the formulation of a new aestheticism. This return to aesthetics certainly does not present a unified phenomenon, but what is common to all such critiques is an attempt to reclaim the transformative function and specificity of aesthetics beyond its complicity with power. Reassessing the arguments about the end of art and aesthetics, Lydia Goehr argues that some of the most compelling of these arguments, like Adorno's, "are in fact *for* continuation, liberation, and survival."[15] John Joughin and Simon Malpas underscore the critical potential of art and literature and "want to put the case that it might be time for a new aestheticism."[16] For his part, Jonathan Loesberg, in his *A Return to Aesthetics*, reclaims the complexity of the aesthetic categories and shows that cultural critiques of modernity are themselves indebted to the legacy of aesthetics. In his *Aesthetic Democracy* Docherty asks to what extent democracy itself depends on aesthetic experience, insofar as such experience opens the possibility of the encounter with alterity and self-differentiation.[17] Writing from the Deleuzian ontological perspective, Elizabeth Grosz makes a powerful case that art is an enhancement of bodily sensations, intensities, and sexual attractions. As she puts it, "art proper . . . emerges when sensation can detach itself and gain an autonomy from its creator and its perceiver, when something of the chaos from which it is drawn can breathe and have a life of its own."[18]

The tension between aesthetics and the politics of race and gender is also crucial in feminist critiques of aesthetics and in modernist studies. Both the canon of high modernism and its ideology have been called into question by materialist, feminist, and cultural studies scholars at least since the 1980s.[19] These new "modernist studies" have recovered neglected women writers, analyzed the institutional and transnationalframeworks of modernisms, and examined the politics of cultural production. In a different development, African American literary critics and race theorists, for instance, Houston Baker, Mae Gwendolyn Henderson, Hazel Carby, Fred Moten, David Marriott, and Kevin Bell,[20] have in different ways theorized radical traditions of black aesthetics, elaborated the specificity of black modernism, recovered black women writers, and contested the exclusion of the Harlem Renaissance from Anglo-American and British modernisms.

Despite these achievements, the various projects of rethinking aesthetics from the perspective of race and gender are still characterized by the entrenched opposition between the political critique of aesthetics and the recovery of the aesthetic potential of freedom. On the one hand, as Hein and Korsmeyer, point out, the project of the "gendering of aesthetics" contests the separation of aesthetic values from political power, economic exchange, and "instrumental values."[21] On the other hand, writers like bell hooks, Kevin Bell, and Fred Moten passionately argue for the transformative role of black art in the practice of freedom. Writing about the relation between aesthetics, black visual arts, and black liberation politics, hooks, for example, proposes rethinking the very project of black revolution so that "we create collective awareness of the radical place that art occupies within the freedom struggle and of the way in which experiencing art can enhance our understanding of what it means to live as free subjects in an unfree world."[22]

It is certainly one of the ironies of history that the beginnings of feminist aesthetics coincide with feminist arguments about its impossibility. In her 1989 *Beyond Feminist Aesthetics: Feminist Literature and Social Change* and her 2000 *Doing Time: Feminist Theory and Postmodern Culture,* Rita Felski claims that the very project of feminist aesthetics is inherently contradictory because there are "no legitimate grounds for classifying any particular style of writing as uniquely or specifically feminine."[23]

According to Felski, the project of feminist aesthetics tends to ascribe gendered meanings to literary forms on the basis of either the expression of distinct female subjectivity or the textual disruption of patriarchal norms of signification. As she concludes, "my dissatisfaction with feminist aesthetics does not stem from a belief that there are no connections between art and gender politics. Rather, I do not think that feminist aesthetics helps us understand these connections adequately."[24]

Even this brief engagement with the debates on the relation between aesthetics and politics in modernism and feminism foregrounds several closely intertwined difficulties in the revision of aesthetics from the perspective of gender, race, and cultural studies: We are confronted with the persistent difficulty of redefining the specificity of aesthetics with regard to the politics of race and gender without falling into the trap of either apolitical formalism or the political overcoming of aesthetics. How can we contest the separation between political and aesthetic spheres, *as well as* the entrenched divisions between sexual difference and "the color line" fracturing these spheres from within, without either reducing art to a reflection of historical conditions or ascribing gendered meanings to subversive aesthetic forms? My approach to these questions is twofold: first, I underscore the complexity of early feminist debates about literature and politics in modernism, which subsequently have been underappreciated in feminist and aesthetic theories. Second, I develop my own theoretical perspective, which draws upon diverse theorists of race and gender, on the one hand (in particular Kristeva, Arendt, Irigaray, Agamben, Moten, and Spillers), and on Adorno's aesthetic theory, on the other.

Why is this encounter between Adorno, feminism, and race theory crucial for modernist studies? What is important in Adorno's work is his account of the contradictory relation between modern artistic practice and politics. Without such a trenchant analysis of the historical status of literary practice in modernism, feminist thinking about sensibility, bodies, resistance, or literary language might indeed be either misread as political analysis of the content, fall under the shadow of essentialism, or be discounted as the fetish of formal subversion. Nonetheless, what is missing in Adorno is, first, an analysis of race and gender as conditions of literary production, second, a consideration of women and black writers, and, finally, an emancipatory political praxis. It is around these pivotal issues that the interventions of feminism and race theory have been decisive both to my own theoretical orientation and to the formation of modernist studies.

The starting point for my formulation of feminist aesthetics is Adorno's definition of the paradoxical status of literary practice in modernism, or what he calls the heteronomous autonomy of art. Such a definition means that modern literature both depends on and is independent from its social material conditions, which, in my interpretation but not in Adorno's, include gender and race power struggles. As a force "that originates in history and then is separated from it,"[25] literature is both autonomous and a product of the social division of labor; it both reproduces and departs from capitalist relations of production. This contradictory status of modern art situates women's modern literature *between* economic exchange and utopian political praxis, *between* political domination and the possibility of freedom. Another consequence of the ambivalent function of modern literature, its subversion of and complicity with domination, is a new approach to formal experimentation in modernism: Such experimentation not only contests obfuscated historical contradictions and antagonisms, which also include gender and racial antagonisms, but also produces the emancipatory "schema of social praxis" (*AT*, 228).

This juxtaposition of gender, race, and capitalism with women's experimental literature means that contestation of the gendered hegemony of white supremacy has to be analyzed not only in the context of the sociology of art or the political critique of aesthetics but also within the structure of women's literary works. For Adorno, such "immanent" critique of literature and aesthetics means that "social concepts should not be applied to the works from without"—that is, not from the sociology of art or the political critique of aesthetic ideology—"but rather drawn from an exacting examination of the works themselves."[26] Sociology or political critique can well diagnose class, gendered, and racist relations of power, which exclude women from the institution of art and politics, but they fail to address how this exclusion manifests itself and is contested within women's literary practice.

The choice of Adorno's work as the starting point for a feminist aesthetics might seem both compelling and problematic. Despite his still tenuous position in Anglo-American literary criticism, Adorno, as Jay Bernstein suggests, is widely regarded as one of the most important theorist of modernism and modern philosophical aesthetics.[27] For Bernstein, Adorno remains a source of a "philosophical defense" of late modernism in painting.[28] From a different theoretical perspective, Frederic Jameson claims that Adorno's aesthetic theory is "the expression of the distinctively modernist Marxism."[29] Yet, for feminist critics, Adorno's work is also problematic. Based almost exclusively on white male artists, Adorno's aesthetic theory seems to reproduce the gendered bifurcation of subjectivity, diagnosed most explicitly in *Dialectic of Enlightenment*, into the self-constituting, masculine subject represented by Odysseus and the feminized, repressed nature and sensibility represented by the Sirens. As Sabine Wilke and Heidi Schlipphacke point out, although Adorno offers a radical critique of the hegemonic formation of masculine subjectivity, he unreflectively repeats patriarchal constructions of the feminine as the excluded or repressed nature, sexuality, and sensibility, that is, as the other of culture and politics.[30]

Despite these limitations, I nonetheless argue that a feminist reformulation of the heteronomous autonomy of modern literature and art is the condition of possibility of a feminist aesthetics since it allows us to examine artistic practice in the context of the politics of capital, race, and gender—which constitute the heteronomous aspect of women's literature—without negating its aesthetic specificity—that is, its autonomy. Furthermore, the heteronomous autonomy of art underscores both the political limitations and the critical function of modern literature—its complicity with and its contestation of racist, economic, and gendered structures of exploitation. By rethinking Adorno's aesthetic theory in the context of feminist theories of politics and modernism, I analyze gendered and racist structures of power, which constitute the heteronomous aspect of women's modern literature, and show how they "contaminate" the purity of the aesthetic autonomy and alter aesthetic conceptuality.

Nonetheless, my project of feminist aesthetics also departs from Adorno's theory of modernism in fundamental ways. By refocusing my analysis on the work of white and black modern women writers, I argue that race and gender, in addition to capitalist modes of production, are crucial, if heteronomous, categories of modern aesthetics. The introduction of these categories into philosophical aesthetics changes, first of all, the analysis of the politics of modernism. The collusion of white supremacy with patriarchy reveals new forms of domination that require supplementing Adorno's Marxism and his trenchant critique of totalitarianism with feminist critiques of commodification, on the one hand, and with feminist critiques of biopolitics, on the other. More importantly, feminist analyses of gender and race politics theorize in different ways possibilities of resistance and, in so doing, contest claims of total political domination, whether it is Adorno's thesis of administered society or Agamben's notion of the camp as the hidden paradigm of modern biopower.

Following Arendt's notion of transformative action, my analysis of the political focuses on the contradiction between subjugation and democratic struggles for freedom by oppressed groups—for the purposes of this study, on the militant suffrage movement in Britain and the struggle against antiblack racism during the Harlem Renaissance in the U.S. It is this contradiction between freedom and domination that opens new questions about the relation between the experimental character of women's literature and the innovative aspect of democratic struggles. What does the heteronomous autonomy of modern literature mean when transformative potential is associated not only with art but also with political action? And conversely, how can we think the innovative aspect of gender and the racial politics of modernity vis-à-vis experimental aesthetics?

What I propose as an alternative to the overcoming of art by either politics or philosophy is an investigation of the divergence and convergence of aesthetic and political forms, their gendered, racial configurations, and their respective relations to violence and materiality. Such a relation between feminist politics and aesthetics is already staged in the main topics of this book: the notions of revolt, melancholia, materiality, commodification, violence, and experimental forms that belong neither to the classical lexicon of aesthetics nor to politics but are widely used in the study of modernism and in feminist theories of the political. However, despite the importance of these concepts in feminist theories, they have not been interrogated as points of intersection, as entanglements and contradictions between feminist politics and aesthetics, problematizing the autonomy of each of these spheres of praxis. As hybrid concepts, these categories not only attest to what Adorno calls the loss of the self-evidence of aesthetic terminology, but, more importantly, imply the productive intersections between gender politics and aesthetics without collapsing the crucial differences between them.

The intersection between gender/race politics and experimental aesthetics is also reflected in the heterogeneous and interdisciplinary contents of this book, as it moves from the historical reconstruction of the importance of suffrage militancy for a feminist theory of revolution and modernist experimentation to revisions of melancholia in terms of the psychoanalytic genealogy of historical domination, from engagements with political philosophy (Arendt, Agamben, Du Bois) to the philosophical aesthetics of modernism (Adorno, Hegel, Kristeva), from the gender and racial implications of the Marxist theory of the commodity (Marx,

Irigaray, Moten) to specific literary analyses of women's literary texts (Woolf, Larsen).

Reformulated in the context of the gender and race politics of modernism, my approach to feminist aesthetics accounts for both the literary specificity and the political significance of diverse literary practices. It examines the formal complexity of women's literature as a disclosure of new types of antagonisms: those between the modern ideal of democratic freedom and imperialist, economic, racial, and gender domination, between the autonomy of art and its commodification, between damaged remnants of materiality and the abstraction of social relations, and, finally, between the pessimism of white cultural elites and the proclamations of the emancipatory potential of art by numerous black and female artists. By taking into account the unprecedented literary production of black and women writers in modernism and the emergence of new political and cultural movements that called for the liberation and political participation of women, African Americans, and colonized peoples, I examine complex relations between political and aesthetic transformations, their relation to gender and race differences, and the role of materiality in political contestation and aesthetic invention. The theory of feminist aesthetics I present traces what has been violently erased from history and asks how this erasure can be transformed into the inauguration of new possibilities of writing, sexuality, and becoming. Moving beyond critique, such aesthetic transformation of loss and violence into new multiple possibilities of signification does not tell us what women's modernism was but rather asks how it might mean otherwise.

PART I

Revolutionary Praxis and Its Melancholic Impasses

1   On Suffrage Militancy and Modernism

Femininity and Revolt

In studies of Western modernism and modernity we encounter
an unresolved and endlessly replicated contradiction between "revolutionary" and melancholic politics and art. How should we interpret this
contradiction rather than reproduce it by privileging either the revolutionary or melancholic side of modernism? How is the divide between
revolt and melancholia implicated in gender and race politics? And what
are its implications for the status of women's literary practice in modernism? I argue that the exclusive focus on melancholia is a symptom of the
forgetting of the revolutionary tradition in modernity. By contrast, the
celebratory insistence on revolution and subversive art forgets loss and
domination, which persist despite ongoing particular struggles for freedom. Consequently, the oscillation between revolution and melancholia
reveals the unresolved political contradiction between particular struggles for freedom coexisting with multiple forms of domination—what
feminist theory has theorized as the intersection of race, gender, class,
and sexuality.

   In this chapter I offer a new interpretation of the revolutionary side of
modernism by reconstructing the import of British suffrage militancy
for political and aesthetic theories of modernity. In particular I analyze
suffragettes' insistence on the female right to revolt in the context of

Hannah Arendt's political philosophy and Theodor Adorno's modernist aesthetics. By reconstructing the political discourse of female revolt in the first section of the chapter, I develop its implications for rethinking women's literary practice in the second section. This juxtaposition of suffrage militancy with aesthetic and political theory allows us to rethink the pervasive modernist preoccupation with the new beyond mere formal experimentation for innovation's sake and address it instead in the context of political struggles. Without this intersection between political and aesthetic struggles, it is all too easy to dismiss the rhetoric of the new as a symptom of either the aestheticization of politics or the commodification of art instead of recognizing it as the transformative political and aesthetic force.

Right to Vote or Right to Revolt?: Arendt and the British Suffrage Militancy

Although the feminist reception of suffrage has moved beyond Elaine Showalter's dismissive claim that "the suffrage movement was not a happy stimulus to women writers" because it failed to produce a "real manifesto of female literature,"[1] British suffrage militancy (1903–1914) still remains marginalized in feminist political and aesthetic philosophies of modernity, and it seems that feminist theory has yet to catch up with this unprecedented female militancy. As a result, suffrage militancy remains a crucial event in the history of feminism without an extensive philosophical or aesthetic elaboration and as such demonstrates a certain failure of thinking and remembrance. As far as political theory is concerned, the role of suffrage militancy is still confined primarily to a historical and controversial intervention. Regrettably, there is little discussion of the contributions of suffrage militancy to feminist political philosophy, ranging from Carole Pateman's *The Sexual Contract* to Judith Butler's *Gender Trouble*. Denise Reily's and Joan Scott's works are notable exceptions because they underscore the implications of suffrage movements for the unsolved dilemmas of feminist theory today. Reily's *"Am I That Name?"* analyzes the British nineteenth- and twentieth-century suffrage movement through her account of the theoretical implications of the unstable collective category of "women" for feminist politics, whereas Scott's *Only Paradoxes to Offer* inquires into the implications of the

French suffrage movement for the still unreconciled contradiction between the feminism of equality and the feminism of difference.[2]

The most important work on the British suffrage militancy has been produced by feminist historians and cultural and literary scholars of modernism.[3] Socialist historians, such as Sheila Rowbotham or Jill Liddington,[4] have reconstructed the initially neglected or forgotten contributions of working-class and labor women to the suffrage movement both on the regional and national levels. Feminist cultural critics, like Jane Marcus, Lisa Tickner, Janet Lyon, and Barbara Green, have moved from a reconstruction of the history of the suffrage movement in the twentieth century to the analysis of the forms of its political activism, its diverse artistic and literary productions as well as its visual iconography. In the context of modernist literature, Jane Marcus and Janet Lyon have revealed parallels between the suffragettes' interruptions of male political discourse and the iconoclastic impulse of the artistic avant-garde movements.[5] Building on these studies, I want to raise a new question, one that has not yet been addressed by feminist critics of modernity—namely, the question of the political and aesthetic implications of the suffragettes' redefinition of the right to vote as the right to revolt. In other words, what is at stake in my analysis is a conflicting relation between women's political and literary discourses of revolution and the inaugural force of innovation. In contrast to the studies devoted to the history of the movement, iconography, or artistic and literary activities, I want first of all to reconstruct the political theory of revolution produced by suffrage militancy. Such a redefinition means that suffragettes' contributions to political modernity and modern aesthetics are not limited to the enfranchisement of women, although historically this has been an enormous victory. Equally significant is the suffragettes' discourse of revolution, which, to paraphrase Hannah Arendt's insights, reveals the inextricable connection between freedom, the emergence of female political and artistic subjectivities, and the creation of new forms of political life. It is only by reconstructing the political discourse of female revolt that we can develop the implications of suffrage militancy for rethinking the status of women's literary practice in modernity.

In order to develop the suffrage political discourse of revolution, I will focus on the militant stage of the British suffrage campaign because it is the experience and justification of female militancy that propelled suffragettes to redefine the right to vote as a more fundamental women's right to revolt. British suffrage militancy is mainly associated with the political activism of the Women's Social and Political Union, a British suffrage organization founded in 1903 by Emmeline Pankhurst and her daughters, Christabel and Sylvia, and, to a lesser degree, with the Women's Freedom League, which emerged out of the split in the WSPU in 1907 over a disagreement about strategy, internal governance, and connections to the labor movement.[6] As Rowbotham argues, although the militants were a controversial minority within the suffrage campaign, they nonetheless "set the pace" and "challenge[d] all the prevailing assumptions about womanhood."[7] The first militant protest organized by the WSPU occurred in 1905, when two of its leaders, Annie Kenney and Christabel Pankhurst, interrupted the Liberal political meeting in Manchester and subsequently provoked an arrest on the charge of an "assault" on a policeman in order to end the press blackout on suffrage political agitation. Indeed, the first task of suffrage militancy was to break the "conspiracy of silence" and force an entry of women as speaking subjects into the political arena of discourse and action. In fact, such a forced entry and insistence on women's active participation in the political can be seen as the first militant act of the suffragettes. In response to the British Liberal government's continuing refusal to consider woman's suffrage legislation and in protest of the increasingly violent repressions of the suffragettes, the WSPU's militant tactics escalated from the "interruption" of male political discourse to large-scale demonstrations, deputations to the prime minister, hunger strikes,[8] window-smashing campaigns, the destruction of letter boxes, property, commodities, and shopping windows, the slashing of paintings in museums, and finally, to isolated acts of arson.[9] After having claimed access to political space through their street demonstrations and marches, the suffragettes responded to the refusal of the vote by contesting and destroying the public circulations of letters and commodities that blocked their access to citizenship. As their window-smashing campaign in London's fashionable shopping districts suggests, they also turned against the new techniques of advertising, display, and consumption, techniques that positioned middle-class women primarily as commodities and consumers rather than political subjects of speech and action. At the same time, in order to justify their militancy, suffrage activists produced in their numerous speeches, letters, manifestos, and journalism unprecedented redefinitions of femininity, revolution, and politics. In skillful quotations of historical precedents of militant protest and revolutionary struggle in the formation of British law and constitutional reforms, from the Magna Carta to male suffrage campaigns in the nineteenth century, suffragettes not only drew upon the tradition of male political radicalism asserting the right to oppose a despotic government, as Laura Mayhall points out,[10] but through this practice of citationality produced an original notion of women's revolutionary politics, the implications of which have yet to be fully appreciated and articulated by feminist political theory today.

Emerging from the practice and justifications of female militancy, the centerpiece of suffrage political praxis lies in the redefinition of women's right to vote as the right to revolt. As Teresa Billington-Greig (who refers to herself as TBG), the founder of the Women's Freedom League,[11] eloquently puts it, "our revolt itself was of very much greater value than the vote we demanded."[12] Contesting the opposition between militant and constitutional methods (that is, the methods of protest that either respect or break the law), Billington-Greig's defense of "the duty . . . to rebel" (TBG, 116) or "the right to rebellion" (TBG, 147) finally culminates in the claim that the deeper meaning of militancy lies not in the fight for the vote but in the defense of women's right to revolution: "Militancy," she writes, is not "the mere expression of an urgent desire for the vote, but . . . an aggressive proclamation of a deeper right—the right of insurrection" (TBG, 147). Despite all the differences between the two main British militant suffrage organizations, the WSPU and WFL, and despite all the internal debates about militant tactics, internal governance, and relations to the labor movement within both these organizations, "the right to insurrection" is in fact the paradigmatic expression and legitimation of suffrage militancy. We see the same definition of militancy as revolution again and again in numerous suffrage speeches and manifestos. In her 1908 speech at St. James Hall, "The Militant Methods of the N.W.S.P.U.," Christabel Pankhurst proclaims that suffrage militancy "is seeking to work the most beneficent revolution in human affairs that the world has yet seen."[13] Similarly, Emmeline Pankhurst, in her 1913 New York speech "Why We Are Militant," skillfully appeals to the ideals of the American and the French Revolutions in order to claim legitimacy for suffrage militancy as a new revolutionary movement: "I want to ask you whether, in all the revolutions of the past, in your own revolt against British rule, you had deeper or greater reasons for revolt than women have to-day?" (SP, 159).

How should we understand this revolutionary supplementation of women's right to vote—a signifier of gender equality and female autonomy—with the right to insurrection? What kind of revolution is implied in suffrage proclamations? This appeal to the revolutionary tradition takes us beyond the logic of identification with the nation-state suggested, for instance, by Julia Kristeva, who associates the first generation of feminism with the feminism of equality.[14] On the contrary, the redefinition of the women's right to vote as revolt announces women's participation in a transformative, creative praxis, its inaugural temporality, and the plurality of political agents. As Arendt argues in her book *On Revolution*, "the modern concept of revolution, inextricably bound up with the notion that the course of history suddenly begins anew, that an entirely new story, a story never known or told before, is about to unfold. . . . Crucial, then, to any understanding of revolutions in the modern age is that the idea of freedom and the experience of a new beginning should coincide."[15] That is why she argues that in order to understand the role of revolution in modernity we need, together, to think political freedom, the creation of the "new story," and the institution of a new beginning in history.

This convergence of freedom, novelty, and revolution changes the meaning of all three of these terms. First of all, revolution in Western modernity has to be distinguished from historical change, resistance, or the restoration of lost liberties, as it refers to the occurrence of an unprecedented event, inaugurating a new course in history. The "revolutionary pathos of the absolutely new" (*OR*, 37) distinguishes modern revolutionary struggle from previous forms of protests. As Arendt writes, "only where this pathos of novelty is present and where novelty is connected with the idea of freedom are we entitled to speak of revolution" rather than the struggle for the restoration of lost liberties (*OR*, 34). Second, novelty also acquires a new sense in the context of the eighteenth-century revolutions. Prior to the revolutions of the eighteenth century, novelty was associated with discoveries in science and with new ideas in philosophy. It is the migration of the "new" from the realm of scientific and philosophical thought to the public realm of political action that radicalizes this notion and links it with the praxis of the multitude rather than with the achievements of a chosen few. Likewise, the revolutionary novelty has to be distinguished from the modern desire for consumption of commodities. It is precisely this revolutionary, collective sense of novelty that is critical for rethinking the status of women's innovative literary practices in modernism.

Finally, revolutionary struggles change the meaning of freedom itself. Political freedom in the contingent historical world is different from liberation, even though liberation is its necessary precondition (*OR*, 33–34). Liberation is primarily negative—it is the struggle to end oppression— while freedom is positive, implying the creation of a new way of life. Furthermore, freedom is neither given by nature nor is it the property of the individual subject, but is relational, contingent, and created by acting with others in the polis. As a modality of being with others, freedom, Arendt argues, implies a participation in public speech, action, and government. And, most importantly, freedom in the positive and revolutionary sense reveals for the first time the capacity to create with others new forms of political life: revolutionaries are "agents in a process which spells the definite end of an old order and brings about *the birth of a new world*" (*OR*, 42, emphasis added). This configuration of revolutionary freedom as an intersubjective, relational, political agency to create new political structures with others —to enact the "birth" of a new world—is even more shocking and unprecedented when claimed by femininity, which is associated in Western modernity either with reproductive necessity and commodified objects of sexual exchange, in the private sphere, or with consumerism, labor, and philanthropy in public life, but never with political agency or revolutionary praxis.[16] Because such agency is relational, created through and for action, it does not require or presuppose a common gender identity.

At the same time, Arendt stresses the fragility of the convergence of revolution with positive freedom, collective praxis, and the inauguration of new forms of political life. It is this fragility that links revolutionary hopes with melancholy. She shows how, in the course of the nineteenth century, the notion of revolutionary freedom was divorced from political action and novelty and associated instead either with the concept of historical necessity (of which the Hegelian dialectic of necessity and freedom [*OR*, 53] is the most famous philosophical articulation) or with its opposite, with the liberation of natural, prepolitical equality and liberty. When freedom is transformed into historical necessity or displaced into the realm of natural violence or evolutionary force, revolution falls under the "sign of Saturn" (*OR*, 49) and gives rise to melancholic despair: "'The revolution devouring its own children,' as Vergniaud, the great orator of the Gironde, put it" (*OR*, 49). This connection between revolution and melancholy shows the loss of freedom and the abdication of agency— that is, the power to inaugurate the new beginning—to historical necessity, natural development, or systemic contradictions in the capitalist mode of production. Melancholy is an effect of forgetting that revolution was not a historical necessity or organic development, but rather an inaugural act, "the foundation of freedom." (216).

When suffragettes reinterpret the right to vote as the right to revolt, they not only contest their exclusion from existing liberties but also demand a positive right to freedom understood as the engagement in transformative praxis inaugurating new gender politics. Although dependent on the struggle against women's exclusion from the political, the freedom implied by the right to revolt exceeds negative contestation because, according to Arendt, it manifests itself primarily as the capacity to create new relations in political life. Thus, in order to understand the implications of suffragettes' redefinition of the vote as the right to revolt, we have to analyze the double aspect of their militancy: its iconoclastic side, negating women's exclusion from the political, and its creative side, inaugurating the unforeseeable. Associated more frequently with suffrage militancy, the iconoclastic side manifests itself, in a manner evocative of the iconoclastic impulse of the artistic avant-garde, as destruction and disruption: as the "breaking" of silence (in particular, the press blackouts of suffrage coverage); as the contestation of derogatory signs of femininity (the political activist as a hysteric); as the interruption of male political discourse; as the shattering of the shopping windows, the destruction of private property and fetishized and commodified art objects; as the self-starvation of the hunger-striking suffragettes exposed to the extraordinary brutality and violence of forcible feedings; and, finally, as the jamming of the circulation of letters, commodities, and signifiers. Yet the escalating destructive force of the suffrage campaign is inseparable from the creation of the new, unprecedented changes in political life and from positioning women as political subjects. Indeed, as the historians of the militant suffrage movement document, suffrage activism launches into the public space new representations and signifiers of femininity, new theories of the political, new rhetoric of public persuasion (enacted, for instance, through its spectacular marches, processions, advertising, and journalism), and, finally, new modes of circulation of bodies, signs, and images between and within public and private spaces.

The destructive aspect of suffrage militancy is intertwined with the contestation of women's exclusion not only from the vote and human rights but more fundamentally from political subjectivity. Given the tenacity of this exclusion, which failed to be redressed by the rational arguments of the constitutional suffrage societies in the nineteenth century, suffragettes could not merely identify with the democratic principles of

equality without a prior "act" negating women's exclusion from the public sphere and the limited political system of representation constructed
on the basis of this exclusion. As suffrage activists frequently point out,
the exclusion of women from political rights deprives them of agency
and de facto puts them in a position of "outlaws" in the existing political
order. In her 1906 essay written in Holloway prison, "The Militant Policy
of Women Suffragists," TBG declares that in order to remove "the bar" to
women's citizenship, one needs first "expose the outlawry to which
women were subjected" (TBG, 111). In an ingenious reversal of the law/
outlaw opposition, suffragettes claim that it is by obeying the law that
they perpetuate "the outlaw" position of women, whereas militancy, by
contesting the law, can give women the status of a legitimate political
subject. The "outlaw" status of women is limited not only to the public
sphere of politics and work but is even more pronounced in the private
sphere. In fact, the most frequently cited evidence of women's exclusion
from political rights is taken from marriage, divorce, and family law
regulating the private sphere. For strategic reasons, suffragettes especially stress the paradox that even the most idealized social vocation of
femininity—motherhood—does not give women parental rights over the
future of their children: "Our marriage and divorce laws are a disgrace to
civilization," proclaims Emmeline Pankhurst in her New York speech
"Why We Are Militant."[17]

As suffragettes never tire of pointing out, the unacknowledged consequence of the exclusion of women from political equality signified by
the vote is the loss of the status of the subject as such. According to TBG,
"there is not consciousness in the mind of many men that women are
human beings. They are regarded merely as sex-beings, segregated wholly,
and not always honorably, for sex uses" (TBG, 115). Or, as Emmeline
Pankhurst puts it, "[a] thought came to me in my prison cell . . : that to
men women are not human beings like themselves" (SP, 160). Whether
idealized or denigrated, women, as long as they are excluded from the
political, do not have the status of the human, are not treated as ends in
themselves, but merely as means of sexual exchange or as sexual commodities. And this is a significant shift in the argument for human
rights—such rights do not depend on a presupposed human nature or
particular attributes of that nature, but, on the contrary, constitute the
possibility of political subjectivity for women.

The suffragettes' struggle against women's exclusion from subject-
hood and citizenship can be read, as Joan Scott, for instance, argues, as

the exposure of the unacknowledged "paradox" of liberal democracy, which guarantees universal equality to all "persons" while excluding women and other subjugated groups from the status of the subject on the basis of "difference" construed as inequality or inferiority. This contradiction between universal equality and the exclusionary gender difference is doomed to be repeated in suffrage struggles for equality. Emerging at the site of this contradiction, suffrage, according to Scott, not only exposes but also reproduces this contradiction in the very demand for human rights (universal equality) for and in the name of women (gender difference). Furthermore, contemporary Western feminism, split between the feminism of equality and the feminism of difference, is still caught in the historical legacy of this performative contradiction. In her account of the British nineteenth- and twentieth-century suffrage movement, Denise Reily analyzes a similar instability of the collective category of "women," vacillating between the claims of sexed particularity and sex-blind humanity. Deployed by the proponents as well as the conservative opponents of the vote alike, this vacillation had been used as either the disqualification of or a support for women's political aspirations.[18]

However, by redefining the equality symbolized by the vote as the right to revolt, suffrage militants also reformulate this contradiction, or the "abyss" between the sexed particularity and universal equality inherited from liberalism, as an enabling condition of revolutionary practice. In suffrage agitation, the contestation of women's exclusion from the political and the very instability of the signifier of "women" leads to the reclaiming of the right to an ongoing revolt, without which the vote loses its political value and becomes a "banal," "respectable little thing" (TBG, 142) or, even worse, another commodity. By redefining the vote as the right to revolt, suffragettes reinterpret the contradiction between equality and difference as the justification of transformative political struggle. Through their contestation of gender inequality, suffragettes discover that "difference" can be linked not only with the exclusion and subjugation of women but also with positive freedom, with women's capacity to make a difference in political life, with the inauguration of what Hannah Arendt calls "an entirely new" and, therefore, entirely different "beginning" (OR, 37). In other words, the crucial implication of suffrage militancy is the redefinition of the logical contradiction between universality and difference in terms of the creative novelty of positive freedom.

The unpredictable novelty of revolutionary struggle is strongly emphasized in suffrage writings. In her 1908 speech at St. James Hall, Christabel Pankhurst proclaims that suffrage militancy is *"the most beneficent revolution* in human affairs *that the world has yet seen"* (*SP*, 42, emphasis added) and links this emergence of the unprecedented novelty of female militancy with the irrepressible movement of freedom: "did you ever know a great movement for human freedom that could be crushed by repression and coercion?" (*SP*, 50). Suffragettes themselves are struck again and again by the "strange" novelty of the new historical beginning their activism created. For instance, in 1903 Anne Kenney, a mill worker, Labour activist, and later one of the leading members of the WSPU, stresses the overwhelming sense of the new when she for the first time agrees to organize a meeting of the factory women of Oldham and Lees to discuss women's suffrage: "The following week I lived on air. . . . I instinctively felt that a great change had come."[19] When in 1905 Emmeline Pankhurst comments on the tactics of heckling Liberal politicians, she, like so many other suffragettes, stresses the sense of an unprecedented beginning not only in the suffrage movement but in history itself: "This was the beginning of a campaign the like of which was never known in England, or, for that matter, in any other country."[20] TBG captures perhaps the most essential aspect of the new revolutionary beginning when she connects militancy with the emergence of new thought and compares revolution to a new political birth: "[A] great rising of new thought, a great seeking after freedom, has manifested itself around the suffrage agitators wherever they have worked. . . . *'We have been born anew'* said one to me—a suffragist of thirty years standing—'It has been a revolution'" (TBG, 116, emphasis added).

The creative freedom of women's militancy both evokes and redefines another paradox of revolutionary action, namely, the incommensurability between constituted and constituting power, articulated for the first time in the course of the French Revolution by Sieyès in terms of "his famous distinction between a *pouvoir constituant* and a *pouvoir constitué*" (*OR*, 163). The problem this distinction presents for political theory in general and for feminist politics in particular is double: As both Agamben and Arendt argue in different ways, one has to differentiate constituting power from national sovereignty, on the one hand, and, on the other hand, from the existing political order (Agamben) and various forms of historical determinism (Arendt).[21] If constituting power is identified with national sovereignty, then its excess is interpreted, as has been historically the case, with the transcendence of the sovereign will and disconnected from the multiplicity of contingent political struggles. If constituting power is confused with the constituted order, or with historical development, then it falls under the provenance of historical necessity and is disconnected from political freedom. Although Hannah Arendt shares with Agamben the critique of sovereignty and historical necessity, she distinguishes constituting force both from sovereign will and historical necessity by focusing directly on the "grammar of action" and the "syntax" of political power. Such grammar and syntax underscore the multiplicity, plurality, contingency, and intersubjective character of political praxis. For Arendt, constituting power emerges when divergent actors come "together for the purpose of action," and it disappears with their dispersion: "The grammar of action: that action is the only human faculty that demands a plurality of men; and the syntax of power: that power is the only human attribute which applies solely to the worldly in-between space by which men are mutually related" (*OR*, 175). The only possible legitimation of such relational capacities stems from the very act of beginning, which contains its own principle.

It is in the context of the relational character of political action that we see the greatest limitations as well as the deepest class and race divisions within the British suffrage movement. Both the constitutional and militant campaigns were shaped by the class and empire discourses structuring British citizenship and the right to vote in the nineteenth and twentieth century. Despite the diversity of the suffrage movement emphasized in street demonstrations, suffrage militancy, as many the suffrage historians point out, was dominated by white middle-class women, although, as Liddington, Norris, and Rowbotham show, contributions of working-class women to both constitutional and militant organizations were significant. Conflicts over the coalition with the labor movement, which was reluctant to grant women's suffrage priority, as well as the debate over adult (that is, universal) suffrage versus women's suffrage on the same terms with men, not only was a dividing issue between the Pankhursts and Charlotte Despard, a socialist and cofounder of the Women's Freedom League, but also one of the reasons Sylvia Pankhurst, also a socialist, left WSPU in 1913.[22] Nonetheless, despite these persisting class conflicts and divisions, there were significant, if limited, instances of collaboration and solidarity among British middle-class and working-class women. As Rowbotham puts it, "in the context of the British class structure the very existence of such cross-class collaboration [in the suffrage movement] was extraordinary."[23] Such collaborations have been far more difficult if not impossible in the colonial context of the British Empire. As

Antoinette Burton points out, "like contemporary class and gender systems, imperialism was a framework out of which feminist ideologies op-
erated and through which the women's movement articulated many of its
assumptions," just as the vote "represented the conferring of formal political power in the imperial nation-state."[24] Although far less frequently
analyzed by suffrage historians, the imperialist discourse was not only a
legacy of the Victorian feminism coming to age at the height of the British Empire and not merely a response to the imperial anxieties, skillfully
used by antisuffrage propaganda, which implied that granting the vote to
British women at home would instigate revolts in the colonies.[25] The
imperialist framework of the Edwardian suffrage movement also was
symptomatic of its implicit or explicit sense of British cultural and racial
superiority and the expression of its civilizing mission with respect to
"Oriental" women. In particular, the constitutional suffrage organizations, as Burton argues, represented Indian women as "helpless victims
awaiting the representation of their plight and the redress of their condition at the hands of their sisters in the metropole."[26] Although militant
suffragettes constructed "an 'Oriental woman' who was less passive than
the suffragists version of her," and although they might have had some
influence on Gandhi's struggle for independence,[27] they still saw themselves as the center of the women's revolutionary movement around the
world. The "Oriental woman" was therefore not granted the same right to
insurrection and was not seen as an equal partner in suffragettes' revolt.

Antoinette Burton's analysis raises a larger question of the role of race
in suffrage political discourse. In addition to the colonial context, suffrage agitation in Britain had adopted the liberal rhetoric of slavery and
used it to generate feelings of moral outrage and public sympathy for the
suffrage cause. That rhetoric underscores the subjection of women in the
family and represented prostitution as the white slave trade. Laura Mayhall traces the genealogy of the rhetoric of slavery in suffrage struggle all
the way to John Stuart Mill's 1869 *The Subjection of Women* as well as to
Guiseppe Mazzini's (who was a proponent of Italian nationalism and the
emancipation of working-class men) 1858 *The Duties of Men*.[28] Both these
texts were widely read by suffrage political activists in the late nineteenth
and early twentieth centuries. In particular, John Stewart Mill underscored a double analogy between slavery and women's subordination in
the family and political despotism in the state. Despite the changing
ramifications of the rhetoric of slavery, this persisting analogy emphasized the outrage of women's oppression at home and subjugation in the

political sphere but did not see enslaved peoples' struggle for freedom as a model for women's liberation. Consequently, the rhetoric of slavery implicitly emphasized the whiteness of suffragettes' rebellion, as it associated blackness and colonized people merely with subjugation and not with political struggle or agency. Not surprisingly, such rhetoric failed to create interracial solidarity among white British militants, colonized women, and black women. And this failure to see an interconnection between gender, class, and race oppression as well as between different struggles for liberation continues to haunt Western feminist theory today.

In the context of Arendt's work on revolution, the suffragettes' demand for inclusion within the British state and the gendered, class, and imperial power of its institutions—the demand for the vote—challenges and reproduces the *constituted* power of the law. At the same time, the more fundamental political right to revolt reclaims for women *constituting* power and the capacity to create a new beginning that would exceed established power structures. In fact, suffragettes' justifications of militancy reclaim constituting power on the two fundamental levels of political praxis, namely, as "deeds" and "words," as political discourse and action. As Emmeline Pankhurst explains in her summation to the jury during the 1912 "conspiracy trial" following her arrest after a window-smashing campaign, "we did not content ourselves merely with discussion . . . we were not merely content with words . . . but we felt that we were distinct as a militant class . . . determined not only to talk about our grievances but to terminate them. . . . In fact we adopted a motto, 'Deeds, not words.'"[29] Pankhurst implies that women's political agency and subjectivity depend not on their common gender identity but on their capacity to act in the public sphere, on their "deeds" in relation to words. Such a relative priority of action suggests that the identification with the inherited structures of the democratic discourse of equality is an insufficient basis for female political subjectivity and transformative political practice. In the case of excluded groups, political action only negates their exclusion but also inaugurates new forms of political power and language. Consequently, to inscribe themselves within the institutional structures of parliamentary democracy as political subjects, suffragettes claim for themselves the *novelty* of revolutionary power that exceeds existing political and linguistic frameworks.

Despite their famous rallying cry, "Deeds, not words," suffragettes' "deeds" never cease to contest and reinvent words themselves so that the domain of political and public speech becomes an important area for suffrage militancy. Paradoxically, the collective organization of the suffrage movement as "a militant class" cannot proclaim the priority of deeds over words without the prolific creation of political discourse, that is, without creating new speech acts. Consequently, political speech, in its performative and innovative dimensions, is itself characterized by the tension between constituted/constituting power from within, as it were. Whether it is the brilliant rhetorical tactic of quotations, which wrestles and reappropriates the words from the "mouth" of liberal politicians advocating male militancy (as Christabel Pankhurst puts it, "we are prepared to take the words of one Cabinet Minister from his own mouth, and apply them to our agitation" [SP, 42]) or the strategy of "heckling" and ridiculing liberal candidates or the making and publishing of their own numerous public speeches, suffragettes transform speech acts into militant acts, which, in the domain of language, reappropriate old words and create new explosive significations. Indeed, the law recognizes this militant transformation of political speech, as the suffragettes are frequently charged and sentenced for "incitement to riot." Consider, for instance, the suffrage stone-throwing campaign, mostly at the windows of parliamentary buildings, in response to the Liberal government's refusal to receive women's deputations and hear their grievances. In one of the most symbolic gestures of protest against the government's violation of the Bill of Rights, in 1909 Lady Constance Lytton threw stones at a government car (aiming low to avoid injuries to the passengers) wrapped in paper on which she wrote quotations from one of Lloyd George's speeches. One of the inscriptions on the stone that hit the car was as follows: "To Lloyd George—Rebellion against tyranny is obedience to God—Deeds, not words."[30] In this militant act of protest against the suppression of women's public speech, the stone is both a missile and a political letter, aimed at liberal politicians with their own words reappropriated for the suffragettes' ends.

Such militant redefinition of language for the purposes of a new revolutionary act is especially striking in the rhetorical war over the meaning of politically charged words, such as "revolt," "conspiracy," "rush," or "militancy." In a characteristic gesture, Emmeline Pankhurst, charged with conspiracy, begins her address to the jury with a stunning linguistic reinterpretation of the very word *militancy:* "I want to call your attention to some of the definitions of the word 'militant.' It is a word which is liable to be misunderstood, my lord. . . . I find in Webster's dictionary militancy defined as 'a state of being militant, warfare.' Well, that sounds like violence, doesn't it? . . . Then, again, it is defined as meaning 'a conflict, to fight.' In Nuttal, I find it is 'to stand opposed, or to act in opposition.' In the Century dictionary I find a quotation . . . which refers to a 'condition of militancy against social injustice.' . . . And so I could go on showing you that the word 'militant' is not necessarily interpreted to mean only violence."[31] In these twists and turns of various definitions, the word *militancy* itself becomes militant, indeterminate, giving rise to new conflicting interpretations.

Pankhurst's militant legitimation and deployment of "militancy"—that is, of the signifier of suffragettes' political action—reveals two different performative effects of militancy. On the one hand, militancy is intertwined with opposition or taking a stand against social injustice—in this case, with the contestation of class and gender inequalities. This is a negative and iconoclastic meaning of militancy, closely related to the negative struggle for liberation. On the other hand, militancy, though feared as violence, is a new event, the inaugural act of revolutionary struggle. It is a force of invention that exceeds positionality, agency, articulation. The transformative force of such an act cannot be integrated without a remainder either into the constituted framework of power or into the notion of negation. In this sense militancy does not have a clearly defined agent: it vacillates between activity and passivity, it is a transitive force that women as much undergo as put into practice. As a verbal deed exceeding the letter of the law, militancy in fact undoes the classical opposition between the political act and speech—it makes uncertain whether the origin of the political lies in words or in acts. Such contradictory meaning of militancy as both the negative and transformative force, articulation and inaugural act, embodies what Julia Kristeva aptly calls the "sense" and "non-sense" of the revolt.[32]

The suffragettes' defense and legitimation of both the negative force and creative novelty of revolutionary praxis, of its destructive and constituting power, lead them to reflect on the relation between such acts and their institutionalization into law. Implicitly, such reflection posits revolutionary action rather than the juridical notion of social contract as the origin of law and the cause of its historical transformations. As TBG eloquently argues, every law, every political right, originates in the constituting power of revolt and is only retrospectively transformed into an institutionalized articulation of human rights and liberties: "all history is full of examples of the fact that liberty is only won by revolt. The political liberty of men, religious liberty, liberty of speech have all been finally obtained by conflict with existing authority" (TBG, 114). Thus, the split between words and revolutionary acts characterizes not only women's militant action but law itself. Revolt and conflict threaten the law and the specific form of political power embodied in it not from the "outside," as it were, but, in fact, reveal the forgotten, disavowed origins of the law and the source of its historical transformations. This is the great "historical lesson" suffragettes draw from previous revolutionary struggles by excluded groups, in particular, the militant struggle for male suffrage, in order to justify their own revolt against the government. The emphasis on the role of revolutionary struggle in the constitution and the history of the law not only challenges its neutrality but opens the possibility of its transformation. Thus, what provokes women's insurrection is indeed their historical exclusion not only from the vote and citizenship but even from the negative status of political offenders; yet what enables and legitimates their revolt in the first place is the fact that revolutionary struggle, always already inscribed within the law as its origin and principle, makes the law open to further transformations. Thus militancy is not a purely external opposition to the law but rather a new reactivation of its founding revolutionary principles (and I use the term *principle* in Arendt's sense of *principium*, that is, in the sense of a beginning giving rise to its own rule) in service of the ongoing struggle for the transformation of the legal system and the realization of a more expansive notion of freedom (*OR*, 212–214).

By stressing the revolutionary foundation and the ongoing transformations of the law from the Magna Carta to the nineteenth-century reforms bills (1832, 1867, 1884) that expanded male freedoms and suffrage, suffragettes argue that the seeming neutrality of the law, misrepresented as the social contract, represents an unstable compromise between two kinds of power: between the insurrectionary forces struggling for a new and more expansive conceptions of freedom and the conservative force of the government aiming to subjugate these forces in order to reproduce the already constituted political order and its imperialist, gendered, and class hierarchies. In other words, it is a struggle between the constituting, inaugural force of the revolutionary act—the capacity to create a new beginning—and the constituted, conserving power of law.[33] According to TBG, "Government authority and the law represent at any given time not the progressive ideals of liberty of which the people are capable, but the amount of liberty the forerunners of the people have been able to wrest from earlier and equally unwilling governments" (TBG, 114–115). TBG refers here to the forgetting of what Hannah Arendt describes as the two sides of every revolutionary event—the act of founding the new beginning and the task of the preservation of this new structure of freedom. On the one hand, there is "exhilarating awareness of the human capacity of beginning . . . the birth of something new on earth;" on the other hand, "the act of founding the new body politic, of devising the new form of government involves the grave concern with the stability and durability of the new structure" (*OR*, 223). In the revolutionary "act of foundation" these two aspects of power "were not mutually exclusive opposites but two sides of the same event, and it was only after the revolutions had come to their end . . . that they parted company" (*OR*, 223). The two sides of praxis are repeatedly disavowed in order to preserve social stability and to prevent the irruption of new revolts in the present. The fetishistic disavowal of the ongoing struggle for a more capacious freedom aims to obliterate the gap between words and acts, between the constituted power of the law and the constituting, inaugural force of revolt.

To prevent this forgetting of the revolutionary spirit, and to legitimate their militant activism, suffragettes not only assert their right of revolt against the despotic government—the right, as Laura Mayhall points out, well established in British political radicalism[34]—but, in more radical ways, justify the necessity of women's ongoing revolutionary struggle by stressing the temporal delay, or disjunction, between revolutionary acts and their belated political institutionalization.[35] In other words, women reclaim the right to militant revolt not only because the despotic government has overstepped the bounds of the social contract but because the law itself is disconnected from its past revolutionary conditions and from the new aspirations of freedom of current and future generations. As TBG argues, current laws are the institutionalized effects of forgotten male struggles for liberty in the past, and therefore their articulation is limited, belated, and insufficient for the political aspirations of the new generation, in particular for women's aspirations of freedom and equality. Because the law articulates and preserves the historical victories of past generations, there is an irreducible temporal lapse between institutionalized rights and new demands for freedom: "Government . . . rests upon and acts in accordance with the limited foundations of liberty which have already been laid. These foundations have been laid by the rebels of the past. The wider foundations of greater liberty must be laid by the rebels of the present" (TBG, 115). The conservative force of preservation of the status quo separated from the principle of a new beginning, the belatedness and nonsynchronicity of the law with new aspirations for freedom, show the necessity of an ongoing struggle to expand the outdated formulations of political rights. It is this temporal belatedness of the law vis-à-vis new demands of liberty that justifies Billington-Greig's seemingly aporetic association of "duty," usually understood as the respect for the law, and "rebellion," usually understood as the contestation of the law. Rather than leading to anarchy, or apolitical violence, suffrage militancy reenacts the democratic duty of revolt in order to reactivate its own revolutionary principles and thus save the law from ossified obsolescence. In so doing, suffrage militancy also protects the future of freedom, which cannot be limited to contemporary political forms created by former male generations.

The final complication that suffragettes introduce, albeit very cautiously, to their justification of revolt refers to the libidinal, sexual aspects of the law and revolt itself. The caution and reticence regarding the politics of sexuality was no doubt partially an effect of hostile stereotypes of suffragettes as uncontrollable hysterics, fanatics, repressed spinsters, or "masculine" women as well as the persisting Victorian legacy of the "sexual purity" arguments used to legitimate women's citizenship. Nonetheless, despite this reticence about sexuality and politics, suffragettes manage, on the one hand, to expose the brutal violence of sovereignty as an obscene, "savage" passion and, on the other hand, to admit the joyous passion of revolt. In the most provocative section, "Man Still a Semi-Savage," of her article "The Woman with the Whip," TBG diagnoses the "savage," "primal passions" of the guardians of the law—passions barely hidden by "an artificial garment of culture" (TBG, 127). And she adds that "party passion is itself a strong unreasoning force" (TBG, 127). Emmeline Pankhurst, by contrast, affirms the joy and "exultation" of the rebellion directed against this irrational force of law: "If there are any men who are fighters in this hall . . . I tell you, gentlemen, that amongst the other goods that you, consciously or unconsciously, have kept from women, you have kept the joy of battle. We know the joy of battle" (SP, 162).

What is the libidinal nature of "the exhilarating awareness" of creative capacities and "the joy of battle and the exultation of victory" that women have been excluded from? And how to explain the libidinal, "savage" irrational force of the law unleashed by the militants? These questions about the libidinal aspects of revolt and political authority reveal the limitations of Arendt's theory and the necessity of its supplementation through feminist interpretations of psychoanalysis. In particular I would like to refer briefly to Carole Pateman's and Julia Kristeva's critical revisions of Freud's theory of the son's revolt against the primal father, the figure of unlimited phallic power and enjoyment, in *Totem and Taboo.* This text famously diagnoses how the libidinal aspects of paternal power and filial revolt—the originary crime of parricide—are transformed into moral law and symbolic authority, which is nonetheless haunted by the specter of the "savage" libidinal passions of its origins.

How should we read Freud's narrative of the origin of the law in sons' revolt against the primal father and suffragettes' justification of female joy in revolt against equally "savage," unbounded violence represented by the patriarchal figure of the "Tzar"? Despite the fact that Freud is writing his story of filial rebellion at the height of the militant phase of the suffrage movement, that is, in the very midst of female rebellion against the "savage," primal passions of the law, Freud, as Kristeva notes, fails to analyze the role of femininity, which could have provided an alternative for or modification of the phallic logic of revolt.[36] As she points out, the social bond formed through the transformation of the patricidal violence into political authority forms a homosocial order, predicated on a double renunciation of femininity, evident not only in the exchange of women but also in the repression of brothers' homosexual erotic desires.

Kristeva not only diagnoses the repressed origin of the law in the unlimited phallic jouissance of the primal father that still haunts sovereign power but also the possibility of the reactivation of the jouissance of the revolt—"the joy of the battle"—whenever a group finds itself excluded from the libidinal/symbolic profits of the social bond under the weight of oppression. In her revision of Freud, Kristeva associates femininity not only with the reactivation of the jouissance of revolt but also with the demystification of the fixity of the law and "a cult of the phallus."[37] The revolutionary potential of femininity in Kristeva's account thus is intertwined less with the reactivation of the oedipal rebellion, which, sustained by phallic jouissance and violence, contests exclusions in order to reconstruct a new figuration of the symbolic paternal authority, but more with an ironic exposure of the persistence of the infantile, phallic illusion in various forms of authority and revolts against this authority. Consequently, as the suffragettes' parodic tactics of citationality and ridicule of liberal politicians suggests, feminine logic is associated both with jouissance and the ironic adherence and nonadherence to any form of authority, with the refusal of the fetishistic fixity of the law.

As my interpretation of suffrage militancy in the context of Arendt's theory of revolution shows, suffrage writings, far from being merely a historical precedent, make a significant theoretical contribution to current feminist discussions of agency, gender, human rights, and power. Despite all the limitations of the suffrage movement, its reinterpretation of the right to vote as the right to revolt reclaims and redefines, in the context of gender politics, an important legacy of the revolutionary tradition, namely, the productive tension between the constituted, institutionalized character of power and its inaugural, constituting force. This split (as well as its libidinal character) is either forgotten or reproduced in contemporary discussions without a clear awareness of its origins in revolutionary praxis. Because of this separation from praxis, the constituted/constituting power appears more frequently as the opposition between historical determination and contingency. As Ernesto Laclau and Chantal Mouffe, Michel Foucault, Giorgio Agamben, Judith Butler, Joan Scott, and other poststructuralist theorists argue, the historical relations of power/knowledge constitute political identities, discourses, and institutions in a contingent and indeterminate manner and therefore do not preclude possibilities of political transformation. Yet the emphasis on the incompleteness and contingency of historical reality is not necessarily and not always linked to agency and freedom. That is why we observe so many misinterpretations of these theorists in terms of either determinism or voluntarism. By contrast, Arendt's theory of revolution and suffrage militancy demonstrate that the split between constituted power and constituting, transformative capacities emerges from praxis itself and reveals, therefore, not only the contingency of political relations but also intersubjective, relational agency and its unpredictable force of radical novelty.

Suffrage Militants and Modernism: Toward a Feminist Theory of Heteronomous Autonomy of Art

I have argued that suffrage militancy's redefinition of the right to vote as the right to revolt makes a significant contribution to feminist political theories of agency, praxis, and freedom. Most important, it redefines the meaning of femininity from the sex object, reproductive body, or the nonhuman being to the political subject, the bearer of political innovation, and the new beginning in the political life. Yet what are the implications of the suffrage militant movement for feminists' theories of aesthetics and modernism? In an answer to this question, feminist historians, cultural critics, and literary scholars of modernism have proposed three different approaches. Aiming to recover marginalized suffrage literature and art, the first, thematically oriented approach analyzes the propaganda function of suffrage literary and visual productions in support of the movement. Influenced by a cultural studies methodology, the second approach examines the role of suffrage and suffrage art in the revision of the broader cultural discourses of modernity and, in so doing, makes a crucial contribution to the "gender of modernity" studies. The third approach focuses more directly on the relation between suffrage activism and modern experimental literature. Yet none of these approaches goes far enough to address the political inventiveness of the suffrage movement, on the one hand, and its impact on the redefinition of feminist aesthetics and the status of women's literary practice in modernity, on the other. The first of these approaches deastheticizes art altogether and subordinates it to instrumental political uses; the second subsumes both art and politics within the larger cultural discourse of gender in modernity; the third investigates analogies between experimental literature and suffrage contestation. The model of the analogy, however, does not account for the redefinitions of the status of the work of art in the light of the inaugural force of the new beginning in history and in art.

The effort of the recovery and analysis of the literary, theatrical, and visual production of suffrage artistic organizations (for instance, the Women Writers' Suffrage League founded in 1908) has produced important collections of primary texts, such as *Voices and Votes: A Literary Anthology of the Women's Suffrage Campaign*, edited by Glenda Norquay. These often propagandistic literary works, for example, Elizabeth Robins's *The Convert*, adapt popular and conventional literary genres of melodrama, autobiography, conversion narrative, or more direct polemical tracts for the instrumental political purposes of persuading the audience, gaining new converts to the cause, and changing social structures.[38] Yet, though Norquay conceives of this anthology as a kind of supplementary literary "documentation" of the suffrage movement, she nonetheless points out that even within the confines of conventional genres the language of suffrage texts is "strikingly unstable," marked by "the struggle to define and redefine terms such as woman, martyrdom, and the vote. Rejecting the "elite" notions of experimental writing, Wendy Mufford similarly privileges the representational and propagandist modes of writing to articulate sex and class oppression.[39] The instrumentalism of this approach is particularly evident in the claim of the priority of the political significance of literary production and literary organizations over the aesthetic value of the work of art.

By contrast, feminist critics, like Jane Marcus, Lisa Tickner, Janet Lyon, and Barbara Green have moved from a historical reconstruction of the suffrage militant movement and its artistic productions to an analysis of the new cultural discourses of femininity, political activism, and its visual iconography. Tickner's groundbreaking study, *The Spectacle of Women: Imagery of the Suffrage Campaign, 1907–1914*, is primarily devoted to the visual iconography and artistry of suffrage activism and its elaborate street theater, such as the Women's Coronation Procession of 1911, the largest of the suffrage marches.[40] Also concerned with the spectacle, Barbara Green's work, *Spectacular Confessions: Autobiography, Performative Activism, and the Sites of Suffrage, 1905–1938*, examines the diverse autobiographical and confessional writings of suffragettes. Green locates the intersection between modernism and suffrage—what she calls modernist feminism—in the new cultural discourses of femininity, spectacularity, advertising culture, and the discipline of females' bodies. Both Tickner and Green recover the importance of suffrage visual and literary productions for feminist revisions of the culture of modernity and its obfuscated gendered mechanisms.

In turn, Jane Marcus and Janet Lyon focus more specifically on the similarities between the suffragettes' contestation of male political discourse and the iconoclastic impulse of artistic avant-garde movements. In the introduction to her pioneering collection, *Suffrage and the Pankhursts*, Jane Marcus emphasizes the parallels between suffragettes' interruptions of male political discourse and the textual interruptions practiced by experimental women writers. Interruption becomes for Marcus a key rhetorical strategy of obtaining a voice and assuming the position of the speaking subject in the political and aesthetic arenas.[41] She finds a similar formal practice in Virginia Woolf's *A Room of One's Own*: "Constructed brilliantly around the literary tropes of interruption and absence, *A Room of One's Own* eloquently enacts the history of struggle."[42] While Marcus tends to deemphasize militancy, stressing instead the violence suffered by women, Janet Lyon examines the revolutionary rhetoric produced by suffrage and English avant-garde movements. Rejecting the thesis of a simple appropriation of the suffrage revolutionary energy by male experimental writers, she demonstrates instead many semantic links between suffrage and vorticism, both of which share an iconoclastic anti-bourgeois stance and the rhetoric of defamiliarization.

Yet, what is at stake in the discourse of revolt in suffrage militancy and modern aesthetics is more than shared rhetorical strategies; more fundamentally, the convergence and divergence between the struggle for freedom in the political and aesthetic praxis enables us to redefine the status of the work of art in Western modernity. As we have seen, suffrage militancy links women's revolution both with negative freedom—that is, with the destruction of oppressive gender structures—and with "positive" freedom—that is, with the creation of new gender relations and forms of life. The juxtaposition of suffrage militancy and experimental literature by women writers allows us, first of all, to rethink the pervasive modernist preoccupation with the new and the "subversive" beyond mere formal experimentation for innovation's sake and address it instead in the context of the struggle for freedom. Second, formal invention in experimental women's literature radicalizes the function of freedom in politics by connecting freedom with the unforeseeable, inaugural force of the new beginning, which exceeds determined goals of liberation. In so doing, women's experimental writing enables us to distinguish transformative freedom—the creation of the new and unforeseeable beginning—from the instrumentalism of politics. And, finally, the common question of freedom interrogates the autonomy of both literature and gender politics, exposes each of these activities to its other without abolishing important differences between them. Consequently, my approach to feminist aesthetics not only refocuses on the artistic production of modern women artists—in this study on Woolf's and Larsen's texts—but also revises the very concept of the autonomy of art in the context of women's political struggles for freedom.

To analyze the struggle for freedom in suffrage militant and modernist texts, I would like to recall and revise Theodor Adorno's theory of the heteronomous autonomy of modern literature.[43] Through this paradoxical concept, Adorno addresses both the irreducible specificity of art—that is, its autonomy—and its historical relation to the political—that is, art's heteronomy. According to Adorno, the autonomy of modern art is heteronomous because art both depends on and is independent from oppressive social conditions. As "a productive force" "that originates in real history and is then separated from it," art is both autonomous and a product of the unjust division of labor; it both reproduces and contests capitalist relations of production (*AT*, 228, 226). Heteronomous autonomy thus underscores the contradictory status of art in modernity: as both a commodified object and "the plenipotentiary of what is free from domination," (*AT*, 227) modern literature is situated *between* political domination and the aesthetic promise of freedom. As I have argued in the introduction, the heteronomous autonomy of literature is a crucial term for my theory of feminist aesthetics because this approach avoids the instrumental subordination of art to gender identity politics or the collapse of artistic innovation into formalism.

Although essential for a nonreductive approach to the art/politics divide, Adorno's theory of artistic practice's heteronomous autonomy has nonetheless to be revised in the context of feminism for two reasons: first, and more obviously, because Adorno's notion of the political is too narrow—it focuses on labor but ignores gender and race as categories of political and aesthetic analyses. Second, and more fundamentally, because he primarily stresses art's contradictory relation to economic domination—its subversion and complicity with the structures of power—he does not address numerous political struggles for freedom by subjugated groups. Yet, once we take into account an emergence of new political and cultural movements, such as suffrage, labor unrest, decolonization movements, or the "black radicalism" of the Harlem Renaissance, all of which called for the liberation and political participation of women, African Americans, and colonized peoples, we are compelled to criticize the Frankfurt school's thesis that administrated society is totally dominated by commodity exchange and instrumental rationality. Developed in *An Ethics of Dissensus*, my concept of the political is necessarily broader than Adorno's because it stresses the emergence of new antagonisms and new political struggles against multiple forms of domination of marginalized groups.[44] Consequently, I argue that the importance of the suffrage campaign for feminist aesthetics is that women's contradictory artistic production in modernism cannot be considered only as a utopian semblance of revolutionary practice, which is as yet impossible in reality, but also has to be analyzed in relation to existing political movements.

By contrast, Adorno's famous thesis that the freedom of the Enlightenment reverses into its opposite, namely, the barbarism of domination, suggests that the promise of freedom is associated primarily with the aesthetic side of the art/politics divide. Thus, if the heteronomy of modernist literature reveals its complicity with domination, the autonomy of art, its separation from oppressive political and economic structures, is intertwined with the promise of freedom. From the first page of *Aesthetic Theory* Adorno reminds us that aesthetic autonomy is not a manifestation of indifference to the political but, on the contrary, a historic achievement of freedom understood, first of all, as the independence of art from religious values: "For absolute freedom in art, always limited to a particular, comes into contradiction with the perennial unfreedom of the whole. . . . The autonomy it achieved, after having freed itself from cultic function and its images, was nourished by the idea of humanity" (*AT*, 1). Yet this principle of freedom in modern art arrives at a crisis in modernism not only because art's autonomy depends on the unjust division of labor but also because the aesthetic principle of freedom "comes into contradiction with the perennial unfreedom" of capitalist society as a whole.

Because of this contradiction between art and political domination, for Adorno aesthetic freedom is primarily negative: it manifests itself first of all as the opposition to, separation from, or "revolt" against injustice. Modern art can maintain its contradictory relation to freedom only by negating capitalist structures of production on the level of aesthetic form. Second, art negates its own utopian promise of freedom as soon as this promise degenerates into an ideological consolation. Arts' opposition to the "barbarism" of modernity thus turns into an internal negation of art's promise of a better practice once this promise gains an affirmative essence: "The revolt of art, teleologically posited in its 'attitude to objectivity' toward the historical world, has become a revolt against art" (*AT*, 3). Even in its relation to aesthetic novelty, the freedom of the work of art is "destructive" (*AT*, 20) and is a privative rather than positive manifestation of a new beginning. "Historically inevitable," the concept of the new in modernism is "privative; since its origins it is more the negation of what no longer holds than a positive slogan" (*AT*, 21).

Both Adorno and Arendt stress the historical authority of the new and its relation to aesthetics, yet they derive aesthetic novelty from different, contradictory traditions of modernity: revolution and commodity production. As we have seen, for Arendt political novelty in the public realm arises from the fundamental interrelation between the revolutionary struggle for freedom, language, and the emergence of the unprecedented event in history. However, her consistent but unexamined deployment of literary terminology—such as the invention of a "new story"—already implies a close relation between politics and aesthetics. By remarking this relation more explicitly in the context of suffrage militancy, we could say that one of the fundamental intersections between feminist aesthetics and gender politics in modernity focuses on the revolutionary discourse of the new. Indeed, the connection between the creation of the new and freedom is also pivotal to theories of modern aesthetics—the "new" and the "subversive" belong to the most familiar slogans of modernism. In twentieth-century Europe the only other discourse that could rival the revolutionary rhetoric of the new was modernist art associated with Ezra Pound's famous dictum, "Make it new." As Marinetti puts it in his "Manifesto of Futurism" (1909): "Courage, audacity, and revolt will be essential elements of our poetry. . . . We will sing of great crowds . . . we will sing of the multicolored, polyphonic tides of revolution in the modern capitals."[45] The fact that modern artists and literary critics of modernism could so easily link aesthetic novelty with the discourse of "revolution" suggests an unacknowledged, and perhaps even unnoticed, debt of the modern avant-garde, in particular, futurism and vorticism, to the revolutionary tradition revived in twentieth century by new liberation movements such as the October Revolution and decolonization movements. Even less frequently, the modernist discourse of the new is examined in the context of the suffragettes' militant struggle for the vote. And yet the intertwined rhetoric of the new and revolt in suffrage agitation is a crucial starting point for thinking through the possibilities of freedom in women's aesthetic and political praxis. Without this intersection between political and aesthetic freedom, it is all too easy to dismiss the rhetoric of the new as a symptom of either the aestheticization of politics or the commodification of art, both of which, in Adorno's words, "[bind] the new to the ever same" (AT, 22).

By contrast, Adorno derives the predominance of the new from the expansion of capital and increasing commodification rather than from the revolutionary tradition: "Since the mid-nineteenth century and the rise of high capitalism, the category of the new has been central, though admittedly in conjunction with the question whether anything new have ever existed" (AT, 19). It is because of art's contestation of the character of commodity that the aesthetic concept of the new in modernism, according to Adorno, is in the first instance negative and destructive: "consumer goods [are] appropriated by art by means of which artworks distinguish themselves from the ever-same inventory . . . of capital" (AT, 22). Through privation, negativity, and "irritating" indeterminacy about its purpose and meaning, the work of art reappropriates and transforms the ever same "novelty" of consumption into an enigma of inassimilable otherness. Despite its uncanny similarity to commodity fetishism, aesthetic novelty maintains its promise of freedom by provoking shudder (*AT*, 20) rather than consumer satisfaction. Thus, unlike Arendt's politics of natality—the birth of the new world through praxis—for Adorno, the violence of aesthetic novelty, in its break from the past, resembles the "ominous aspect" of death. Ultimately, the violence of the new is reflective of "the negative self-reflection of identification with the real negativity of the social situation" (*AT*, 21). The novelty of the work of art also contests subjective originality and imagination, since it arises from the demands of the art object, the experimental process of making, and the social relations embedded in the artistic materials: "The violence of the new, for which the name 'experimental' was adopted, is not to be attributed to subjective convictions or the psychological character of the artist. When impulse can no longer find pre-established security in forms or content, productive artists are objectively compelled to experiment" (*AT*, 23).

Nonetheless, if we read Adorno against the grain of his main argument as well as against the dominant interpretations of his work,[46] we are also able to detect the inaugural force of transformation in the violence of the new. This is especially the case since Adorno stresses the dynamic "processual" aspect of the artwork, which creates its own "force field" (*AT*, 178–179). The interconnection between freedom and aesthetic novelty not only negates capitalist structures of domination and explodes the "gapless continuum of tranquil development" (*AT*, 19) of history but also offers a utopian promise of a better praxis that is as yet impossible in reality. Thus, the inaugural force of the new enacted in the work of art exceeds the determinate negation of historical reality and the gendered, imperialist structures of power imbedded in it. Such a constituting force points beyond the "real negativity of the social situation" toward a new beginning. To be sure, the aesthetic presentation of such inaugural force is indeterminate because, in its radical alterity and nonidentity, the new resists symbolization, aesthetic judgment, and communicability: The modern experimental artwork "is unable to speak what has yet to be, and yet must seek it" (*AT*, 22). The new cannot be determined even through the negation of existing power relations; on the contrary, its constituting force and utopian promise manifest themselves in the cryptic and enigmatic character of experimental art.

The aesthetic configuration of novelty and freedom is defined by Adorno as a utopian promise of a better praxis: "Art is not only the plenipotentiary of a better praxis than that which has to date predominated, but is equally the critique of praxis as the rule of brutal self-preservation at the heart of the status quo and in its service. . . . [It] opts for a form of praxis beyond the spell of labor" (*AT*, 12). Despite its implication in economic and political domination, the negative autonomy of literature, achieved through separation from the social, initiates a new beginning. It offers, in Adorno's terms, "the schema of social praxis: Every authentic artwork is internally revolutionary" (*AT*, 228). This "revolutionary" aspect of the artwork does not provide guidelines for political action but manifests itself "immanently" within the structure of the work of art. Respecting the autonomous aspect of art, an "immanent" interpretation of the work of art means that "social concepts should not be applied to the works from without but rather drawn from an exacting examination of the works themselves" (*NT*, 39). Such an immanent or aesthetic manifestation of revolution is reflected, on the one hand, in the experimental form of the work of art and, on the other hand, in the critique of aesthetic categories such as genius, beauty, aesthetic autonomy, or the death of art. Yet, in the context of the suffrage movement, we also have to investigate the heteronomous aspect of this "internally revolutionary" artistic praxis, namely, its relation to women's political contestation of power.

If a feminist approach to Adorno's aesthetic theory allows us to underscore the import of suffrage for the studies of modernism in a new way, feminist interpretations of suffrage also make a critical intervention in Adorno studies. As we can see, Adorno's defense and redefinition of the autonomy of modern literature, based on art's internal negation of political domination and its own complicity with oppressive power, in the last resort exceeds the negative. Nonetheless, Adorno's redefinition of the autonomy of modern literature in the context of freedom fails to address the relation between "internally revolutionary" aesthetic praxis and political struggles for freedom. Because Adorno focuses primarily on the economic character of exploitation and on rational instrumentality, he does not investigate the question as to whether "the plenipotentiary of the better praxis" reenacted in art could be intertwined with the inaugural force of positive freedom—what Arendt calls the freedom of the new beginning—in revolutionary political praxis. Yet, as the political implications of suffrage militancy suggest, it is not only art that is a "plenipotentiary" of a better practice as yet impossible in reality but also women's political revolt, similarly based on the contradiction between the inauguration of a new beginning in history and the reproduction of old patterns of domination, in particular, class and colonial domination. As the revolutionary struggle for a more expansive notion of freedom by militant

suffragettes, "black radicals" of the Harlem Renaissance, or decolonization movements suggests, the heteronomous aspect of literary practice
has to be considered not only in terms of art's capacity to negate gendered, racist structures of domination but also in relation to the transformative force—as well as the grammar and syntax—of political praxis.
That means that the heteronomous autonomy of modern literature has to
be thought beyond the negative, even though the critical function of negation, just as the negative stage of the contestation of domination, is in-
dispensable for any transformative practice. What feminist aesthetics has
to address, therefore, is how aesthetic novelty and the promise of a better
praxis in women's writings is intertwined with the inaugural force of
freedom in the political.

Through the juxtaposition of suffrage militancy and Adorno's aesthetic theory, I propose to redefine the heteronomous aspect of aesthetic
autonomy, that is, art's relation to the political, in two new ways. First of
all, the transformative capacity of art and literature, their ability to contest gender domination, imperialism, and the gendered division of labor
on the level of form, is intertwined with the transformative modality of
women's political praxis. Conversely, art's relation to the political reveals
the destructive impact of gender domination on the very possibility of
women's art. Art might be internally revolutionary, but gender oppression can prevent it from coming into being at all. The main dilemma that
Woolf and Larsen, the two women writers discussed in this study, confront is how to transform a persisting legacy of the destruction of wom-
en's art into its revolutionary possibility. For Woolf, this transformation
of the paralyzing effects of gender domination into the possibility of
women's literature is intertwined with women's collective political struggles. For Larsen, it entails the communal transformation of the entire
register of "cursed" racist and sexist language, a transformation supported by, as Alain Locke famously puts it, "a unique social experiment"
of the New Negro.[47] The heteronomous autonomy of art presents, therefore, a far more complex relation between women's art and gender, racial
politics: the destructive effects of domination and the revolutionary possibilities characterize both the domain of literary and political praxis.
Consequently, the feminist theory of modernist aesthetics I elaborate in
this study not only refocuses on the artistic production of modern women
writers but also revises the status of the work of art—its heteronomous
autonomy—in the double context of persisting domination and women's
political struggles for a more expansive notion of freedom. Thus the main

question I address is how aesthetic novelty and the promise of a better praxis in women's writings can emerge from the destruction of women's art and lives and the ways in which this emergence is intertwined with the inaugural, intersubjective force of freedom in the political.

Adorno is right to argue that "freedom in art, always limited to a particular, comes into contradiction with the perennial unfreedom of the whole" (AT, 1). Yet the same argument can be advanced with respect to gender and race politics—here too freedom is limited to particular movements and particular events, and they come into contradiction with persisting unfreedom. We have seen this contradiction between the struggle for women's freedom and the persistence of class and race inequalities among women within the suffrage movement itself. Consequently, the conflict between freedom and domination not only characterizes the relation between art and politics but also manifests itself within political and artistic practices. As we shall see, this conflict produces and reproduces a split in the studies of modernism between "subversive" and revolutionary aesthetics, on the one hand, and its diametrical opposite—the politics of melancholia and the aesthetics of mourning, on the other hand.

The feminist theory of aesthetics I propose refuses this uncritical either/or binary and thinks through the political and aesthetic implications of the unresolved historical contradiction between freedom and domination. In the context of women's struggle for political and economic freedom, this contradiction exposes the inaugural possibility of a new beginning despite persisting racism, imperialism, and gender domination. One implication of my approach is the reinterpretation of the formal disruptions of aesthetic harmony, so frequently stressed by Adorno as "an immanent" expression of suppressed social antagonisms, as the aesthetic manifestation of the unresolved contradiction between particular struggles for freedom and diverse forms of domination. And, conversely, in the context of the gendered, racialized history of modern literature, the contradiction between freedom and domination threatens art's promise of a better praxis with the destruction of the very possibility of women's writing by class, gender, and racist domination. In other words, the "disaster" not only afflicts political life but destroys the possibilities of art itself. The Hegelian thesis of the death of art, which proclaims the loss of art's social relevance in Western modernity, is therefore not merely the threatening end of art, but the impossible beginning of women's writing. The main question Woolf and Larsen pose for the history and theory of Western aesthetics is how the possibility of women's art can emerge from the site of its destruction and this destruction's persisting legacy. Consequently, the heteronomous autonomy of women's artistic practice means not only that art negates structures of domination, not only that it finds aesthetic means to express invisible social contradictions, including labor, gender, and race contradictions, and to offer alternative models of liberating political praxis. The decisive aspect of heteronomous autonomy, ignored by Adorno, is that the inaugural force of women's political revolt might enable the transformation of the historical impossibility of women's writing into its future possibility.

2 Melancholia, Death of Art, and Women's Writing

Like its uncanny double, melancholia follows closely in the footsteps of the "revolutionary" side of modernism. Not surprisingly, many influential critics of modernism, like Gregg Horowitz, examine not "the affirmative achievements of aesthetic theory" but rather its mournful encounters with the past.[1] Such an analysis is necessary because the oscillation between revolution and melancholia reveals the contradiction between multiple forms of domination coexisting with particular struggles for freedom. In the context of politics, melancholia reveals an impasse of the revolutionary struggle, a destruction of the very grammar and syntax of practice. In the context of aesthetics, melancholia responds to a crisis of literary practice: it either laments the loss of art's political significance or, on the contrary, revives its importance by ascribing to art the task of mourning.

Like "revolt," melancholia is a hybrid concept, frequently used in both aesthetic and political theories of modernity, although it does not belong to the classical lexicon of either of these "disciplines." This hybridity manifests not only the interrelation between the political and the aesthetic but also marks the struggle between universality and particularity within both of these domains. Within aesthetics it is a tension between general concepts in aesthetic theory, like modern literature, and the excluded particular works—for instance, the experimental novels by women of color—that do not figure in the elaboration of Western aesthetic theory. Consequently, it is not just the unavoidable tension between aesthetic concepts and the specificity of literary texts but the struggle between excluded women's writings and the hegemonic conception of modernism based on such exclusion. Within politics it is a struggle between multiple gendered and racialized forms of political emancipatory movements—such as British militant suffrage and the Harlem Renaissance—and the construction of the universal agent of liberation, which excludes these movements. Since the melancholic paralysis blurs the conventional boundaries between political and aesthetic praxis, it undermines most accounts of the relationship between politics and art, from aestheticism to the sociology of art.

To address women's literary practice in the context of melancholic crisis, I begin with the question Balibar addressed to Marxist theory: What if history "not only advances by its 'bad side,' but also *to the bad side*, the side of domination and ruin" and in so doing shows an impasse of dialectic?[2] Balibar's concern with the catastrophic impasses of the dialectic resonates with Arendt's claim that revolution reverts to a melancholic spectacle of Saturn devouring its own children once the multiple struggles for liberation are misinterpreted as the unifying law of history. By engaging Freud's theory of melancholia, I will offer a psychoanalytical genealogy of such a sadistic "law" of history, devouring its own children. Articulated at the moment of late modernism, the Freudian "modernist" theory of melancholia might be read as the dangerous incorporation of the sadistic historical law as the cruel superego and, eventually, as the unconscious substitution of political antagonisms by the internal self-destructive struggle of its victims. By turning from a psychoanalytic genealogy to women's literary practice, I will examine the writing of melancholia in Nella Larsen's and Virginia Woolf's fiction in the context of Adorno's and Kristeva's theories. Far from focusing merely on the subjective expression of female suffering, such an inquiry involves first of all a rethinking of the status of literary practice, femininity, and race in modernity.

Melancholia, the End of Art, and the Limits of Political Aesthetics

As a paralyzing encounter with loss and finitude, in the long history of its cultural and philosophical elaborations, melancholia has produced contradictory approaches. As Juliana Schiesari argues in a feminist classic, *The Gendering of Melancholia*, in the Western cultural tradition melancholia is associated not only with a mental disorder but also with the exceptional, if paradoxical, status of genius and creativity. From Renaissance to modernism, melancholia "came to be perceived as . . . a special, albeit difficult gift," indicating artistic or spiritual grandeur.[3] This tradition of melancholic greatness is neither sexually nor racially neutral. According to Schiesari, the grandeur of male melancholic philosophers and artists contrasts sharply with women's cultural expressions of loss and sorrow, which, associated with the ritual work of mourning, "is not given the same . . . representational *value* as those of men within the Western canon of literature, philosophy, and psychoanalysis."[4] A similar argument has been made by Ranjana Khanna concerning the racial and colonial difference: colonial psychiatrists like J. C. Carothers, who stressed a heightened sense of moral responsibility and introspection among melancholiacs, could argue as late as the fifties and sixties that Africans and Algerian Muslims were "constitutionally violent" and thus "less prone to introspective melancholia . . . than the Europeans."[5]

Yet, this gendered and racialized tradition of melancholic grandeur also undergoes a crucial reversal in modernity: Rather than an enabling condition, melancholia also becomes a symptom of the paralysis of aesthetic and social praxis. In the context of politics, numerous cultural and political critics, for instance, Paul Gilroy, Judith Butler, Ranjana Khanna, and Anne Anlin Cheng treat melancholia as a destructive effect of heteronormativity, racism, and power. In the context of aesthetics, the melancholic crisis of artistic practice, I would like to propose, is intertwined with the Hegelian legacy of the "end" of art. Hegel himself has recognized that the so-called end of art in modernity might provoke a melancholic lament over the loss of art's seriousness.[6]

In this section I will focus on the melancholic crisis of artistic praxis the death of art represents in Western philosophical aesthetics and on the responses to this crisis in Marx and Adorno. For a feminist critique of aesthetics, it is important to revisit the "end of art" thesis, because it founds the very distinction between aesthetic autonomy and the politics of art, a dualism feminism seems to reproduce. Needless to say, the famous Hegelian notion of the death of art and the long history of critical engagements with this thesis do not announce the end of artistic production in modernity but rather point to the eclipse of the social function of Western art, which, for this reason, is no longer an essential source of collective self-understanding and thus "no longer satisfies our supreme need."[7] Because of the loss of the social significance of art in the culture of modernity, the formal beauty of art offers merely aesthetic enjoyment. And if art still carries social meanings, they are, according to Hegel, no longer in harmony with the sensuality of its form and thus their complexity can be more adequately expressed by the conceptual language of philosophy. Thus, as Hegel famously claims, art, as the source of collective self-understanding, is a thing of the past: "In all these respects art, considered in its highest vocation, is and remains for us a thing of the past" (A, 11). In her analysis of the end of art, Eva Geulen points to the ambivalent and contradictory meanings of the Hegelian insight: The end of art vacillates between the fulfillment of art and the loss of its meaning; between something that has already happened and is still to come; between revolutionary triumph and melancholic lament.[8]

Yet the endless repetitions of the death of art are not gender neutral. They fail to take into account what is excluded from the hegemony of Western art, namely, the ghostly clamor of racialized and feminized subjectivities. As we shall see in our analysis of Virginia Woolf and Nella Larsen, the history of art is haunted by lost possibilities, which have never been "a thing of the past." Thus, one of the feminist interventions in the discourse of the end of art is the analysis of the destruction of aesthetic possibilities prior to art's death, of the unknown and unremarked deaths that constituted the hegemony of Western art. Although feminist interventions into aesthetics are sometimes all too quickly associated with antiaestheticism or discredited as another instance of the sociology of art, they show that binary opposition between the aesthetic autonomy and the politics of art fails to take into account the racialized and gendered destruction of art's possibilities.

The shift from the philosophical overcoming of art to the political aesthetics is no doubt a logical conclusion of Marx's attempt to transform philosophy itself into an element of social praxis. In the celebrated last thesis of his *Theses on Feuerbach*, Marx proclaims the necessity of overcoming philosophy by transformative practice: "The philosophers have only *interpreted* the world, in various ways; the point, however, is to *change* it."[9] The strongest opposition to the political aesthetics within Marxist theory comes from Theodor Adorno, who not only defends the heteronomous autonomy of modernist art against critiques from both the right and the left, but also contests the very dualism between aestheticism and antiaestheticism. In chapter 1 I have already advanced a feminist critique of the subordination of experimental art to the aims of women's revolutionary praxis in the context of suffrage militancy. However, Adorno's critique of the direct politicization of art takes into account the opposite historical conditions, namely, domination. In this context, the negative autonomy of art assumes the full ethical import of the contestation of historical injustice—it wants to "destroy the destroyer"[10]—and conveys, on the level of aesthetic form, that the world "should be otherwise" (C, 194). Adorno's critique of political art contests in particular capitalist economy and commodity exchange. To subordinate art to the instrumental needs of politics when practice in capitalism is determined in large measure by the instrumentality of the market would not only reinforce the death of art but also obscure the "death" of praxis in commodity culture: the integration of art into "a profit driven industry . . . by its smooth functioning obscures the fact that it [practice] is already dead" (AT, 18).

Ultimately what contests the Hegelian death of art is the persistence of domination. Historical catastrophes and the disavowed suffering of victims transform the death of art into a "radically darkened art," which, despite all its ambiguities, "protest[s] against [Hegel's] . . . verdict on art" (AT, 19). Even though Adorno's aesthetics begins with the Hegelian end of art, "it is self-evident that nothing concerning art is self-evident anymore, not its inner life, not its relation to the world, not even its right to exist" (AT, 1), his own diagnosis of the contradictions of modern art and literature is different from Hegel's. Hegel's proclamation that art is a thing of the past is based on the quasi-theological assumption of a freedom realized in the state and on the privilege of self- reflective rational culture. By contrast, Adorno's defense of art's heteronomous autonomy underscores the loss of freedom produced by imperialism, fascism, anti-Semitism, white supremacy, and recurring genocide. Second, Adorno shows that the Hegelian privilege of philosophical knowledge is incompatible with the testimony to suffering. Thus, contra Hegel's claim that the reflective culture of modernity demands a merely conceptual interpretation of art, Adorno argues that the importance of modern art lies in its preservation of freedom and in its fidelity to suffering, which remains foreign to knowledge.

If Adorno's hypothesis is correct, then the impatient calls for the politicization of art might be treated as the melancholic denials of the persisting suffering, gender and racial domination, and commodification in modernity. Yet, although Adorno's critique of political art responds to the historical conditions of the Second World War and high capitalism, he is suspicious of a direct political message under any circumstances. This is the case because "aesthetic reduction for the sake of political truths" (C, 183) fails to take into account the role of form in artistic production, namely, the transformation of nonaesthetic material and meaning into the struc-ture of the work of art. Despite the limitations of Adorno's aesthetics, his critique of a direct politicization of art is relevant for feminist theories of aesthetics, and it is a welcome intervention in studies of gender in mod-ernism precisely because it contests the binarism between historicism and aesthetic formalism.

Does Adorno's work represent therefore a kind of Marxist reversal of Marx back to Hegel? Not exactly; Adorno's defense of the heteronomous autonomy of art, his suspicion of the unmediated politicization of art, is in fact based on Marx's own distinction, often forgotten or rejected by his followers, between transformative praxis and its degradation into com-modity production. What is important in this distinction is that the dif-ference between liberating and alienating practice is articulated through aesthetics. Thus, if the end of art marks the antiaesthetic moment within the tradition of aesthetics, the appeal to aesthetic sensibility, and espe-cially to the sensibility of suffering, preserves the necessity of aesthetics within supposedly antiaesthetic Marxist politics. Most clearly elaborated in Marx's early, so-called humanist texts, especially *Economic and Philo-sophic Manuscripts of 1844*, practice in a liberated society would not be limited to production in a narrow sense but would encompass the entire process of self-constitution, transformation, and creation of freedom in community: "The *rich* human being is simultaneously the human being *in need of* a totality of human life-activities—the man in whom his own realization exists as an inner necessity, as *need*" (*MER*, 91). By transform-ing physical needs into "human" needs for freedom and self-realization, liberating praxis intensifies the richness of being in the active sense of "coming-to-be" and reconciles the subject and the object. Exceeding the production of goods, praxis not only cultivates sensible subjectivity but in fact transforms sensibility: it "produces man in this entire richness of his being—produces the *rich* man *profoundly endowed with all the senses*" (*MER*, 89).

What is significant for aesthetic theory is that for Marx the liberation and cultivation of the sensible character of practice manifests itself, according to the etymological meaning of aesthetics as a science of feeling and sensation, through aesthetic sensibility. This is in sharp contrast to Hegel's claim that the sensible aspect of art comes into conflict with the abstract reflective culture of modernity and therefore has to be overcome by philosophical reflection. For Marx, however, aesthetics is untimely: on the one hand, aesthetic sensibility is produced through practice, on the other hand, such sensibility preexists practice as the standard according to which we can distinguish between social and nonsocial sensibility, between freedom and historical necessity: "just as the most beautiful music has *no* sense for the unmusical ear . . . the *senses* of the social man are *other* senses than those of the non-social man. Only through the objectively unfolded richness of man's essential being is the richness of subjective *human* sensibility (a musical ear, an eye for beauty of form . . .) either cultivated or brought into being" (*MER*, 88–89). Emancipated through practice, human senses are transformed into social, that is, aesthetic, sensibility—into musical ears, into eyes capable of perceiving beauty. Conversely, practice can enrich the human sensorium only when it transcends the standard of needs and already produces "things in accordance with the laws of beauty" (*MER*, 76). As these references to creation, aesthetic sensibility, and especially to the process of "coming into being" suggest, liberating practice for Marx is not limited to the paradigm of production, or historical necessity, as Arendt, Agamben, and Gadamer in different ways claim, but in fact encompasses all three aspects of practice distinguished by Aristotle: work, action, and *poesis* (understood in the Greek sense of the word of bringing something new into being). So, in one sense, the full richness of aesthetics is still to come. Yet, in another sense, a certain autonomy of aesthetics, not completely dominated by the market, is always already presupposed in order to set up "beauty" as an alternative standard of human activity. As we shall see, the main limitation of Marx is that the poetic aspect of praxis is still limited to the freedom of the masculine subject and thus can be interpreted as the process of male self-realization rather than as a disclosure of otherness.

One of the devastating effects of capitalism is that commodity production suppresses action and poesis and limits praxis to degraded work and dispossession. As if in anticipation of Adorno's critique of the Enlightenment, Marx claims that the capitalist mode of production reduces freedom to the instrumental means of maintaining "physical existence": "In degrading spontaneous activity, free activity, to a means, estranged labour makes man's species life a means to his physical existance" (*MER*, 77).

As the dominant form of praxis, estranged labor deprives productive life of freedom and desire and reduces it to the activity of self-preservation. In so doing, capitalist production turns the liberating practice into its opposite—into a production of privation, poverty, self-sacrifice, and overwhelming loss concealed by political economy (*MER*, 73). The scale of such loss is truly monumental: it encompasses not only the worker's alienation from his product and productive capacity, but, more fundamentally, a loss of being, community, and love. "The greater this activity, the greater is the worker's lack of objects . . . the greater this product, the less is he himself" (*MER*, 72). The final "product" of capitalist labor is, therefore, not only exploitation, commodity, and the structure of misrecognition intertwined with it, but privation, destruction of culture, and "the denial of life" itself (*MER*, 95), culminating in "a sacrificed and empty being" (*MER*, 101). Paradoxically, what Marx calls the "absolute poverty" of being (*MER*, 87) is intertwined with the greedy "sense of *having*"—that is, with the reduction of the human sensorium to rapacious possessiveness. As Marx puts it, "The less you eat, drink, and read books; the less you go to the theater . . . the less you think, love, theorize, sing, paint, fence, etc. . . . The less you *are*, the more you *have*; the less you express your own life . . . the greater is the store of your estranged being" (*MER*, 95–96). The obverse side of the accumulation of capital is the growing impoverishment of sensibility, thought, desire, and, finally, of being itself. In the context of Marx's critique of capitalist production, it becomes clear that the reintegration of art into political economy would not overcome the death of art. In addition to the reenactment of the Hegelian end of art, the project of political deaestheticization would impoverish the idea of praxis itself and, in the last resort, augment the melancholic denial of the increasing poverty of being to which art bears witness.

From the Poverty of Being to Prostitution and Social Death

For Marx as for Adorno, the universal figure of the absolute poverty of being and the loss of freedom is the worker. Because the worker's deprivation encompasses all other losses, it has the status of the universal experience of dispossession. That is why the proletariat, through the dialectical overcoming of capital, can become the agent of universal liberation: "The emancipation of the workers contains universal human emancipation—and it contains this, because the whole of human servitude is involved in the relation of the worker to production" (*MER*, 80). In Balibar's words, the proletariat can overturn the "negative universality" of dispossession into a positive universality of freedom for all (*PM*, 37–40). Yet, Marx cannot express the universality of human privation and suffering without analogies to other forms of dispossession, in particular to slavery and prostitution. Even though slavery and prostitution might appear as more drastic forms of human degradation, they are nonetheless always treated as merely particular cases of injustice that fail to encompass the whole of human subjugation and thus serve merely special interests. Female prostitution, for instance, is merely "a *specific* expression of the *general* prostitution of the *labourer*" (*MER*, 82). Nonetheless, such rhetorical supplements contaminate the universality of workers' oppression and their agency of liberation. Once inscribed in the chain of analogies, the negative universality of human suffering hegemonized by the proletariat becomes merely one part in the sequence of diverse forms of domination.

What is at stake in Marx's appropriation of slavery and prostitution is not only a crucial historical instance of the entanglement of the competing claims to the universality of class, race, and gender, the legacy of which still troubles feminist political theories today, but also a symptom of a melancholic incorporation of the suffering of the other. We have seen another instance of such melancholic incorporation in suffragettes' appropriation of slavery and "Oriental" women. A similar mechanism of the melancholic incorporation of the suffering of others characterizes the proletariat's negative universality of dispossession and the manic reversal of suffering into the positive universality of liberation. However, if the identification with slavery (*MER*, 73, 78–79, 100) appropriates and subordinates racial difference to class difference, the feminization of the worker's subjection is much more ambivalent. Fluctuating between the commodification of all human beings and the particular sexual commodity, prostitution marks both the analogy and irreducible difference between class (universal subjectivity) and gender (the particular object). For instance, Marx suggests that in the transitional period of "crude" communism, the prostitution of the worker and the prostitution of women will undergo different transformations: in that stage, a woman, no longer the private property of her father and her husband, will become the "*communal* and *common* property" of all men (*MER*, 82). Conversely, men will act as the universal capitalist, possessing all women in common. Only when the feminization of the worker is overcome through this violent fantasy of the collective rape of all women and gender hierarchy is reestablished, the figure of the *"woman* as the spoil and handmaid of communal lust" can once again be used as the analogy of "the *infinite* degradation in which man exists for himself" (*MER,* 83). Through the series of analogies and melancholic appropriations of the oppression of others, Marx reserves the universality of suffering for the working class, and the particularity of oppression for slavery, race, prostitution, and femininity, which, because of this particularity, are excluded from the agency of universal emancipation.

Needless to say, the universality of the proletariat as the bearer of the whole of human suffering and liberation has been contested by numerous feminist, postcolonial, and race theorists. We have seen such a contestation and controversial appropriation of the universality of the worker's revolutionary struggle by mostly middle-class British militant suffragettes. In his polemics with Sartre's revision of the Marxist dialectic, Frantz Fanon famously displaces universal revolutionary agency from the Eurocentric notion of the proletariat to the African decolonization movements. Likewise, Orlando Patterson critiques Marx's appropriation of racialized slavery to signify labor as the universal human bondage. In his *Slavery as Social Death,* Patterson argues that the widespread explanations of slavery in terms of production, compulsory labor, private property, commodity, and disposable capital, though correct in a narrow sense, fail to account for the most devastating social and political consequences of slavery, namely, for the social death it inflicts on enslaved peoples.[11] For Patterson, the term *social death* exceeds the Marxist notions of alienated labor since, in addition to economic exploitation and the loss of freedom, it expresses the most extreme delegitimation and destruction of social life. The association of slavery with social death already stems from the precapitalist origins of slavery, where it was instituted as a substitute for the death inflicted by war, execution, or starvation. Such an expropriation of a slave's life constituted him or her as a nonperson or a socially dead person. Akin to "secular excommunication," slavery in all its different historical formations from antiquity to modernity functioned as an extreme destruction of the social and symbolic constitution of human subjectivity, aiming to destroy not only human freedom but also the claims of genealogy, cultural memory, social worth, and language. As a mark of illegitimacy and exclusion from the realm of symbolization and social life, this extreme mode of deracination reconstituted an enslaved person as a nameless, invisible nonbeing. Thus, although both slavery and alienated labor in capitalism signify unfreedom, what unsettles the analogy between the slave and the worker is the spectrality of social death.

According to Patterson, such an extreme negation of being destroys natality itself. In fact, even the concept of social death is not sufficient to express the most drastic destruction of being—hence its supplementation by "natal alienation." By signifying the erasure of both biological and social origins, "the term 'natal alienation' . . . goes directly to the heart of what is critical in the slave's forced alienation, the loss of ties of birth . . . a loss of native status, of deracination" (SSD, 7). As the exclusion from ancestors and descendants, from the past as well as from the future, the loss of natality means, according to Patterson, primarily the loss of kinship and the lack of the symbolic and social recognition by the law of the father, so that the enslaved person neither "recognized" nor was recognized by the "father and . . . fatherland" (SSD, 40). Yet, if this nonrecognition by the law of the father constitutes symbolic death, natal alienation also negates the symbolic and semiotic relation to the maternal body, which mediates the first organization of the libidinal body of the child and constitutes the prototype of object relations. Although not developed in Patterson's analysis, the destruction of the relation to the maternal constitutes the enslaved person not only as socially dead but also as unborn being (SSD, 38).

In an implicit competition with Marx, Patterson's notion of social death offers a historical and sociological rewriting of the Hegelian master/slave dialectic, which allows us to contrast the extreme dispossession of the slave with that of the proletariat. The proletarians, as Marx and Engels famously write in *Manifesto of the Communist Party*, "have nothing of their own to secure and to fortify" and, because of this dispossession can lead the universal revolutionary struggle for the abolition of private property (MER, 482). By contrast, enslaved people were deprived not only of all possessions and the means of production but, more fundamentally, of social life, being, and natality. Perhaps one reason for Marx's appropriation of slavery to describe the dispossession of the proletariat is that he agrees with Hegel that only such absolute negation of being can be dialectically transformed into a universal struggle for freedom. In a way, as the ending of his book suggests, Patterson also concurs with the possibility of such dialectical transformation of servitude into freedom: "without slavery there would have been no freedmen" (SSD, 342).

What is most compelling about the diverse strands of dialectical thought, from Hegel and Marx to Fanon, is that they posit the dispossessed as the agents of liberation rather than passive victims. Nonetheless, the dialectical transformation of exploitation into a universal revolutionary struggle for freedom raises several questions. First of all, is such a revolutionary transformation possible without mourning the devastating losses suffered by the dispossessed? In the words of W. E. B. Du Bois, the awakening of a dispossessed group as an agent of liberation has to maintain a tension between mourning for the past and revolutionary hopes for the future: "as though in this morning of group life we had awakened from some sleep that at once dimly mourns the past and dreams a splendid future."[12] Second, as Balibar puts it, what if instead of the transformation of the "bad side" of history into revolutionary struggle, history regresses even further into domination and in so doing reveals an impasse of dialectic? (*PM*, 99). What if revolution itself, as Arendt suggests, reverts to a melancholic spectacle of Saturn devouring its own children? What are the effects of the melancholic disavowal of multiple losses in the construction of the universality of suffering and emancipation? What if the negative universality of suffering regresses into dispersed melancholic afflictions? Consequently, the tension between revolt and melancholia represents not only the difference between the past and the future but, in fact, the ongoing conflict between particular struggles against racism, imperialism, misogyny, and homophobia and persisting domination.

This Melancholia Which Is Not One: On Gender and the Psychoanalytic Genealogy of "the Bad Side" of History

I have proposed that the conflict between particular struggles and the universal liberation make mourning and melancholia into intimate companions of political praxis. It is hardly surprising, therefore, that in contemporary cultural theory of gender and race, from Paul Gilroy and Judith Butler to Anne Anlin Cheng, among others, we find the wide-ranging appropriation of melancholia as a symptom of domination. Yet, more frequently, it is Freud rather than the dialectical tradition that provides an explanatory paradigm of power. The import of the Freudian analysis of melancholia is, according to Butler, an unconscious substitution of the internal conflict "for the world in which it dwells. The effect of melancholia, then, appears to be the loss of social world, the substitution of psychic parts and antagonisms for external relations among social actors."[13] According to Kristeva, what might be specific for Western modernity—the age of imperialism, colonialism, world wars, and the ongoing erosion of the practice of freedom in the public realm—is precisely such unconscious absorption of political crisis by private suffering rather than its transformation into political struggles.[14]

Given the wide-ranging appropriation of melancholia as a symptom of domination, such as in Anne Anlin Cheng's suggestive *The Melancholy of Race*, we have to consider how it is possible to read melancholia as the crisis of political practice. In my answer to this question I propose to interpret melancholia as a modernist, psychoanalytic genealogy of Balibar's "bad side" (*PM*, 97–99) of history. Haunted by the unconscious repetition of the struggles of the dead, this notion of historical suffering cannot be dialectally transformed into the overall project of liberation. What allows for such an unorthodox reading of Freud's 1917 "Mourning and Melancholia" and his 1923 *The Ego and the Id* is his claim that the disorder of melancholia is a reaction not only to the loss of a loved person but also to the loss of "liberty," and, we should add, the losses represented by social death and the poverty of being. Perhaps even more suggestive is Freud's persistent use of economic terminology, such as *poverty, work,* and *money,* to describe the psychic depletion of melancholia, reminiscent of the erosion of political practice in capitalist economy. For instance, the reversal of melancholia into mania resembles the unexpected gain of money "when some poor devil, by winning a large sum of money, is suddenly relieved from perpetual anxiety about his daily bread."[15] Based on the mirage of individual gain, which leaves social relations unchanged, the blind chance of gambling is the antithesis of collective transformative practice. The psychic depletion of melancholia is therefore analogous to a degradation of praxis so severe that the only possibility to overcome its destitution is by gambling—that is, the very opposite of praxis as such.

Yes, despite these suggestive remarks, Freud in his 1917 essay does not develop the relation between melancholia and the loss of freedom, since he focuses almost exclusively on the loss of the love object. By extending Freud's analysis, I would like to propose three forms of melancholia, all of which are necessary to feminist political projects and to feminist theories of aesthetics. The first one is characterizes by the replacement of the lost object of love by unconscious identification with that object. In her suggestive reading of Freud with Nietzsche, Judith Butler has modified this model to account for the melancholic formation of compulsory heterosexuality. Yet, although melancholic gender formation can result in losses of freedom, it does not explain how the crisis of practice or the history of gender and racist oppression can lead to melancholia. To account for the transmutation of the "bad side" of history into mute private suffering, we will have to make sense of two other forms of melancholia. First, we will have to consider the relation between the sadism of the superego and the unconscious repetition of historical disasters from the past and, second, we will have to analyze the melancholic disturbance of language, which undermines both literary practice and what Arendt calls the grammar of political action.

The classic Freudian theory of melancholia is characterized by three features: by the psychic denial of the lost object through its incorporation into the ego, by the internalized love-hate relation to the other, and by the narcissistic character of object relations. The melancholic ego seeks to preserve the lost love through the incorporation of loss—that is, through a narcissistic regression from object relations to an identification. The narcissistic identification replacing object relations explains the ambiguity of loss in melancholia: in grief the loss is in the world, in melancholia that loss, denied in the world, reappears in the ego itself. Even more important for our purposes is the unconscious transformation of "the struggle surging round the object" (MM, 170) into the conflict between the ego and the superego. By identifying with the lost object, the ego becomes a substitute target for the cruelty of the superego—the ego satisfies its hatred of the forsaken object in an indirect way, by putting itself to death: "The self-torments of melancholiacs . . . signify . . . a gratification of sadistic tendencies and of hate, both of which relate to an object and in this way have both been turned round upon the self" (MM, 162). The ego becomes, therefore, an unconscious substitute for the aggressivity of the death drive. And this unconscious substitution in turn calls for a new paradigm of political theory and a new genealogy of history.

The sadism of the superego is the first step toward a reading of melancholia as a psychoanalytic genealogy of the bad side of history. To develop this genealogy further, I would like to link Freud's remarks on the superego as a "culture of the death instinct" with his speculations on the unconscious transmission of historic conflicts. In *The Ego and the Id* Freud repeats the same question—how is it that in melancholia "the super-ego can become a kind of gathering place for the death instincts?"[16]—but gives a different answer. Now it is no longer an identification with the lost object that turns the destruction upon the ego but the melancholic origins of the superego. Based in part on the primary identification and in part on the postoedipal identifications replacing first objects of love, the formation of the superego involves "a desexualization" of Eros, "instinctual diffusion," and the release of the death drive, which is the source of the sadism of the super-ego (*EI*, 56). Freud suggests therefore that by liberating "the aggressive instincts in the super-ego" the melancholic genealogy of the superego exposes the subject "to the danger of . . . death" (*EI*, 59), prior to any subsequent (postoedipal) identifications with lost objects: "The excessively strong super-ego . . . rages against the ego with merciless violence, as if it had taken possession of the whole of the sadism available in the person concerned. . . . What is now holding sway in the superego is, as it were, a pure culture of the death instinct [*eine Reinkultur des Todestriebes*],[17] and in fact it often enough succeeds in driving the ego into death" (*EI*, 54–55). What a strange formulation this is: "a pure culture of the death instinct." Is not the death instinct, which lacks a representative and tends toward the inorganic, the very antithesis of culture?

Since, in this new account of "a pure culture of the death instinct," melancholia characterizes the internal relationship between the ego and the sadism of the superego from the start, any subsequent losses— whether the loss of the object or the wounds suffered by the ego—only exacerbate this "originary" melancholic affliction. In fact, in *The Ego and the Id* Freud reinterprets melancholia as an affliction of the deserted, wounded, and abandoned subject who gives itself up in the face of the excessive dangers of death. Haunted by the traumas and violent conflicts of past generations, threatened by dangers from three directions, the sociopolitical world, the id, and the superego, the melancholic subject suffers from and eventually gives in to the fear "of being overwhelmed or annihilated" by death (*EI*, 60). Freud's speculations on the libidinal aspect of the fear of death—whether the threat of death stems from the hostile external world, from the extreme sadism of the superego, or is inherited from the past generation—suggest that this new form of melancholia can be explained only by the ego relinquishing its own narcissistic libidinal cathexis: the melancholic ego "gives up itself, just as it gives up some external object in other cases in which it feels anxiety" (*EI*, 61). This self-abandonment of the ego provides quite a different understanding of melancholia from the one provided in the 1917 "Morning and Melancholia." If, in the previous case, the melancholic ego was unable to give up its narcissistic attachment to the lost object, now the ego abandons itself under the conditions of unbearable danger. As Freud writes, "the fear of death in melancholia only admits of one explanation: that the ego gives itself up because it feels itself hated and persecuted by the super-ego, instead of loved. . . . When the ego finds itself in an excessive real danger . . . it is bound to draw the same conclusion. It sees itself deserted by all protecting forces and lets itself die" (*EI*, 61). This is a poignant account of the melancholic subject deserted by "all protective forces," which can include social structures, kinship, love, relations with others, and the symbolic universe. Would not such a condition of psychic death resonate with Patterson's notion of social death?

The association of social death with the danger of melancholia is justified, I think, by Freud's speculations on the unconscious aspect of the "bad side" of history or "the pure culture of death instinct" evident, for instance, in the relationship between the sadism of the superego and the unconscious conflicts and traumas of past generations. The situations of danger and abandonment, conducive to melancholia, repeat not only castration anxiety, "the first great anxiety" of birth, and "the infantile anxieties of being separated from the mother," but also the losses and conflicts of past generations. The past is transmitted not merely through by the agency of memory, culture, or counterculture but, more importantly, through the historical unconscious. Freud repeatedly makes the hypothesis that the former generations are haunting the id and, by forming the superego, the ego "resurrects," as it were, former generations and their conflicts. By acting as a representative of the id, the superego is also a haunted representative of the dead. In a stunning historical extension of the melancholic genealogy of the superego into the immemorial past, Freud argues that "in the id . . . are harbored residues of the existences of countless egos; and, when the ego forms its super-ego out of the id, it may perhaps only be reviving shapes of former egos and be bringing them to resurrection" (*EI*, 35). This ghostly reincarnation of the past suggests that the struggle between ego and the superego repeats not only the earliest conflicts of the ego with the objects of the id but also the deadly conflicts of past generations. As the destructive repetition of the battles fought by the dead, the melancholic condition exemplifies the impossibility of what Arendt calls *inicium*, or the inauguration of a new beginning.

The historical but unconscious genealogy of the superego enables us to reread Freud's suggestive reference to Wilhelm von Kaulbach's mural, *The Battle of the Huns* (circa 1834), painted for the Neues Museum of Berlin. The historical referent of the painting is the bloody defeat of the Hun army by Romans in AD 451. The composition of the painting is inspired by the ancient legend dating also to the fifth century, according to which the dead warriors were continuing their bloody slaughter in the sky above the battlefield. For Freud the painting of the bloodshed reenacted by the dead is an allegory of the way the cruel unconscious conflict between the ego and the superego repeats the ancient conflicts of the immemorial past. Freud's brief mention of Kaulbach's painting offers us, therefore, a condensed and quite amazing insight into the psychoanalytic genealogy of the "bad side" (PM, 97–99) of history. The dead repeat the bloodshed of the living, the living in turn repeat, without knowing, the struggles of the dead. The struggle of the multitudes, the multitude of struggles, the past haunting the present, the present leaving a deadly residue for the past of the future. When such struggles of the multitudes are misinterpreted as the unified law of history, Hannah Arendt argues, then it can only appear as a sadistic melancholic law, which, like Saturn, devours its own children. Freud in his turn diagnoses a dangerous melancholic incorporation of such a sadistic law as the cruel superego, but tells us to seek its genealogy in the innumerable immemorial and often deadly antagonistic residues of the past.

By turning to Julia Kristeva, I want to stress the repetition of another struggle from the immemorial past, the traces of which haunt the historical unconscious but are usually erased from most genealogies of history. In contrast to Freud's figure of the dead warriors on the battlefield, for Kristeva this ancient struggle is associated with the crisis of the separation from the maternal body, a separation particularly painful for female subjectivities. Consequently, we are invited to consider that which has never been—a "maternal" genealogy of history, which is nonetheless crucial both to feminist politics and aesthetics. At the same time, by locating such improper "origins" of melancholia at the zero degree of symbolism, Kristeva wrestles with the difficulties of the linguistic analysis of such a genealogy. Melancholia is a symptom of the disturbance of the preoedipal, preverbal, violent, and precarious process of separation from the maternal body. The unnamable narcissistic wound of the melancholic subject stems the archaic refusal to lose the maternal as a narcissistic wrapping of the body and the subsequent failure to symbolize the mother in language as a separate, desiring, and speaking subject. Because of the crisis of differentiation, neither the mother nor the child is constituted as a separate subject. Instead of being a love object, the maternal body remains the unnamable, unbearable Thing, not yet separated from the child, but both a narcissistic support and the unbearable carrier of waste/

violence/death. Retrospectively, the Thing is felt as the supreme good, the loss of which renders the world, language, and social relations worthless. This primary melancholic crisis of separation from the maternal can be reactivated at each subsequent loss, including the traumatic loss of freedom.

Another implication of melancholia for a theory of political and literary practice is a crisis of the signifying capacity of language. Kristeva explains the melancholic distrust of speech in terms of the disavowal of negation ["le déni de la dénégation"][18]: "Depressed persons . . . *disavow the negation*: they cancel it out, suspend it" (*BS*, 43–44). What is then at stake in melancholic discourse, approaching, in extreme cases, silence and asymbolia, is the disavowal of the negativity fundamental to the functioning of language, because it enables the separations between the signifier, signified, and referent. Needless to say, Kristeva's interpretation of the melancholic disavowal of the negative moves beyond Freud's classical interpretation of fetishistic disavowal as the defense against castration. What is disavowed in melancholia is the value of the signifier, its capacity to signify loss and to carry affect into the field of signification. In other words, what is disavowed is the symbiotic and symbolic inscriptions of women's loss, pain, and affect in the signifying process. For Kristeva, such inscription is the most basic operation of metaphor, that is, of the capacity to transpose, transfer, or translate mood, pain, and loss into signification. That is why she calls melancholic subjects "incompetent translator[s]" (*BS*, 41–42) who become foreigners in their own native language. Because of the disavowal of such translation or transfer between two heterogeneous poles—suffering and the signifier—melancholic language appears not merely arbitrary but alien, dead, and without reference. Such an abridgment of symbolic negativity in melancholia not only exacerbates individual suffering but presents a political problem. Since the disavowal of negativity makes it impossible to signify the repressed losses, it undermines any interpretation of the historical unconscious. Second, it points to a regression from the symbolically mediated oppositional force of politics to the aggressivity of the death drive turned upon the ego. Consequently, the melancholic crisis of language disintegrates the grammar of political action, which depends on the intersubjective, symbolically mediated contestation.

The melancholic suspension of the negativity of the signifier can be reinforced by an ambivalence toward oppressive cultural ideals, say the ideal of whiteness, or the masculine ideals of citizenship and genius that ra-

cialized and feminized subjectivities are deemed incapable of embody-
ing. If identification with linguistic signifiers is mediated through the
ideals of the masters, or the hostile voice of the other that repeats with
monotonous insistence "you cannot write," "you cannot vote," "you cannot be human," then rejection of these ideals can lead to women's melancholic distrust of the signifier as such. What such melancholic devalori-
zation of language undercuts is *"(semiotic and symbolic) inscription[s] of the
want [manqué]"* (BS, 44). As a result, melancholia creates an unbridge-
able cleavage between devalorized, empty language and the mute suffering transmitted through generations. By denying the negativity of language, by protecting loss against betrayal in hostile language, melancholic
speech also obliterates any possibility of the transfer/transposition of
meaning to the site of loss, to the nontopos of psychic and social suffering.
Thus, melancholic language is deficient not only in the operation of negation but also in the possibility of translation and protometaphor. Since
this blockage of the movement of language—of the originary "translation" between the affect and the sign—fails to acknowledge psychic and
historical losses, it makes writing the genealogies of the unconscious side
of history impossible and confines the wounded subjects to mute, private
suffering, which reproduces the phenomenon of social death. Such a
truncated and deficient operation of language fails to constitute what Arendt calls the grammar and syntax of political action, that is, the creation
of new possibilities of signification and being in the world with others.

Radically Darkened Art

The turn from the revolutionary to the melancholic side of wom-
en's modernism confronts us with new impasses of aesthetic and political praxis. In my readings of Freud, Butler, and Kristeva, I have interpreted melancholia as a genealogy of what Balibar calls "the bad side" of
history, which manifests itself when unacknowledged political domination is incorporated into the private suffering of the isolated subject and
its gendered "character." According to Hannah Arendt, the melancholic
condition of modernity reveals the destructive misinterpretation of the
multiplicity of political conflicts as the unified, impersonal (dialectical or
structural) law of history "devouring its own children." By contrast, the
Freudian account of melancholia points to the dangerous incorporation
of such a sadistic historical law as the cruel superego and, eventually, to

the substitution of political antagonisms by the internal self-destructive struggle of its victims. The psychoanalytic analysis of such internalized political losses far exceeds the classical Marxist notions of alienation or reification since it points not only to the substitution of the relations between subjects by relationships between commodities but also to the opposite tendency—to the unconscious substitution of social crisis by internal suffering. Such melancholic incorporations are more likely to strike those gendered and racialized peoples who are excluded from the hegemonic subject positions determined by heteronormativity, whiteness, and Western imperialism.

Given this genealogy, writing melancholia in modern women's literature cannot be limited to the subjective expression of suffering, but rather entails multiple migrations of pain, the crossing of uncertain thresholds between the inside and the outside, political and aesthetic, past and present, subjects and objects. These unconscious migrations are often secret companions of other, more readily discernible, political and economic displacements of people that recent transnational studies of modernism and feminism are committed to following.[19] Nonetheless, melancholic displacements of silenced suffering are irreducible to geographic, cultural, or diasporic movements. In fact, neither subjective nor materialist/historicist approaches to modernism, though both important in modernist studies, can do justice to women's melancholia in literature. Interpreting melancholic crossings in women's writings entails asking different questions: How can women's writing possibly convey melancholic internalizations of political conflicts? How does writing melancholia invent new transfers between subjects and objects, past and present, form and pathos, without suppressing the antagonism and multiplicity of these relations? And how does it contest the hegemony of modern literature in the name of an experimental aesthetics of race and gender? As these questions suggests, my discussion of melancholia in modern women's writings is not limited to the subjective expression of suffering, rage, or, in Woolf's case, resentment. On the contrary, it involves a deeper inquiry into the relationship between aesthetics, femininity, and race, the artistic practice, literary language, and affect.

Such an inquiry into the status of the work of art and language is crucial because melancholic displacements of women's suffering sabotage not only political but also literary praxis. Although Freud does not discuss the impact of melancholia on art extensively, the melancholic disavowal of negativity undermines the oppositional force of art and politics. In the context of language, melancholic speech creates the abyss between mute sensation and the empty signifier. In the context of philosophical aesthetics, melancholia disintegrates the mediation between logos and pathos, intelligibility and sensibility. Consequently, melancholia undercuts any possibility of the metaphoric transfer of signification into mute suffering and, vice versa, of affect into language. This severance of the affective/symbolic connections subverts the traditional meaning of aesthetics as sensible experience or subjective expression that speaks to and through the senses. As we have seen, the sensible aspect of aesthetics is critical for Hegel, Marx, and, in a different way, also for Adorno, who associates the meaning of art not only with rationality but with the pathos of suffering as well. The erosion of mediations between political praxis, subjective experience, and aesthetic process undermines any possibility of the full expression of women's suffering in art.

If the melancholic aspect of modernism points not only to political but also to aesthetic impasses, how can women's writings respond to the degradation of aesthetic praxis and the crisis of subjective expression? That the ethical and political stakes of modern literature are intertwined with the articulation of suffering is certainly not a new insight in modernist studies or philosophical aesthetics.[20] Nonetheless, despite the enormous interest in melancholia in feminist political and literary theory, there are few studies that interrogate the devalorized suffering of women in relation to the crisis of literary praxis and language. I will discuss the melancholic crisis of subjective expression, practice, and language in women's modernism by engaging Kristeva's and Adorno's approaches to suffering. The articulation of art's testimony to the repressed "bad" side of history and suffering is one of the most compelling contributions of Adorno's and Kristeva's theories for feminist aesthetics, despite justified critiques of Adorno for his failure to address gender oppression, the disaster of slavery, or the violence of antiblack racism—and of Kristeva for her failure to analyze racism and heteronormativity. Yet, although Kristeva and Adorno underscore the expression of melancholic suffering as one of the most important tasks of modern art and literature, their approaches differ. While Adorno stresses the migration of forgotten or disavowed historical disasters into the structure of the work of art, Kristeva traces such migration into melancholic subjects and asks how literary texts can respond to this mute subjective pain. In other words, Adorno is primarily interested in the status of the art object in relation to political domination, whereas Kristeva—in the relation between affect, sexual difference, and language. By bringing these two theorists together, yet ultimately moving beyond the limitations of their approaches, I address the affective, aesthetic, and political aspects of female suffering in women's writings.

For Adorno the aesthetic expression of suffering is intertwined with the analysis of the relationship between politics and the status of artistic practice. As he famously argues, the "politically dead" practice migrates into art: "it is to works of art that has fallen the burden of wordlessly asserting what is barred to politics. . . . Politics has migrated into autonomous art" (C, 194). Such a migration is at stake in Adorno's enigmatic claim that art speaks the disaster by "taking it upon itself": "The darkening of the world makes the irrationality of art rational: radically darkened art . . . In its pleasure in the repressed, art at the same time takes into itself disaster" (AT, 19).The ethicopolitical task of enunciating the disavowed disasters is one of the greatest strengths of Adorno's work and his contributions to modernism. Kristeva, by contrast, diagnoses the migration of the disaster into the mute suffering of melancholic subjectivities. For her, one of the major stakes of literature in the aftermath of the horrors of the twentieth century is the articulation of the changed economy of psychic grief, which "was experienced as an inescapable emergency, without for that matter ceasing to be invisible, nonrepresentable" (BS, 222). Consequently, the ethical and the political demand that art "enunciates the disaster" repressed by hegemonic culture is complicated by the subjective incorporation of gender and racial oppression. Paradoxically, it is the subjective incorporation of oppression that undermines the expression of women's grief, since such suffering is not available as a social or a subjective referent.

Since the very capacity of linguistic and subjective expression is undermined in melancholia, writing female suffering in modern literature entails neither an objective nor subjective enunciation of loss. Yet how can we move beyond these entrenched oppositions in modern studies— beyond the binarisms of objectivism/subjectivism, form/content, formalism/materialism—while preserving their best insights? In contrast to these oppositions, my own approach to melancholia in women's writings stresses unpredictable, conflicting migrations of pain between subjects and objects, political oppression and literary practice, language and affect. I begin with the paradoxical status of aesthetic practice and the historic contradiction between the resources and injustices it represents for women writers. On the one hand, the autonomy of literature is linked with the enabling role of negativity, which can be turned against the silent work of death and against political oppression. Yet, on the other hand, such autonomy is also intertwined with the destructive exclusion of femininity and racialized subjectivities from the hegemony of modern art. So the question is how this negativity and this exclusion are negotiated in the composition of literary texts. By placing this question at the center of my analysis, I offer a new way of reading the inscription of women's historical struggle and pain in the structure of the work of art—an inscription so often obscured by the formalism/historicism debate. Such inscription of the feminine and blackness, even in the negative form of their erasure, turns the composition of a literary text into a struggle against both external gender and racial antagonisms and against the internal struggle raging within melancholic subjects. Consequently, modern literary works render the destructive "work" of melancholia "unworkable" by absorbing its destruction into their own language. In so doing, literary practice brings the mute subjective incorporation of the political crisis into the language of literary texts. Writing melancholia in women's texts therefore creates an interconnection between literary form and sensibility, between composition and affect, without abolishing their heterogeneity. Such aesthetic transfer between logos and pathos is crucial not only for modern literature but also for all intersubjective communication and action.

In what sense can the negativity of literary practice contest the subjective incorporation of gender and racist domination? As we have seen, art's autonomy, according to Adorno, does not imply a neutral separation from social life but the determinate negation of political domination, which, as feminist critics of modernism stress, includes white supremacy and gender oppression. The negative autonomy allows art to have a different historical development, diverging not only from capital, political power, and the culture industry but also from the melancholic impasses of modernity. Differentiated from other domains of social praxis, oppositional art contests the degradation of the political, in which, as Marx already pointed out, increased productivity coincides with the consumption of the loss of being. We can say that women's experimental literature, though not immune to politics and melancholic impasses, can nonetheless negate ever expanding commodification and persistent gender and racial domination. It is only in the context of such negative possibilities of artistic practice that Adorno's claim about a temporary migration of the "politically dead practice" into the domain of oppositional aesthetics makes sense. Consequently, the negativity of art creates the possibility of a migration of the disaster from the subject into artistic process. By taking disaster into itself, the work of art performs a substitution of the artistic practice for the suicidal incorporation of the historical disaster by the subject.

Yet, as Adorno is first to point out, this autonomous status of modern art is implicated in numerous contradictions. Its negativity notwithstanding, such autonomy is suspect of formalism and political impotence, of reproducing unjust divisions of labor, and, finally, of providing quasi-theological consolations for suffering. Because of such contradictions, the work of art both assumes and negates its autonomy, on which its critical function as well as its distance from politics and subjective suffering depends. In addition, I want to stress gender and racial contradictions ignored in Adorno's aesthetic theory. In the West, the autonomous status of artistic practice is based on not only unjust divisions of labor but also on the racist and gender hegemony of art—that is, on the exclusion of women and other subjugated groups from artistic production. To make this gendered and racial aspect of modernist hegemony visible, Woolf, for example, constructs in *A Room of One's Own* a parable about the destruction of Shakespeare's imaginary sister, who in pursuit of her artistic career is raped and eventually commits suicide. Similarly, the destruction of the artist figures as the crucial component of the narrative structure of Nella Larsen's fiction. As Larsen and Woolf show, the destruction of the feminine, racial other is constitutive of art's "greatness." Since this invisible exclusion of women from the institution of modern experimental literature renders the expression of women's suffering impossible, the aesthetic task of female mourning has to contest the gender hegemony of modernist art and, at the same time, appropriate the historical achievements of artistic autonomy.

Such persistent blindness of Western aesthetics to questions of race and gender undermine the critical function of the negative autonomy on which the aesthetic reworking of melancholia depends. In the context of women's modernism, it becomes apparent that the historical achievements of Western artistic autonomy are structurally and politically intertwined with the exclusion of women, colonized peoples, and subjugated groups from what counts as the Western tradition of autonomous art. As Sabine Wilke and Heidi Schlipphacke point out, *Aesthetic Theory* uncritically reproduces these exclusions.[21] The most obvious instance of gender blindness is the paucity of modern women writers mentioned in *Aes-*

thetic Theory. A more crucial consequence of the exclusion of women from *Aesthetic Theory* is the failure to analyze the systematic destruction of the possibilities of women's art—in fact, for modern women, artistic practice is hardly more feasible than gender politics. On the contrary, as Virginia Woolf and Nella Larsen—the two modernist women writers discussed in this study—show, the autonomy of Western art has been shattered not only by political oppression but also by the exclusion of women and black artists from the domain of art. Consequently, the hegemonic status of modern art, based on gender and racist domination, is intertwined with the destruction of the very possibility of women's art. Autonomous modern art might provide a refuge from suffering, but gender oppression destroys its existence.

To address the contestation of the artistic hegemony of modernism in women's texts, I want to refer briefly to Virginia Woolf and Nella Larsen. I will analyze their texts in greater detail in chapter 3 (Woolf) and chapter 6 (Larsen); for now I would like to discuss briefly the allegories of erased women's suffering and the destruction of women's art in their writings. Woolf's *To the Lighthouse* (1927) and *A Room of One's Own* (1929) and Larsen's *Quicksand* (1928) and *Passing* (1929) are striking examples of a literary practice that incorporates and contests the destructive effects of the modernist hegemony of art in order to invent a female art of mourning. Despite all the differences between the historical circumstances and formal characteristics of their works, Woolf and Larsen confront again and again the dilemma of how to transform the persisting legacy of the destruction of women's writing into the possibility of female art and female mourning. For example, in *A Room of One's Own*, Virginia Woolf, like Marx before her, refers to Greek slavery as the paradigmatic destruction of women's political and aesthetic praxis. The devastation of poverty, imperialism, and sex inequality in modern England puts aspiring women writers, especially poor women writers, in a condition similar to that of the ancient Athenian slaves: "we may prate of democracy, but actually, a poor child in England has little more hope than had the son of an Athenian slave to be emancipated into that intellectual freedom of which great writers are born" (*RO*, 107–108). For Larsen, however, slavery is not merely a metaphor for class and gender exploitation. On the contrary, the destructive historical legacy of slavery and continuing antiblack violence haunts Larsen's novels *Quicksand* and *Passing* and eventually leads to the destruction of the main characters, Helga and Clare, who are implicit figures of black aesthetics, taste, beauty, and writing. What Woolf and

Larsen foreground is the invisible death of the feminine in the midst of their respective cultural renaissances—the destruction of Shakespeare's imaginary sister during the British Renaissance in the sixteenth century and the death of Larsen's mulatto characters in the Harlem Renaissance of the twentieth century—as if to suggest that cultural rebirth not only excludes femininity but in fact takes place through the destruction of female bodies.

Woolf often describes *To the Lighthouse* as a modern elegy, since the text engages the question of mourning on multiple levels: autobiographical (the death of Woolf's parents), political (the devastations of the war), economic (the unjust gendered division of labor evident, for instance, in the contrast between old cleaning women and the young female artist), aesthetic (the exclusion of women from the institution of art), and, finally, formal (the experimental process of artistic composition). The novel's main protagonist, Lily Briscoe, cannot complete her painting until she metaphorically "kills" and subsequently mourns the death of her symbolic mother, the ambivalent object of love and hate, Mrs. Ramsay. This symbolic act of matricide is intertwined with the contestation of gender ideology internalized by Mrs. Ramsay, who invalidates Lily's art and considers it trivial in comparison with marriage. In the third part of the novel, Lily's work of mourning, her contestation of Victorian gender ideology, British imperialism, the exclusion of women from the tradition of painting, and the composition of the painting are so closely intertwined that one cannot be accomplished without others. Inscribed into the fabric of the painting and the novel, the work of mourning presents a threat to Lily's art. Just before the completion of her painting, Lily contemplates and accepts the risk of the destruction of her painting: "[the picture] would be hung in the attics, she thought; it would be destroyed. But what did that matter?"[22] And she cannot finish her artwork until she finds a way to inscribe multiple losses, political violence, and the threat of the destruction of women's art into the composition of her work: "She looked at the steps; they were empty; she looked at her canvas; it was blurred. With a sudden intensity, as if she saw it clear for a second, she drew a line there, in the center. It was done; it was finished" (*TTL*, 208–209). One has to appreciate the ambiguity of the final lines of Lily's painting and Woolf's novel. Just as the line in the middle of the canvas unifies and divides, cuts the canvas with the "razor blade" and transforms the violence of that cut into a concluding brushstroke, so too the final sentence in the novel announces the ambiguous end of women's art. The doubling and the internal division marked by the semicolon in the phrase—"it was done; it was finished"—implies both the completion of female art and the persisting threat of its destruction.

The destruction of black female aesthetics is even more devastating in Nella Larsen's novels. In her texts, exclusion from the hegemonic Western aesthetic tradition is figured as a radical form of disinheritance—an exclusion that evokes Orlando Patterson's social death—from cultural institutions, kinship, and the black renaissance. In her first novel, *Quicksand,* the narrative structure yields no progression, no migration, but circles ever more closely around the vortex of the internal wound of the main heroine, Helga Crane. The short-lived outburst of happiness and hope are drained and drowned in that vortex of destructive sorrow and death until no ideals, no consolations remain. Desire for possessions, social status, love, aesthetic taste, and beauty are set up in the novel as if to show their seeming, disillusioning, and sinister character as they are implicated in white and patriarchal power. After tearing apart all the ideals and possibilities of art, the novel ends in the unbearable condensation of birth and death. Inverting the meaning of black renaissance, the novel, instead of rebirth, gives "birth" to the death of black femininity. In so doing, it implicitly negates the image of the black madonna on the cover of Alain Locke's manifesto-like collection titled *The Harlem Renaissance.* The unbearable birth of death at the end of the novel is anticipated by the destruction of the female tongue—the organ of subjective expression, song, and what Fred Moten calls "black mo'nin."[23] Helga Crane experiences a suffocating sensation in her throat when she remembers the violence of lynching—her tongue becomes an alien suffocating thing. Despite her association with taste and beauty, Helga's body disregards aesthetic distance and mimetically responds to the horror of the tortured black body by experiencing herself the asphyxiation of lynching. Larsen's novel asks: How it is possible to write from within such suffocation? How is it possible to transfer, or transpose, that sensation that destroys not only subjective expression but also language itself and its musicality into writing? How can the novel inscribe the trace of that violence and death buried in the female mouth into its own language?

In Larsen's second novel, *Passing,* the death buried in the female mouth is reenacted as the destruction of the illegible black female writing—of the enigmatic scrawl. In the first scene, the main female character, Irene, shreds to pieces a letter from her unacknowledged lover and alter ego Clare Kendry, who is passing for white. In the last concluding scene we witness the destruction of the writer herself. Just as Lily contemplates the destruction of her painting before she puts that final line in the middle—the line of division and "razor blade" connection of opposites—here too the composition of Larsen's novel incorporates into its composition the racist history of the destruction of the possibilities of black art as well as a dangerous countertext of racial, sexual, and artistic freedom: "With an usual methodicalness she tore the offending letter into tiny ragged squares. . . . The destruction completed . . . she dropped them over the railing and watched them scatter" (P, 178). This tearing apart and scattering of the insurgent black text and the desiring female body are inscribed in the composition of Larsen's novel through the proliferation of dashes, ellipses, silences, unexpected abrupt endings, and, finally, through the exclusion and scattering of Clare's letters, which prefigures the violent death of the letter writer herself. Both Clare and her illegible writing are included in the novel only to foreground their catastrophic exclusion from hegemonic art. Like the petrification of Helga's tongue, the exclusion and destruction of the illegible scrawl inscribes within the structure of the novel a testimony to the racist violence of lynching, segregation, and the disavowed traumatic memory of slavery. The risk of death bears witness to the destruction of the possibilities of women's art and to the untimely "death" of female art in white patriarchal culture.

Both Woolf and Larsen associate the process of writing female melancholia with the risk of the destruction of women's writing and confront a political and aesthetic dilemma of how women's art might emerge from the history of its destruction. The political answer to this dilemma, as I have argued chapter 1, is that the very possibility of women's autonomous art, including the art of mourning, might depend on women's revolutionary politics and on women's alternative communities. For Larsen, such possibility depends first of all on what Alain Locke calls "a unique social experiment" and the "iconoclastic" mass movement of the Harlem Renaissance.[24] Even more, it also requires the transformation of the entire register of murderous racist language, which turns the female tongue into a suffocating dying thing. Thus, the juxtaposition of Adorno's *Aesthetic Theory* with women's modernism reveals a chiasmatic and contradictory exchange between gender aesthetics and gender politics: If, as Adorno argues, the degradation of politics is transformed into an autonomous art of mourning, for women the very possibility of such artistic practice in turn depends on revolutionary politics. Thinking through this contradiction is one of the main concerns of this book; it requires a reinterpretation of the heteronomous autonomy of women's literature in relation to both emancipatory movements and the history of women's suffering and destruction.

Yet the emergence of women's writing from the haunting history of its destruction also presents an aesthetic challenge. Such a challenge transforms literary practice into a veritable "battleground" manifesting on the level of its form the discord between meaning and non-meaning, death and re-naissance. In order to bear witness to the psychic disintegration, repressed political conflicts, and exclusion of women from art, the work of art incorporates destruction and antagonism into its own structure. Such a formal struggle by literary means—scattering, fragmentation, ellipsis, illegibility—"externalizes" the subjective incorporations of political conflicts and transforms them into formal construction. By absorbing destruction into their own language, modern women's writings render the invisible and destructive "work" of melancholia "unworkable." In contrast to a direct subjective expression of pain, mediation of women's suffering through literary composition maintains the tension between two antithetical forces: between the opacity of suffering, bodies, and death, on the one hand, and the possibility of signifying such opacity on the level of aesthetic form, on the other—between the death of meaning and its survival in art. According to Kristeva, literary texts shift "back and forth" between unnameable nonbeing and "the proliferation of signs" and, in so doing, "remake nothingness" within their structure (BS, 101, 100, 99).

One of the aesthetic tropes that comes closest to expressing such conflicting relations between political antagonism, mute pain, and formal construction is "dissonance"—a term that for Adorno is the "trademark of modernism" as a whole. Although dissonance might seem a rather familiar modernist figure, it always manifests itself in singular ways in the structure of artwork. As a writing of female melancholia, dissonance, like the tear or the cut in Larsen's and Woolf's novels, inscribes suffering and disavowed disasters on the level of form. Insofar as such tears in the textual fabric manage to leave a trace of repressed social antagonisms and subjective pain, they can be read, as Robert Hullot-Kentor suggests, as "the writing of the historical unconscious."[25] By contesting formalism, historicism, and psychologism alike, the dialectic between subjective expression, historical unconscious, and literary structure paradoxically produces a mimetic enactment of the body in pain on the level of form: "Artistic expression comports itself mimetically, just as the expression of living creatures is that of pain" (AT, 110). As Adorno puts it in a frequently quoted phrase, the fragmentation of form is a scar transferred to the body of language: "Scars of damage and disruption are the modern's seal of authenticity" (AT, 23).

The dialectic between subjective expression, political domination, and formal composition in Larsen's and Woolf's literary texts sets the stage for one of the most difficult tasks of transforming the deadly work of melancholia into the work of art: namely, the mediation between affect and empty melancholic language stripped from sensibility. In order to rework melancholia, modern literature has to contest the affective evisceration of melancholic language and bring the silenced suffering and longing of women into the composition of literary texts. That is why the female painter, Lily, in Woolf's *To the Lighthouse* desires not only a new language of painting, the scripture rescued from the maternal body, but also an impossible proximity to sensuous "intimacy" that could not "be written in any language known to men" yet has to be expressed in the form of her painting (TTL, 51). The concern with sensibility and affect, both in its bodily and political dimensions, has been of course at the center of feminist theory since the seventies, in particular, in French feminist theory. For example, Luce Irigaray contests the gendered hierarchy between the sensible and the transcendental, the letter and the spirit, and proposes a new relationship between affect and language in her notion of the sensible transcendental created through feminine poesis. This relationship is also crucial to Kristeva's theory of semiotics, which examines complex mediations between the drive, affect, and the signifier.

In the context of melancholic modernism, however, the affective and sensible quality of art, traditionally a distinguishing feature of aesthetics as such, has been undermined not only by the melancholic disintegration of the affective and signifying functions of language but, paradoxically, also by the autonomous status of literary practice. The autonomy of art, which safeguards its oppositional force, at the same time distances literature from suffering and affective possibilities of experience. As Adorno puts it, "aesthetic autonomy remains external to suffering. . . . The artwork is not only the echo of suffering, it diminishes it. . . . Art thereby falls into an unsolvable aporia" (AT, 39). The articulation of female mourning in modern literature cannot resolve this aporia and unify affect and signification, sensibility and form. On the contrary, it reveals tension between artistic autonomy and the affective force of suffering: women's literature has to maintain its autonomy in order to contest the forgetting of women's suffering in history, and, at the same time, it also has to negate that autonomy in order to remain in proximity to suffering.

In the political context of Anglo-American modernism, this tension between sensibility and the negative force of aesthetic autonomy contests the political regulation of sensibility by the confluence of white supremacy, heteronormativity, and patriarchal culture. As Woolf argues in *A Room of One's Own*, the exclusion of the feminine from subject positions and conceptual knowledge in the hegemonic culture of the West positions white middle-class women between normative, crippling emotional labor in support of the masculine and equally destructive female resentment, which is another form of violent melancholia turned upon female subjectivity. By contrast, Larsen explores the destructive appropriations of black female sensibility by the ideology of primitivism, racist fantasies of unrestrained black sexuality, and the equally destructive counterideology of black female propriety. Oblivious to Helga's inarticulable suffering and despondency, the white artist regards her as his desired model, a key to his artistic "immortality," precisely because she embodies for him the fantasy of the exotic, uninhibited sexuality that can be appropriated in order to revitalize the sterility of European art: "You have the warm impulsive nature of the women of Africa, but, my lovely, you have . . . the soul of a prostitute" (*Q*, 87). Helga regards this appropriation of her suffering and sensuality as the political abjection of black mourning. What she sees in the painting is "some disgusting sensual creature with her features" (*Q*, 89). The white artist's view of Helga as the "soul of the prostitute" indirectly admits the status of hegemonic art, which appropriates and commodifies black sensuality under the guise of the recovery of aesthetic sensibility.

Although it does not directly engage female sexuality or the ideology of primitivism, Adorno's own analysis of the socially regulated repression or regression of sensibility, most evident in the last chapter, "Elements of Anti-Semitism: Limits of Enlightenment" of *Dialectic of Enlightenment*, is especially important for understanding the role of the sensible in art. Adorno argues that in the West the regulation of sensibility (or what he calls the "mimetic" libidinal impulses of the body) is from the outset intertwined with the desire for mastery of internal and external antagonistic forces. Repressed by concept and identity, sensibility is also regulated by consumption and political power, especially by the division of labor, technology, and science: "Civilization has replaced . . . mimetic behavior proper, by organized control of mimesis, in the magical phase; and, finally, by rational practice, by work, in the historical phase. Uncontrolled mimesis is outlawed."[26] Yet, as the history of racism and anti-Semitism shows, in modernity, the social control of sensibility assumes another form, namely, that of the fantasmatic hostile projections of the "unrestrained" libido onto racialized others. In this respect, Adorno's diagnosis of the libidinal aspects of anti-Semitism is also applicable to antiblack racism—both types of racism allow for regression to archaic violence and an obscene enjoyment of the suffering of others: racist crowds, including children, watching a lynching or the violent anti-Semites who "celebrate the moment when authority permits what is usually forbidden."[27] The libidinal economy of fascism and racism becomes an administered "regression" to libidinal violence, a perverted compromise between enjoyment, aggression, and social regulation. Such a regression, to recall Freud's formulation, is a political "culture of the death drive." This analysis of the libidinal aspects of antiblack racism and anti-Semitism intersects with feminist critiques of primitivism and exoticism, which are also socially regulated projections of unrestrained sensuality onto black women.

Thus what makes the expression of sensibility in "radically darkened art" (AT, 19) particularly difficult is not only the contradictions of aesthetic autonomy but also the contradictory tendencies of gendered, racist politics of affect: the administered regression to sensual immediacy and the melancholic evisceration of the sensible. Consequently, the expression of feminine sensibility through literary form has at the same time to contest racist fantasies of the uninhibited sensuality of racialized bodies and empty language severed from the transmission of affect. In other words, the critical mediation of sensibility has to recover the sensuality and pain severed from signification and at the same time negate any illusion of regression to unmediated sensibility. As we have seen in Lily's struggle with the antithetical composition of her painting in Woolf's To the Lighthouse, art's empathy with suffering is neither unmediated nor socially administered; it neither regresses to nor disavows the libidinal economy of the body. Because the task of the aesthetic translation of affect is to bring the obfuscated political and subjective contradictions into the language of art, literary texts do not produce unification between affect and form, but, like the final line in the middle of Lily's painting, reveal the irreducible tension between sensibility and formal construction in the composition of modern artwork. To put it in a different way, the relation between female sensibility and form neither unifies nor separates them but rather produces disjunction and conjunction between form and feeling in the structure of the work of art. Instead of sublating the opposites, the work of art deploys a double negation ("neither nor") in order to preserve the tension between affect and form. Through this internal tension between sensibility and form, literary texts can contest not only any lingering feminist worries about essentialism but, more importantly, fantasmatic projections of unrepressed sensuality and violence onto racialized and feminized others.

Because language and literature is at stake in melancholia, the expression of women's suffering in modern art is indirect, transformed into tears and tensions of literary form. It is through this dialectic between subjective expression and formal composition that women's writings convey affect and suffering and, in so doing, repair the rift between empty language and mute pain at the core of the melancholic crisis. To refer to Kristeva's analysis, the artistic process transfers the signifier to the site of mute pain and conveys affect into signs: "Through its in antithetical essence, through its potential for ambiguity," the work of art conveys "meaning to the very place where it was lost in death and/or nonmeaning" and at the same time presents meaning as illusory (BS, 102, 103). For Kristeva, such an indirect expression of suffering through literary form resembles the work of translation or the movement of metaphor. Needless to say, the terms *translation* and *metaphor* are themselves metaphoric since they do not operate between languages or within language but rather between signs and what is fundamentally alien to them—affect buried in the psyche. Such a restoration of minimal symbolic mediation and translatability for the untranslatable wounds of history transposes the register of individual and social losses from the domain of women's private suffering to the sphere of public (if marginalized) artistic practice.

What restores the transfer of meaning to the place of loss and suffering to language is the possibility of creating a new signifier in place of death. Woven "around and with the depressive void," (BS, 99), the creation of a new signifier for femininity and blackness within the symbolic register resonates with feminist emphases on resignification of the abjected specters expelled from the domain of signification. Such inscription of the feminine and blackness, even if this inscription merely marks the traces of their erasure, contests hegemonic discourse and opens new possibilities of signification. The inscription of traces of death presents the art as what can "withstand" (BS, 100) death and psychic and cultural destruction. It enables the enunciation of the disaster incorporated by the subject and repressed by hegemonic culture. That is why "radically dark-ened" art, in contrast to melancholic paralysis, may disclose "the very universe of the possible" (BS, 101). This possibility is contradictory and ambiguous: it is the possibility of death but also "the infinite possibility of ambivalent, polyvalent resurrections" (BS, 101). Or, as Larsen's fiction suggests, women's art transforms the death of the feminine and the so-cial death of blackness into a possibility of a black female renaissance yet to come.

**

As these diverse encounters with melancholia suggest, it is one of the most unstable and heterogeneous categories, blurring the boundaries between aesthetics and politics, the unconscious and history, subjects and objects, the multiplicity of historical struggles and the cruelty of the superego. It shows both the impasse of dialectics and the importance of aesthetic mediations between mute sensation and empty language, be-tween the historical catastrophes buried within female subjectivities and their expression in the form of the work of art. Feminist interpretations of melancholia uncover again and again the unrecorded lost possibilities of women's art and the erasure of women's suffering in politics. They present the invisible death of the feminine in the middle of historical ca-tastrophes and political renaissance.

The heterogeneity of melancholia as an aesthetic and political phe-nomenon demonstrates once again the importance of Adorno's heterono-mous autonomy of art for feminist aesthetics. However, in the context of melancholia, the heteronomous autonomy changes its meaning: It not only points to art's origin in the unjust economic division of labor but also to the ethical and political task of bearing witness to the suffering of victims of domination. Thus, if in the first chapter I have redefined the paradoxical status of literary practice in relation to women's struggle for freedom and its inaugural force of novelty, in this chapter I emphasized another dimension of aesthetic autonomy, namely, art's testimony to the mute suffering of women cut off from the signifying possibilities of lan-guage. Such testimony to suffering in women's writing does not entail a direct subjective expression of pain. On the contrary, in place of unmedi-ated expression, women's texts radicalize aesthetic negativity. In contrast to the melancholic disavowal of finitude, loss, and the negative, these texts assume the risk of their own death and negate their own complicity with domination in order to contest the exclusion of the feminine and blackness from the hegemony of modern literature. Call it the feminine operation of the negative. It is only through this double negation of political domination and aesthetic hegemony, performed by literature itself, that art stands a chance of keeping its promise of a better practice.

Yet writing melancholia in women's texts ultimately moves beyond the work of the negative toward the creation of new possibilities. First of all, the inscription of the feminine and blackness, even in the negative form of their erasure, changes the status of the work of art. Neither a detached object of aesthetic contemplation nor a product of history, the disjunctive composition of literary texts is an antagonistic practice, a struggle against both external gender and racial antagonisms and against the unconscious internal struggle raging within melancholic subjects. In this way, modern literature renders the invisible and destructive "work" of melancholia "unworkable" by absorbing its destruction into its own language. Second, by inventing new aesthetic transfers between language and affect, subjective and political conflicts, writing melancholia brings the mute subjective incorporation of political struggles into literary language. And, finally, by recording the erased destruction of the feminine and blackness in Western modernity, women's literature also invents fragile possibilities of another renaissance yet to come.

3 Woolf's Aesthetics of Potentiality

"Every Great Book Has Been an Act of Revolution"

The contradictions between revolutionary and melancholic modernism I explored in the first two chapters of this book is central to Woolf's reflections on the possibility and impossibility of women's literature. To explore this contradiction in Woolf's writings, I would like to turn to her literary essays, her best-known aesthetic manifestos on the stakes of modernism and gender politics. Of these essays, recently collected and published in a four-volume set but still only a fraction of the enormous corpus of Woolf's essay writing, the best known is *A Room of One's Own*. An instant best seller since its first publication on October 24, 1929, it has been reclaimed as a hallmark or, in Susan Gubar's words, "a classic—if not *the* touchstone text—in the history" of Western metropolitan feminism.[1] However it has not yet achieved a similar status as a landmark in Western aesthetics or feminist aesthetics, even though the importance of Woolf's reflections on art has been frequently acknowledged and analyzed in Woolf studies.

The form of Woolf essays is itself experimental and iconoclastic, blurring the boundaries between fiction, aesthetic reflection, political polemics, critique, biography, autobiography, and review. According to Hermione

Lee, "essays turn into fictions, fictions into essays; . . . readings of modern fictions may be commentaries on her own processes."[2] Yet despite Woolf's contestation of the divide between experimental literature and gender politics, and despite the fact that at least since the eighties feminist critics have attempted to break down, in Diane Filby Gillespie's words, "the customary distinction between art and politics," these divisions persist in Woolf's scholarship.[3] As Laura Marcus and Hermione Lee point out, critics interested primarily in modernist aesthetics focus on Woolf's aesthetic manifestos, such as "Modern Fiction" or "Mr. Bennett and Mrs. Brown," while more politically oriented feminist and socialist critics tend to favor *A Room of One's Own* and *Three Guineas*. According to Marcus, these tensions between feminist politics and aesthetics in Woolf scholarship reproduce the divide between modernist and realist aesthetics and in a certain way replay "the debates between Brecht and Lukács in the 1930s, which had been newly translated and represented for the 1970s, with Moi on the side of Woolf's modernism and avant-gardism and Showalter standing for a realist aesthetic opposed to textual innovation."[4] Indeed, in 1985 Toril Moi reworks Brecht/Lukács polemics in order to argue for the importance of Woolf's experimental aesthetics for the feminist politics of sexual difference.[5] We hear the echoes of the divide between experimental aesthetics and politics in Naomi Black's reconstruction of Woolf's "radical and political feminism," which focuses on Woolf's involvement in the women's movement of her time, but excludes Woolf's aesthetic practice as "unrelated to politics or to feminism in the normal senses of the words."[6] By contrast, Jane Goldman stresses Woolf's aesthetic innovations and their relation to suffrage art in the streets and postimpressionist art on gallery walls.[7]

The tension between feminist politics and aesthetics in Woolf studies is not entirely surprising given the fact that the question of fiction and its relation to life, freedom, labor, and gender politics is a central preoccupation of Woolf's work. As if anticipating Adorno's sentiment that "every authentic artwork is internally revolutionary" (*AT*, 228), Woolf similarly claims that "every great book has been an act of revolution"[8]—a claim frequently noted by feminist scholars, who, like Jane Marcus, see it as an expression of Woolf's feminism and socialism.[9] And, as she puts it in her 1919 essay, "Modern Novels," at stake in this artistic revolution, just as is the case in gender politics, is the question of freedom: "The problem before the novelist at present, as we suppose it to have been in the past, is to contrive a means of being free" (MN, 34–35). Yet, the "act of revolution" in modern fiction does not mean that novels either illustrate gender struggle or inspire their readers to participate in political struggle; rather such revolution has to be created within the structure of the work of art itself. In Woolf's essays and literary works, that aesthetic manifestation of revolution is reflected in her contestation and transformation of aesthetic categories, genius, originality, death of art, and, finally, literary conventions of the novel. Her choice of these categories is neither arbitrary nor dictated solely by the exclusion of women artists from the history of art, since all of them are associated with the question of aesthetic freedom.[10]

Woolf's first claim that "every great book has been an act of revolution" might be read as a complacent modernist cliché if it were not for her second claim that the aesthetic freedom manifesting itself immanently in the composition of literary texts refers nonetheless to the political struggles of women. Not only an aesthetic negation of political domination, the very possibility of women's artistic revolutionary praxis depends, according to Woolf, on the collective "habit of freedom" (RO, 113) in political life. "When human relations change," Woolf argues, "there is at the same time a change in religion, conduct, politics and literature."[11] In the concluding passage of A Room of One's Own—a text that Jane Marcus reads as a literary feminist response to suffrage political tactics[12]—Woolf argues that women's collective struggle and practice of freedom in political, economic, and intellectual life are the precondition of a revolutionary literary act: "For my belief is that if we live another century or so—I am talking of the common life which is the real life and not of the little separate lives which we live as individuals—and we have five hundred a year each of us and rooms of our own; if we have the habit of freedom and the courage to write exactly what we think . . . then the opportunity will come . . . without that effort on our part . . . that would be impossible" (RO, 113–114). If the possibility of women's writing depends on the ongoing practice of freedom in women's collective lives, such practice requires women's access to political, economic, and intellectual forms of participation—their right to vote, to education, and to the practice of professions. Without such collective preparation, without the creation of new conditions for women's collective lives, women's artistic practice would be impossible.

Consequently, we need to ask about the relation between two seemingly contradictory, yet inseparable, tasks: the task of the female writer to "contrive means of being free" and the collective task of women's struggle for freedom, which in turn assures the future possibility of female art. How can women's fiction be at once autonomous and at the same time depend for its possibility on revolutionary praxis? If, following Adorno, we can describe this paradoxical status of women's literary practice in terms of the heteronomous autonomy of modern art, then we have to stress significant differences in the way Woolf allows us to reformulate this concept. In the context of Woolf's work, the heteronomous aspect of the autonomy of modern art—its relation to the political—has to be thought beyond art's negation of gender oppression in political and social life. Woolf shows that the struggle between freedom and gender domination characterizes not only art but also politics. That is why Woolf situates the transformative capacity of literature—its ability to contest gender domination, imperialism, and the gendered division of labor on the level of form—in relation to women's political aspirations for freedom. And, conversely, she also shows that class, gender, and racist domination threaten the very possibility of art: in fact, the history of women's literary production begins with the utter destruction of women's art and their bodies—a destruction internalized as madness, melancholia, and resentment. Consequently, the main question Woolf poses for feminists aesthetics is how the promise of a better praxis in women's writings can emerge from the contradiction between revolutionary and melancholic modernism and how this emergence is intertwined with an inaugural, intersubjective freedom in the political.

As I have argued in chapter 1, women's struggle for political and economic freedom creates the inaugural possibility of a new beginning despite persisting gender domination. In the context of the gendered history of art, however, this contradiction between freedom and domination means that art's promise of a better praxis is haunted by melancholia, by the destruction of the very possibility of women's writing. In other words, the "disaster" not only afflicts political life but destroys the possibilities of art itself. The Hegelian thesis of the death of art, which proclaims the loss of art's social relevance in modernity, reveals therefore not merely the threatening end of art but the impossible beginning of women's writing. In this context the paradoxical status of women's art means not only that art negates structures of domination, not only that it finds aesthetic means to both express invisible social contradictions, including labor, gender, and race contradictions, and offer alternative models of liberating political praxis. The crucial aspect of heteronomous autonomy, ignored by Adorno, is that the inaugural force of women's political revolt enables the transformation of the historical impossibility of women's art into its future possibility.

Haunted by melancholia, Woolf's deployment of the rhetoric of revolution is neither gratuitous nor limited to aesthetic experimentation for it's own sake. Rather such rhetoric implies that the main intersection between gender politics and gender aesthetics rests precisely on the impossibility and possibility of female freedom. Thus, even if women's revolutionary struggle for freedom is not always reflected in the themes of Woolf writing, it is this struggle that turns the melancholic "impossibility" of women's art into the possibility of its arrival. Revolutionary struggle, therefore, carries with it the possibility of at least two new beginnings. One of them is women's creation of new freedoms in the political realm; the other one is artistic freedom manifesting itself in women's artistic practice.

On Genius, Anger, and the Future of Female Writing

Woolf explores the paradoxical dependence of women's writing on the political struggle for freedom by focusing on the destruction of women's art and its effects: madness, melancholia, and resentment. The destruction of women's artistic practice by gender and class exploitation is at stake in Woolf's philosophical/fictional parable of the tragic fate of Shakespeare's talented sister, who, deprived of education, beaten by her father, raped and impregnated by the theater manager, killed herself in the pursuit of her artistic career. Her corpse was buried anonymously at the crossroads to prevent her future reappearance. In *A Room of One's Own*, Shakespeare's dead sister is a shattering reminder of the monstrous destruction of the possibility of female art by gender, colonial, and class exploitation. By contrast, Shakespeare is evoked as a figure of unsurpassed originality and "incandescent mind." How should we read this stark contradiction between the destruction of the female poet and the unsurpassed freedom of Shakespeare? Woolf claims that "If ever a mind was incandescent, unimpeded . . . it was Shakespeare's mind" (*RO*, 57). The hypothetical form of this sentence creates in fact some doubt as to whether such an incandescent mind ever existed and whether its creations were unconditional. That doubt is further reinforced by the contrast between the completeness of Shakespeare's mind and the missing books (*RO*, 45) about women's lives. Furthermore, Woolf speculates that if Shakespeare's artistic freedom was confronted with his sister's political demand for women's liberation, his awareness of women's political struggle would not have enhanced his artistic practice because he too would have succumbed to the self-conscious resentment so symptomatic of the masculine protest against suffragettes' demand of political freedom in twentieth-century England: "Doubtless Elizabethan literature would have been very different . . . if the woman's movement had begun in the sixteenth century" (*RO*, 101). We should not be surprised, therefore, that in *Moments of Being*, Woolf, in a feigned moment of shock, claims that the overcoming of genius aesthetics is parallel to the "death" of God: "But there is no Shakespeare, there is no Beethoven; certainly and emphatically there is no God; we are the words; we are the music; we are the thing itself."[13]

To expose the gendering of the foundational concepts in the history of aesthetics, Woolf's parable about the tragic death of Shakespeare's sister interprets the relation between genius and femininity as a destructive master/slave dialectic. Like Marx and suffragettes before her, in *A Room of One's Own* Woolf refers to Greek slavery as the paradigmatic negation of both political and aesthetic freedom by economic and class exploitation. She equates the devastation of poverty, imperialism, and sex inequality in modern England with ancient Athenian slavery: "We may prate of democracy, but actually, a poor child in England has little more hope than had the son of an Athenian slave to be emancipated into that intellectual freedom of which great writings are born" (*RO*, 107–108).

Woolf's critique of the aesthetics of genius in the context of the master/slave dialectic can be said to anticipate subsequent Frankfurt school and feminist contestations of the notion of artistic freedom at stake in the concept of genius. As Adorno points out, the concept of genius obfuscates the fact that artistic praxis both depends on and intervenes into social conditions, and, in so doing, it denies the persisting unfreedom in the world: "Privileged genius becomes the proxy to whom reality promises what it denies humanity as a whole" (*AT*, 171). Yet Woolf's association of femininity and slavery contests Adorno's abstract expression of "humanity as a whole," which glosses over the specific differences of exploitation within that whole. By examining the relation between literature, gender, poverty, and slavery, Woolf exposes femininity as the unacknowledged antithesis of genius, which, thanks to this opposition, can become the embodiment of artistic freedom. In other words, the freedom of genius disavows gender oppression, the unjust division of labor, and the destruction of women's writing by projecting political domination as the inferiority of the feminine. It is not only in politics but also in aesthetics that the feminine functions as a magic "looking-glass" reflecting the masculine figure "at twice its natural size" (*RO*, 35). As her parody of Nick Greene in *Orlando* suggests, the aesthetic concept of genius, implicated with the glory of the past, the fame of empire, and the cult of the artist, far from overcoming exploitation, is in fact one of its aesthetic manifestations. Both in *Orlando* and in *A Room of One's Own* the artistic freedom of Shakespeare is juxtaposed with racism, colonialism, and imperialist conquest.

Nonetheless, Woolf's critique of genius is also marked by her own disavowal of racial divisions and inequalities among women, despite the fact that the inscription of racial and Oriental differences between them occurs again and again in her texts, for example, in *A Room of One's Own*, *Orlando*, or *To the Lighthouse* (for instance, Lily's Chinese eyes). Referring to her white female audience, Woolf observes sardonically that the only benefit of women's exclusion from the artistic tradition is their "exclusion" from the barbarism of British imperialism: "You have never shaken an empire or led an army into battle. The plays of Shakespeare are not by you, and you have never introduced a barbarous race to the blessings of civilization" (*RO*, 112). A parody of the antisuffrage argument that women cannot vote because they do not bear arms, this quote suggests that Woolf is critical of the violence of the British imperialism and shows a correlation between the subjugation of women at home and colonial domination abroad. Nonetheless, she fails to imagine solidarity between Shakespeare's white sister and the colonized women. In fact the "other woman" is never the "addressee" or interlocutor of Woolf's writings, never a part of her "community of the outsiders." Thus the master/slave dialectic between Shakespeare and his white sister is complicated by the objectification of black and Oriental women in Woolf's texts. The white female poet fails to address or listen to the black woman, to imagine an interracial solidarity between women based on different but interrelated patterns of exclusion from aesthetics and history. And this failure to contest the racialized concepts of aesthetics repeats the objectification of other women. Although Woolf fails to analyze this objectification, the figures of femininity and race are a shattering reminder of the monstrous destruction of the potential of art by gender, colonial, and class exploitation. As Woolf suggests, art's promise of freedom cannot be separated from the history of political and economic domination that threatens art's own possibility: just as it is impossible to find poets among the exploited working class, so too "it would have been impossible, *completely and entirely*, for any woman to have written the plays of Shakespeare in the age of Shakespeare" (*RO*, 48, emphasis added).

One way the contradiction between revolutionary and melancholic modernisms manifests itself in Woolf's texts is through the antithesis of aesthetic freedom and its destruction. Another way this contradiction is mobilized is through the erasure of gender domination from history, aesthetics, and politics. Rather than being an object of critical analysis, the exclusion of women is reproduced in normative accounts of history: "the life of the average Elizabethan woman must be scattered about somewhere, could one collect it and make a book of it. . . . I thought, looking about the shelves for books that were not there, to suggest to the students of those famous colleges that they should re-write history" (*RO*, 45). The same can be said about the scattered, unrecorded lives of colonized women abroad. Such absence from history implies that the destruction of female creativity has the status of nonevent, of something that has never happened yet haunts and interrupts historical time. In a predictable fetishistic fashion, male poets compensate for the exclusion of white women by creating fascinating female characters, such as Shakespeare's Cleopatra or Lady Macbeth. Woolf links this fetishistic denial to the monstrous contradiction between the absence of ordinary women in historical narratives and the fantasmatic presence of female characters in male poetry: "She pervades poetry from cover to cover; she is all but absent from history. . . . It was certainly an odd monster that one made up by reading the historians first and the poets afterwards" (*RO*, 43–44).

In *A Room of One's Own*, the monstrous antithesis between the fetishistic work of poetry and the obliterating work of history is a symptom of another contradiction between spiritual freedom and enslaving materiality. As Woolf points out, these contradictions are projected as the monstrosity of female beauty, which appears as "a worm winged like an eagle; the spirit of life and beauty in a kitchen chopping up suet" (*RO*, 44). This displacement of the unreconciled, monstrous contradiction between the work of art's materiality and freedom onto white femininity is reenforced by the mocking associations of the female artist with animality in both theology and literature: "Cats do not go to heaven. Women cannot write the plays of Shakespeare" (*RO*, 46). Woolf imagines an angry misogynist writing about the inferiority of women "as if he were killing some noxious insect . . . but even when he had killed it that did not satisfy him; he must go on killing it" (RO, 31). At the basis of this violent analogy between femininity and animality is the absence of soul or the spirit. The spirit of freedom, let us recall, is one of the characteristic features of art. Since woman, associated with enslaving materiality, is deprived of this spirit, we should not be surprised that Dr. Johnson's remark about women preachers is repeated in 1928 about women musicians: "'Sir, a woman's composing is like a dog's walking on his hind legs. It is not done well, but you are surprised to find it done at all'" (RO, 54).

Erased from historical and literary language, and projected instead as the "inferior" female gender, the violent contradictions between freedom and domination, spirit and materiality, writing and destruction are incorporated as the suicidal internal struggle of female melancholia: "Who shall measure the heat and violence of the poet's heart when caught and tangled in a woman's body?" (RO, 48). Unacknowledged as political domination, gender oppression manifests itself as the private suffering of isolated women and their inferior "character." What Woolf diagnoses, therefore, is not only the destruction inflicted on women by patriarchal culture but also the violent substitution of gender antagonisms by the internal suffering of subjugated groups. In the absence of the collective struggle for women's political, economic, and educational rights, the female poet is destroyed not only by the external conditions of gender and class oppression but also by internalized feelings of pain, inferiority, and resentment. Political domination is in fact intensified by the internal self-destructive struggle of the female poet "caught and tangled in a woman's body": by madness, torture, scattering, and the violent tearing and "pulling asunder" of both the artwork and the female poet (RO, 49). The female poet would have been "crazed with the torture that her gift had put her to . . . a highly gifted girl who had tried to use her gift for poetry would have been so thwarted and hindered by other people, so tortured and pulled asunder by her own contrary instincts" (RO, 49). The freedom that art calls for would have presented for the female poet "dilemma which might well have killed her," and if she survived it would have killed or "twisted and deformed" her work and her body. In contrast to a reconciliation signified by aesthetic harmony, the melancholia of the female poet, excluded from history and humanity itself, embodies a dangerous state of war between art and body, matter, and sociopolitical conditions: "[A] woman [is] at strife against herself" (RO, 51). Woolf suggests that the effect of these contradictions associated with feminine melancholia is the invisible, untimely feminized death of art—the invisible destruction of literary practice prior to the conceptualization "the end of art" in modernity.

The destruction of the female writing leaves, nonetheless, dispersed traces in displaced figures of animality, the witch, the madwoman, the mothers of accomplished men, and in the collective anonymous creations.[14] By collecting these traces, Woolf explores the impossible possibility of transforming the violent legacy of destruction into "free" women's writing. Yet she emphatically argues such transformation is not synonymous with the unmediated subjective expression of women's rage. The most controversial part of Woolf's argument for feminist critics is her claim that the literary expression of justifiable female anger is neither a liberation from melancholia nor a manifestation of artistic freedom but rather a crippling and reactive resentment. Under the weight of resentment women betray, compromise, or even abandon their work because they focus on their individual feelings of suffering and anger rather than on the aesthetic mediation of affective, linguistic, and political relations in the process of writing itself: "Her books," Woolf argues, "will be deformed and twisted. She will write in a rage where she should write calmly. . . . She will write of herself where she should write of her characters" (RO, 69–70). Unlike the collective practice of freedom, which teaches women the joy of revolt and of creating new forms of life, solitary anger thwarts the potential of artistic freedom: "It is clear that anger was tampering with the integrity of Charlotte Brontë the novelist. She left her story, to which her entire devotion was due, to attend to some personal grievance" (RO, 73).

Although many critics have read these passages as the suppression of Woolf's own anger,[15] I propose to reinterpret them as Woolf's feminist revision of the Nietzschean critique of melancholic resentment.[16] This might be a counterintuitive claim, since the outward-directed expression of female rage, discouraged through centuries, seems at first glance to be a reversal of the violent self-accusations of the melancholic. Yet, as Nietzsche suggests in Thus Spoke Zarathustra, resentment, though more commonly associated with rage, anger, guilt, and revenge, might be one of the most "secret" names for melancholy, springing from the powerlessness of the will to change the past.[17] As Giorgio Agamben points out, for Nietzsche the impossibility of changing the past "is what torments the will, transforming it into resentment."[18] As a reactive rather than creative affect, resentment is therefore a frustrated and powerless will

riveted to past injuries rather than engaged in the creation of new political or artistic forms of life. As such, resentment might be interpreted as
a symptom of a failed mourning and a failure to participate in the struggle to end the oppression of women. Indeed, as Woolf argues in *A Room
of One's Own*, female writers' rage and defensive protests against im-
puted inferiority perpetuate women's subjugation by riveting them to
their injuries, keeping them dependent on the opinions of others, and,
especially, blocking the possibility of political and aesthetic transformation. Consequently, it is not only oppressive material conditions, the madness of melancholia, and women's exclusion from the literary tradition—
for instance, the absence of "the common sentence ready for" women's
use—but also the culture of resentment that impedes women's creativity.

According to Woolf, the unmediated expression of female anger in
literature remains a reactive force of resentment as long as its violence is
not transformed either into a political action or artistic practice but interrupts and deforms the conception of the work of art from outside, as it
were. This opposition between the reactive force of anger and the creative
force of artistic freedom does not imply that women should simply repress their anger (and that is how Woolf has been more frequently interpreted), but, on the contrary, it means that they should transform rage
into either an artistic practice or a collective struggle for freedom. For
Woolf, the unmediated expression of female anger is the negative counterpart of an unmediated expression of masculine freedom; whether it is
the spontaneity of originality or the spontaneity of female rage, both
deny the mediation of subjective expression through the materiality of
the work of art and the social process of making. At stake in Woolf's
feminists aesthetics is, therefore, not only the critique of the false spontaneity of originality but also the transformation of the crippling, reactive
forces of melancholia and anger into the iconoclastic and innovative force
of art's immanent "revolution," into an element of artistic composition.
In "Professions for Women" Woolf argues that one of the phantoms a
woman writer has to kill in order to write is the Angel in the House—the
phantom of self-sacrifice and chastity; in *A Room of One's Own* she argues for the necessity of slaying the opposite demon, what might be
called the Anger in the House. As she writes in "Professions for Women,"
"indeed it will be a long time still, I think, before a woman can sit down
to write a book without finding a phantom to be slain."[19]

For Woolf the overcoming of the culture of resentment is a necessary
precondition of women's artistic practice. Yet this overcoming of the crip-

pling effects of anger is not an isolated subjective act since it depends on women's collective struggle for and practice of freedom, which teaches them the joy of the battle and the joy of creating new forms of life. It is this joy that allows art to bear witness to the history of destruction without turning that testimony into a subjective expression of anger or resentment. Furthermore, intersubjective relations with other women transform anger into conditions of critique—they enable female writers "to discuss and define" the ideological phantoms impeding literary work: "for thus only can the labor be shared, the difficulties be solved. But besides this, it is necessary also to discuss the ends and the aims for which we are fighting, for which we are doing battle with these formidable obstacles. Those aims cannot be taken for granted; they must be perpetually questioned and examined."[20] Political revolt and a collective culture of freedom are necessary therefore to overcome both melancholia and resentment and to transform them into artistic creation.

This unprecedented possibility of women's art is presented in the concluding pages of *A Room of One's Own* as the parable of the second coming of Shakespeare's dead sister. This future resurrection of the female poet requires, however, a double preparation: women's ongoing struggle for the political and economic culture of freedom, on the one hand, and, on the other hand, the continuous literary struggle against ossified conventions and ideological phantoms on the level of literary composition. Such literary struggle and invention are at stake in the fictional figure of a modern writer, Mary Carmichael. Supported by women's collective political/economic struggle and yet already practicing aesthetic freedom in her art, Mary is a transitional and fictional figure in an otherwise seemingly historical chronology of British women writers. She appears in the hiatus between what is no longer—the anonymous traces of destroyed female bodies and languages—and what is yet to come—the future possibility of female art. At the beginning of *A Room of One's Own* Mary Carmichael is one of three possible pen names the narrator borrows from an anonymous folk ballad about three Marys, one of whom will be sentenced to death for sexual transgression. Marked by the shadow of death and anonymity, Mary Carmichael becomes toward the end of the text an innovative writer who, almost liberated from hatred and fear, has a remarkable and free sensibility. This freedom allows her to laugh at the peculiarities of the other sex, to ignore the admonitions and criticisms of the bishops and the deans, and to focus instead on the process of writing itself. She stretches language to its limit in order to find a way of expressing "unrecorded gestures" of femininity, to uncover "almost unknown or unrecorded things," and to bring to light that which had been buried: destroyed bodies of women, women's unrecorded lives, sexual and professional relations among women, and female political communities (*RO*, 92). By providing an alternative to the destructive freedom of masculine genius, to the madness of melancholia, and to female resentment, Mary transforms the destruction of female art into the contestation of literary conventions. She inscribes on the level of form the historical contradiction between Shakespeare and his imaginary sister, between the aesthetic ideal of freedom and gendered and imperialist violence. To be sure, she writes under an almost suffocating burden of unrecorded lives; yet, because her writing is enabled by relations with other women, she can record that burden without resentment and transform it, as the title of her work suggests, into the joy of *Life's Adventure*.

Mary Carmichael's iconoclastic and transformative practice is one of the preconditions for the future appearance of the female poet. The second precondition, on which I want to focus in greater detail, is the community of women and their struggle for a political culture of freedom. The role of the community of women, so often stressed in Woolf's texts, is especially emphasized in the concluding fable of the second coming of Judith Shakespeare. At the end of *A Room of One's Own*, this fable reenacts the rebirth of the dead female poet, who was buried at a crossroads to prevent her emergence from the invisible underground of social and poetic transactions. Yet for Woolf the future coming of the female poet is intertwined with the possibility of art as such. As a preamble to her vision, Woolf comments on the ingrained indifference of the modern public to "the future of fiction" (*RO*, 95). Against thousands of instructions of what women should be writing and admonitions of what they should not, Woolf offers "a little fantastic" vision of what does not yet exist—of the possibility of female artistic freedom, which so far has been consistently destroyed, thwarted, or blocked in history: "Now my belief is that this poet who never wrote a word and was buried at the crossroads still lives. She lives in you and in me, and in many other women who are not here tonight, for they are washing up the dishes and putting the children to bed. But she lives; for great poets . . . need only the opportunity to walk among us in flesh. This opportunity, as I think, it is now coming within your power to give her" (*RO*, 113). As the rhetoric of the second coming in this passage suggests, the relation between female art and the political practice of the female communities both evokes and displaces male messianism. Julia Briggs finds this messianic rhetoric to be one of "the most subversive" parodies in the text, which began with "a woman breaking patriarchal taboos in an Edenic garden," and ends with the promise of the second coming of the female writer, standing "in the place of the savior of the scriptures."[21] Yet at stake in this feminist displacement of messianic rhetoric is not only irony but also a contestation of historical chronology and causality. Because of its incompletion and interruption of historical sequence, messianic time has been frequently evoked by poststructuralist critics to critique historical necessity and to underscore the possibility of a retrospective revision of history. As Agamben, for instance, explains, messianic time signifies a disruption of the linear by "the paradoxical tension between an *already* and a *not yet*. . . . The messianic event has already happened . . . but, nevertheless, in order to truly be fulfilled, this implies an additional time."[22] The paradox of messianic time reenacts therefore an interminable deferral of the fulfillment of history, which, although it has already happened, has to be repeated again in the unreachable future. By making the meaning of the past dependent on the future completion, the messianic event contests the irreversibility of the past and, in so doing, restores the possibility of change to the past itself.

The possibility of changing the past is one of the conditions of overcoming resentment—which as we recall represents the crippling enslavement of the will by past injury. Yet Woolf's overcoming of resentment depends on a different temporal structure and ultimately calls for a replacement of the messianic event by the transformative practice of female communities. In place of the messianic event, Woolf presents a paradoxical tension between the traces of the worldly event—the destruction of the female poet—radically excluded from history and the restoration of its future possibility through artistic and political practice. The past event—the first coming of the female poet—has never taken place in language and recorded history, but occurred only as the monstrous destruction of the half-female/half-animal body. This displacement from collective historical narrative to the anonymous bodies of women creates the crippling effects of melancholia and resentment, both of which represents powerlessness vis-à-vis past destruction. The second, yet nonetheless unprecedented, arrival of the female poet will be an event of transformative poetic practice. By undermining historical continuity and determination, this temporal disjunction between what has never been (a female Shakespeare) and its

future possibility marks the radical contingency of history and in so doing restores the possibility of transformation not only to the present but
to the past itself. If women's artistic and political practice replaces a messianic event, then such practice not only reclaims the past but, to paraphrase Agamben, saves what has never been (*PCE*, 270). As a precondition of overcoming resentment, the historical recovery in Woolf's text is
intertwined with a strange temporality of the inaugural "second" time,
which was not given a chance to occur as a linguistic, historical event for
the first time. Because the arrival of Judith Shakespeare signifies both
repetition and the unprecedented occurrence, this new beginning nonetheless bears witness to the past destruction and transforms the destroyed flesh of history into future possibilities of poetic language.

As Woolf's references to the bodies of women suggest, what is at stake
in the parable of Judith Shakespeare is the replacement of both the individual "incandescent" mind of genius *and* the transcendent messianic
redemption by the inaugural temporality of the worldly, embodied, and
relational practice of women in politics and art. Woolf figures the future
of art as the rebirth of the anonymously buried female body: "the dead
poet . . . will put on the body which she has so often laid down" (*RO*, 114).
Unlike the spontaneity of individual originality or the messianic transcendence of history, the future possibility of poetry is sustained by the
anonymous communities of women whose unrecorded lives and bodies
transmit the traces of the past destruction and whose practice opens the
possibility of inscribing these traces in language. The aesthetic freedom
symbolized by the female poet is, therefore, not the fetishized spontaneity of the isolated poet because its possibility emerges from the transpersonal, relational, and embodied practice of women: "I maintain that she
would come if we worked for her" (*RO*, 113–114).

Intertwined with women's continued struggle for freedom in the political and private spheres, freedom manifesting itself in artistic practice
is therefore distinguished from the oedipal battle between fathers and
the sons, which, for instance, opens *To the Lighthouse* and continues as a
distant accompaniment of Lily's painting. By gathering isolated women,
by inventing supportive relations among them that are not mediated by
male signature, this collective work transforms privatized and paralyzing
resentment into the possibility of artistic or political praxis. In so doing,
it also enables a transformation of destroyed female authorship into the
possibility of art. Thus, in contrast to Adorno's aesthetic theory, Woolf

argues that the work of art, which negates domination and provides a model for a better political praxis in its own right, is itself intertwined with political struggle and the practice of freedom by subjugated groups. We could say that this paradox represents Woolf's feminist reformulation of the status of literary practice. For Adorno, we recall, the heteronomous autonomy of art is both implicated in and free from political domination. For Woolf, however, such heteronomous autonomy in women's art also implies a mutual interrelation between the possibility of art and the possibility of freedom in women's lives.

What is helpful for understanding Woolf's appeal to the community of women giving "birth" to the female poet is Hannah Arendt's emphasis on the interdependence between political community and relational creative freedom (*OR*, 175). By bringing together dispersed women, Woolf's female community of outsiders "gathers together the isolated strength of the allied partners" (*OR*, 170), increases their capacities, and creates new possibilities for speech and action. These new possibilities emerging from the formation of political communities constitute for Arendt "the world building capacity of man" (*OR*, 175). Despite a certain homosocial rhetoric in her work, "the world building capacity" is also called the birth of a new world. Ultimately what is at stake in Woolf's numerous figurations of women's "communities of their own" is a shift from procreation to the world-building capacity of women. As Woolf puts it, the creative power of women, which "differs greatly" from the power of men, must "harness itself to pens and brushes and business and politics" (*RO*, 87). The world-building capacities of women shed a new light on Woolf's suggestion that the work of art, which might provide a model of a better political praxis without domination, itself depends on the political practice of freedom. The unheard-of creation of the communities of outsiders among women not only augments their capacities but also enact a "birth" of a different world, a world in which a female poet could exist in flesh and in language: "As for her coming without that preparation, without that effort on our part, without that determination that when she is *born* again she shall find it possible to live and write her poetry, that we cannot expect, for that would be *impossible*" (*RO*, 114, emphasis added).

By displacing male messianic redemption and the artistic originality by the inaugural temporality of intersubjective, embodied practice, Woolf suggests a mutual interrelation between the political struggle for freedom and poetic practice. Ultimately, it is this interaction that transforms the "impossible" into the birth of a new world. The task of a poet, whose life and praxis is made possible by the community of the outsiders, is to create new possibilities of language in order to express the unheard-of relation among women themselves. She has to invent a new "grammar" of female speech and action. As Woolf observes, relations between women—political, erotic, or the relations of friendship "unlit by the capricious and colored light of the other sex" (*RO*, 84)—require a transformation of all the resources of patriarchal language unsuited to these purposes. Thus the relation between the female poet and female collectivity, like the relationship between word and deed, is sustained by a mutual gift: on the one hand, the world-building capacities of female community transform the historical legacy of destruction, melancholia, and resentment into a possibility of creative practice. On the other hand, women's relations among themselves cannot take shape without a transformation of language. The formation of female community calls for art, since "the resources of the English language would be much put to the stretch, and the whole flights of words need to wing their way illegitimately into the existence" (*RO*, 87) before one could extract the "creative force" sedimented in unrecorded lives, and the bricks of private rooms, and express the relations among women in language. Thus female community is formed in relation to the activity of the poet who draws her life from the lives of the dead, from "the unknown" lives of "her forerunners" (*RO*, 114) and who, in turn, gives the gift of language.

Ultimately, the relation between melancholic and revolutionary modernism and Woolf's own "aesthetic theory" enables a redefinition of practice in modernism. Such a practice implies a chiasmatic and non-chronological relation between women's political struggle and aesthetic possibilities. The militant struggle for the vote, economic opportunities, and women's rights is one of the preconditions of women's political and intellectual freedom, which transforms the impossibility and the destruction of female art into its future possibility. Yet, as an act of revolution in its own right, women's experimental literature in turn presupposes and creates new possibilities of freedom and signification.[23] This chiasmatic juxtaposition of the destruction of female art with the revolutionary struggle for a new beginning suggests that relations between women's art and politics escape simple causality or chronology and call instead for a rethinking of the art/politics divide in the context of what no longer exists or does not yet exist: the impossibility and possibility of female freedom.

On Production, Female Potentiality, and the Wild Experiment

To approach the relation between art and politics in terms of the fragile possibilities of female freedom is to redefine the stakes of modernism. In this context the familiar divide between realism and experimental writing can be more appropriately defined as the opposition between the aesthetics of actuality (realism) and the aesthetics of possibility (modernism). Woolf's experimental writing is on the side of the "feminine" aesthetics of possibility emerging out of destruction and not on the side of the politically determined "reality," which excludes, disciplines, or damages women's abilities. As she suggests at the beginning of A Room of One's Own, women's experimental writing shifts the emphasis from the representation of ideological "facts" to the exploration of what is excluded from history and the creation of new possibilities in "fiction." The possibility of change reveals the indeterminacy of historical reference, the plurality of events, and the ideological struggles over interpretations of history. By subverting historical causality, "feminine" experimental writing shows that history itself has to be interpreted in terms of possibilities rather than facts, that there is no one specific event that could exemplify a change in human character.

Prior to A Room of One's Own, the aesthetic of feminine potentiality is explored in Woolf's famous essays and aesthetic manifestos, such as "Modern Novels" (1919) and its later version "Modern Fiction" (1925), "Mr. Bennett and Mrs. Brown"(1923) and the 1924 "Character in Fiction" (a revised version of "Mr. Bennett and Mrs. Brown").[24] These aesthetic manifestos are part of Woolf's larger critique of realism and her ideological battle with the "character" of femininity and experimental literature. In fact, the first version of the "Mr. Bennett and Mrs. Brown" essay was written in response to Arnold Bennett's negative and condescending review of Woolf's Jacob's Room, a review which dismissed Woolf's formal experimentation as "cleverness . . . the lowest of all artistic qualities."[25] Symptomatic of the "decay" of the modern novel, such cleverness fails to create "real" characters. By 1920 Bennett, in his Our Women: Chapters on the Sex-Discord, shifts the target of his attack from the literary character to gender politics and makes a sweeping judgment about the "reality" of women's inferior intellectual and artistic abilities. Consequently, when Woolf declares her "war" on Mr. Bennett, the conflict between reality/

potentiality in aesthetics (the dispute over the literary character) and in gender politics (the "abilities" of women) is equally at stake. In her response in the *New Statesman*, Woolf strongly argues for women's unlimited potential for change: "I must repeat that the fact that women have improved . . . shows that they might still improve; for I cannot see why *a limit should to be set* to their improvement in the nineteenth century rather than in the one hundred and nineteenth (emphasis added)."[26]

Woolf defends the unlimited potential of literary experimentation and female capacities in her controversial claim in "Character in Fiction" that "on or about December 1910" human character changed and that this change had been missed by realist writers like Arnold Bennett (CF, 421).[27] The change in human character is intertwined with the political shift in power relations "between masters and servants, husbands and wives, parents and children" (CF, 422) and thus with a veritable reversal of the gendered master/slave dialectic. There are three important aspects of Woolf's analysis of the human potential to change: first of all, Woolf explores this capacity through fictional feminine figures like Mrs. Brown or the ancient militant Clytemnestra. For instance, Woolf writes: "Do you ask for more solemn instances of the power of the human race to change? Read *Agamemnon*, and see whether, in process of time, your sympathies are not almost entirely with Clytemnestra" (CF, 422). Modern audience's sympathetic identification with subversive femininity, with the mother avenging the murderous sacrifice of her daughter for political ends, rather than with the murderous father/king, is for Woolf a manifestation not only of a change in gender relations but of the human capacity to change as such. Is such a change a recovery of the "maternal" genealogy for experimental women's writing?

The second point Woolf makes is that the aesthetics of female potentiality calls for a critique of the paradigm of production and its increasing commodification of literature. As I have discussed in chapter 2, the widespread critiques of praxis in capitalism, advanced, in the wake of Marx, by Adorno, Kristeva, and Agamben, among others, point out that in Western modernity different kinds of human activity, including art and politics, have become subordinated to commodity production. By colonizing art, labor, and political action, production not only perverts self-realization into alienation but culminates in the worldwide domination of nature and exploitation of other peoples. By subordinating all forms of making, speaking, acting, and work itself to alienated labor, Western political and economic praxis obliterates the otherness of the world and the alterity of others by transforming them into the "materials" of the self-production of the hegemonic subject, which, in the last instance, is capital itself. Although Woolf disagrees with this diagnosis of the total colonization of literary and political praxis because she believes in the liberating possibilities of writing and action sustained by the communities of women/outsiders, she is nonetheless very critical of imperial and economic domination. The unjust gendered division of labor, which enables artistic activity, is thematically and formally inscribed in most of her texts, whether it is her claim that the economic exploitation of the working class destroys the very possibility of art in *A Room of One's Own*, her emphasis on the invisible labor of cleaning women in *To the Lighthouse*, or the shame of property in *Orlando*. Woolf is equally critical of the fact that innovation in modernity is all too often synonymous with the production of new commodities and technological progress.

The critique of commodity, property, and production is what is at stake in Woolf's famous but misleading distinction between "materialist" and "spiritual" writers (MN, 32). Given the materialism of the body she advocates in *A Room of One's Own*, it might be surprising that in "Character in Fiction" she criticizes the "materialism" of Edwardian novelists—a materialism of will and commodities. Since, as Woolf argues in *A Room of One's Own*, the work of art depends on material conditions and on embodied relations to others, "spiritual writers" do not deny these conditions but struggle for the invention/recovery of new potentialities rather than reproducing unjust power relations. By contrast, "materialist" writers represent life either through instrumental social reforms or the accumulation and circulation of new commodities. As Woolf sardonically observes, the characters of Mr. Bennett, one of the materialist writers, "spend their time in some softly padded first-class railway carriage . . . and the destiny to which they travel so luxuriously becomes more and more unquestionably an eternity of bliss spent in the very best hotel in Brighton" (MN, 32).

The most original aspect of Woolf's critique of commodity production is her diagnosis of the specular role of femininity that compensates for alienation in capitalism. Prior to Irigaray's famous critique of the specular function of femininity, Woolf argues that femininity has been forced to serve as the unacknowledged, reflective "mirror" supporting patriarchal narcissistic self-production: "women have served all these centuries as looking-glasses possessing the magic and delicious power of reflecting the figure of man at twice its natural size. Without that power probably the Earth would still be swamp and jungle. The glories of all our wars would be unknown" (*RO*, 35–36). In Woolf's diagnosis of gender and racist domination, the alienating praxis can be associated with the self-production of the hegemonic subject because of the supplementary compensating role of white femininity, which functions as a mirror concealing alienation and magnifying the narcissistic effects of the patriarchal will to power. By shattering this specular support of the dominant subject, Woolf stresses nonappropriative, passionate relations to others and to the world, relations that are irreducible to will and domination and yet are a source of creativity. Woolf rejects realism in the name of the feminist struggles for the new possibilities.

What motivates Woolf's critique of realism, historical determination, and production is a feminist aesthetic of potentiality. Yet how should we understand such potentiality? The relation between the feminine, possibility, and experimental aesthetics transforms the very meaning of femininity so that it is no longer is associated with enslaving materiality, melancholia, or resentment but becomes instead the exemplary figure of the human capacity to change. And, conversely, the meaning of possibility changes as well, once it is associated with women's struggle against the destruction of their capacities rather than with agency or will. Furthermore, potentiality also allows us to rethink Woolf's literary "wild experiments," such as stream of consciousness, interior monologue, shifts in gender identity, and the perspectival play of multiple narrative points of view in *To the Lighthouse, Orlando*, or *The Waves*. The main question that I want to consider is the relation between "feminine" potentiality and experimental writing.

What is original in Woolf's analysis of feminine potentiality is the contradiction between women's unlimited ability to change and their experience of powerlessness and subjugation. At stake in this contradiction is not only a redefinition of revolutionary/melancholic modernism but also of potentiality itself. How does the significance of possibility change once it is analyzed in the context of subjugation and destruction rather than in the context of agency or empowerment? In the essays "Mr. Bennett and Mrs. Brown" and "Character in Fiction" the contradiction between powerlessness and possibility is famously embodied in the figure of Mrs. Brown, a "very small, very tenacious; at once very frail and very heroic" old lady (CF, 425). On the one hand, an abused old woman subjected to the "bullying, menacing" power of her male companions and, on the other hand, an impish phantom of "infinite possibilities," Mrs. Brown is Woolf's paradigmatic figure of the unlimited potential of literature and the un-precedented "power of the human race" to change. As a figure of potenti-ality, Mrs. Brown exhibits a fundamental aporia between political power-lessness, produced and reenforced by the recurrent aesthetic/political judgment of "you cannot" addressed to women—"can't paint, can't write," experienced for instance by Lily Briscoe in *To the Lighthouse* (*TTL*, 159)—and the possibility of "we can," presupposed by the human capacity to change. Like Judith Shakespeare in the sixteenth century, Orlando in the eighteenth and nineteenth centuries, Rhonda in *The Waves*, or the daughters of educated men in the twentieth century, Mrs. Brown is sub-jected to male economic, legal, and aesthetic power. This power is signi-fied in Woolf's essay by men of letters and a man of business who has "some power over her which he was exerting disagreeably" (CF, 424). Such subjection of feminine potentiality to political and aesthetic power produces "waste" and "futility," evident for instance in "the horrible do-mestic tradition which made it seemly for a woman of genius to spend her time . . . scouring saucepans, instead of writing books" (CF, 422). Evoking censorship and political and imperialist domination in *Orlando*, class and gender exclusion in *A Room of One's Own* and *To the Lighthouse*, "waste" and "futility" signify a destruction of female potentiality not only by imperialist, class, and gender politics but also by literary institutions. Nonetheless, Mrs. Brown is also a figure of "infinite possibilities, [assur-ing] us that there is no bound to the horizon" (MN, 36) either to literature or to the human capacity of change. She embodies the possibility of revo-lutionary change manifesting itself in the "insurrection" against empire, gender norms, and literary conventions.[28]

Through these contradictions, Woolf explores hitherto completely un-charted territory in modern aesthetics, namely, a feminine modality of possibility that emerges out of "waste" and "futility." To diagnose the origi-nality of Woolf's aporetic formulations of feminine aesthetic potential, I juxtapose her writing with Agamben's philosophical reflection on poten-tiality. For Agamben, the exemplary instance of potentiality is another literary figure, namely, Herman Melville's Bartleby and his famous for-mula "I prefer not to." Agamben makes the powerful argument that pos-sibility exceeds its historical realization. As he puts it, "contrary to the traditional idea of potentiality that is annulled in actuality, here we are confronted with a potentiality that conserves itself and saves itself in ac-tuality. Here potentiality, so to speak, survives actuality" (*PCE*, 184.) Po-tentiality exceeds historical realization because it is distinguished from the will to power, moral law, and individual agency. Historically, philosophers have attempted to restrict the ambiguities of potentiality "by reducing it to the terms of will and necessity. Not what you *can* do, but what you *want* to do or *must* do is its dominant theme. . . . To believe that will has power over potentiality, that the passage to actuality is the result of a decision that puts an end to the ambiguity of potentiality . . . this is the perpetual illusion of morality" (*PCE*, 254). Woolf proposes a similar critique of the ideology of will, which is most visible in her contestation of the imperialist politics of the British Empire. As if in parody of Lewis's "hailing" in *Blast*, the narrator in *Orlando* hails "anything that interrupts and compounds the tapping of the typewriters and filing of letters and forging of links and chains, binding the Empire together" (*O*, 216). One of the most significant links "binding the Empire together" is the political and aesthetic concept of the "real" character in the novel—the "Captain self, the Key self, which amalgamates . . . controls" and imprisons the plurality of being (*O*, 227). Evocative of the aridity of the letter *I* discussed in *A Room of One's Own*, the Captain self is a counterpart of genius—both of them are haunted by the destruction of feminine and colonized bodies.

According to Agamben, what distinguishes potentiality from agency and will is its relation to privation. As Bartleby's formula suggests, the original meaning of the capacity to do something includes the capacity not to act. For instance, the architect's ability to build a house, or the novelist's ability to write, persist even when they do not work; therefore, their abilities include their capacity not to act: "It is a potentiality that is not simply the potential to do this or that thing but potential to not-do, potential not to pass into actuality" (*PCE*, 179–180). Since the potential includes the potential not to act, it can never be fully actualized because what exceeds its realization is the ambiguous capacity of "not-to." It is this excessive potentiality that questions the historical determination of power, marks the contingency of historical reality, and opens a possibility of freedom. Yet, although Agamben's redefinition distinguishes potentiality from agency and will, it nonetheless raises three questions that are crucial to Woolf's conception of experimental writing and femininity. The first question pertains to the relational aspect of potentiality—how is potential related to the capacities/incapacities of others, say, to Woolf's female communities of outsiders and to what Woolf calls "life?" Because Agamben implicitly interrogates potentiality in the context of the isolated subject, the only way he can liberate it from individual will is by relating possibility "to its own privation" rather than to the potentialities of others. The second question is about the relation between potentiality, materiality, and passion. I refer here to materiality in the double sense of the body of the female artist and of the work of art, for instance, the materiality of the house in Agamben's example of the architect or the materiality of the paint, shapes, and colors in Lily's painting or the materiality of literary language in *Orlando*. Ultimately, the most important question for Woolf and feminism is how to liberate potentiality from the most extreme effects of political domination—from destitution and powerlessness, and impossibility—signified in Agamben's own work by "bare life," in Woolf's texts by the destroyed body of Judith Shakespeare, and in Nella Larsen's novels by the death of the black female figures of writing, beauty, and taste (Helga in *Quicksand* and Clare in *Passing*).

Although Bartleby's "I prefer not to" suspends the distinction between possibility and its privation and challenges individual will (*PCE*, 257), it neither suggests how potentiality can survive its systematic destruction by subjugation, which literature is summoned to witness and contest, nor shows how impotentiality can be a source of a creative praxis. Thus, although Woolf also distinguishes the human "capacity for change" from the masculine will to power, she is nonetheless concerned with a fundamentally different problem, namely, with the liberation of potentiality from the impossibility and destruction of human abilities. What is at stake in Woolf's aesthetics is the survival of women's unrealized capacities despite their destruction, despite the perennial oppositions of "you cannot"—"can't paint, can't write" (*TTL*, 48, 159)—masquerading as impersonal aesthetic judgments. In the case of femininity, the politically critical distinctions between the enabling privation (the ability not to act) and destroyed capacities have been systematically erased and equated with powerlessness. Although Agamben begins his essay "On Potentiality" with a reference to the female Russian poet Anna Akhmatova, who, standing outside a prison to hear the news of her imprisoned son, utters "I can" in response to another woman, he does not pursue this feminine, relational possibility in the face of political destruction. By contrast, Woolf's multiple references to female communities in *A Room of One's Own*, *Orlando* or *Three Guineas* suggest that only the relational mode of potentiality can enable its survival in history. Such survival of feminine possibility cannot be explained by its privation, but rather by its relation to intersubjective capacities of "I/we can." Indeed, as Agamben himself reminds us, human beings exist in the mode of potentiality only "insofar as *they know and produce*" (*PCE*, 182, emphasis added). Only if my capacity to write, paint, or act politically is protected and enhanced in my relations with others can I preserve my abilities when I do not act and especially when I'm told that I cannot do so. Because the feminine experience of impotentiality—"I *can* not-to"—has been so often confused with powerlessness and disqualified as inferiority—as "you *cannot*"—the liberating impotentiality of women and other subjugated groups has to preserve its relation to "I/we can." Only then the inferiority projected onto the feminine can be deprived of its necessity and transformed into a *capacity* for not acting, which is inseparable from the capacity for acting with others.

Finally, what enables the distinction between impotentiality—the capacity not to act—and the brunt of failure or impossibility is the existence of the potential associated with what Woolf calls "life itself" (*CF*, 436). This relation between experimental writing and life emphasizes the excess of possibility beyond the opposition between existence and nonexistence. Woolf's frequent references to "life itself" resonate with what Agamben calls the ontological dimension of potentiality. Because it exceeds both its destruction and its accomplishment, potentiality, Agamben argues, emancipates "itself from Being and non-Being alike" and "creates its own ontology" (or existence; *PCE*, 259). Woolf interprets such an ontological dimension as the transsubjective potential of life, which is beyond human capacities. Paradoxically, the relational character of potentiality includes not only intersubjective capacities but also the transpersonal potentiality of life, which exceeds human abilities but nonetheless manifests itself through feminine figures. Mrs. Brown "is an old lady of unlimited capacity and infinite variety; capable of appearing in any place . . . saying anything and doing heaven knows what. But the things she says and the things she does . . . have an overwhelming fascination, for she is, of course, the spirit we live by, life itself" (*CF*, 436). These figures of the "unlimited *capacity* and infinite variety" of "life itself" anticipate Woolf's emphasis in *A Room of One's Own* on the relation between writing and life and not just "the world of men and women" (*RO*, 114). In the long list of Woolf's conditions, one of the crucial prerequisites for the reappearance of the female poet is the capacity to "see human beings not always in their relation to each other but in relation to reality; and the sky, too, and the trees or whatever it may be in themselves" (*RO*, 114). This is perhaps the most exquisite description of the relational aspect of the potential, which includes not only human communities but also historical world, trees, and sky and "whatever" beings might be in themselves.

When interpreted in terms of potentiality, these numerous references to the "phantom" of "life itself" are far removed from any association with biological process.[29] On the contrary, the potential of life contests any natural or political determinism and, in so doing, enables new political action, poetry, and writing. In "Modern Novels" Woolf famously describes this transsubjective dimension of life's potential as "the semi-transparent envelope, or luminous halo, surrounding us from the beginning of consciousness to the end" (MN, 33). This spectral aura of life, as the figure of the "envelope" suggests, is not far removed from writing. In fact, in the same passage Woolf describes the impressions of ordinary life on the surface of the mind as an "engraving" made "with the sharpness of steel" (MN, 33). Like the "life" of the dead female poet sustained by the collectivity of women, life's engravings in "Modern Novels" anticipate the title of Mary Carmichael's novel, *Life's Adventure,* while the "envelope" of potentiality recalls the "envelopes" of political letters Woolf was addressing during her work for "People's Suffrage" in 1910.[30] As writing and engraving, the spectral potential of life, exemplified by Mrs. Brown and sustained by the communities of women, is inseparable from the potentiality of language and experimental literature.

The relational potentiality associated with femininity and freedom enables Woolf to redefine experimental writing. As she puts it, in the work of art "nothing—no 'method,' no experiment, even of the wildest— is forbidden, but only falsity and pretense."[31] Although the word *experiment* might be associated with the worn-out clichés of modernism, for Woolf the stakes of experimental writing are intertwined with the status of praxis, femininity, and potentiality. In contrast to commodity production or historical determination, Woolf's literary experiment rescues from stultifying literary conventions potentiality exemplified by Mrs. Brown. It is not by accident, therefore, that the essay "Character in Fiction" begins with the relation between potentiality and experimental writing: "It *seems to be possible, perhaps* desirable, that I *may be* the only person in this room who has *committed* the folly of writing . . . a novel. And when I asked myself, as your invitation to speak to you about modern fiction made me ask myself, what *demon* whispered in my ear and urged me to my doom, a little figure rose before me . . . who said, 'My name is Brown. Catch me *if you can*'" (CF, 420, emphasis added). The proliferation of terms like *possible, perhaps, apparition,* or *if you can,* suggests that experimental writing both emerges from and rescues the phantom of possibility.

The aporia of female potentiality—the contradiction between power-lessness and unlimited capacity—is reflected in the two aspects of women's experimental writing: the iconoclastic and innovative. Woolf fundamentally redefines the familiar iconoclastic impulse of modernism as "the rescue" of female possibility from waste and destruction: "At whatever cost of life, limb, and damage to valuable property Mrs. Brown must be rescued, expressed, and set in her high relations to the world before . . . she disappeared for ever. And so the smashing and the crashing began" (CF, 433). The task of iconoclastic writing is to transform waste and im-possibility, associated with the feminine, into an enabling capacity to ne-gate destructive power relations and literary conventions. As Kevin Bell argues, Woolf"s "smashing and the crashing" is "the most shattering evi-dence of the text's principle of non-identity."[32] Like the iconoclastic aspect of the escalating suffrage militancy, the negativity of experimental art, which Woolf expresses in terms of a revolutionary rhetoric of "toppling down" the house of fiction (MBMB, 387), destroys ideologically discred-ited literary conventions, including linear plots, syntactic unity, and the coherence of literary genres: "if one were free . . . there would be no plot, little probability, and . . . the clear cut features of the tragic, the comic, the passionate, and the lyrical were dissolved beyond the possibility of sepa-rate recognition?" (MN, 33). Yet, since it is intertwined with the experi-mental artistic process, Woolf's iconoclasm ultimately moves beyond the negative aspect of modernism and leads to explorations of the unpredict-able relations between female potentiality, passion, writing, and life. In-deed, as Gayatri Spivak suggests, "unmaking" is as important in Woolf's novels as the invention of a new paradigm of aesthetic/erotic making.[33]

As we have seen, this contestation of aesthetic conventions is what is at work is Woolf's figures of modern artists, from Lily in *To the Lighthouse* to Mary Carmichael in *A Room of One's Own.* Turning negation into an aesthetic principle, Mary Carmichael destroys the continuity of the sen-tence and narrative coherence in order to inscribe on the level of form the destruction of women's capacities in history: "First she broke the sen-tence; now she has broken the sequence. Very well, she has every right to do both these things if she does them not for the sake of breaking, but for the sake of creating" (RO, 81). Reminiscent of Orlando's own mode of writing poetry through unwriting, Woolf's tearing apart of Shakespeare's name ("Or was it Sh—p—re?" [O, 229]), experimental writing performs the destruction of the literary universe announced in "Modern Fiction." More fundamentally, the breakdown of conventions of the realist fiction is associated with the inaugural temporality of the new beginning in the work of art. In "Modern Fiction" Woolf tells her audience to be patient with the sounds of destruction in the literary universe, even if the excessive noise of literary "axes" disturbs our desire to sleep; she pleads for her reader to tolerate "the spasmodic, the obscure, the fragmentary" because such destruction will inaugurate a new era in literature. As this emphasis on the new and unpredictable implies, the practice of freedom in literature is not only a negative struggle against sterile conventions but also an experimental disclosure of unprecedented and unimaginable potentialities—the emergence of a "different outline of form . . . difficult for us to grasp, incomprehensible to our predecessors" (MF, 632).[34]

Such an inauguration of a new beginning in literature cannot be accomplished by the iconoclastic destruction of "the very foundations and rules of literary society" (CF, 434) alone, since it requires the creation of a new "habitable dwelling place" for feminine potential in literature. Paradoxically, Woolf defines such innovation as the movement of "following" potentiality—the "new age" in literature can be brought about only by the poet's determination "never, never to desert Mrs. Brown" (CF, 436). Following potentiality is neither an original nor a derivative process, it is neither the actualization of the writer's capacities nor their abandonment. Rather, it means that writing engages in multiple and unpredictable transactions: with potentiality (or its destruction) in the historical world, with "life itself"—variously figured as phantom, "a will-o'-the-wisp," or "the gleams and flashes of this flying spirit" (MBMB, 387–88)—as well as with literary process.

The first implication of this strange fidelity to feminine relational potential is that the creation of new possibilities in experimental literature emerges from the exigency of literary form. Woolf's emphasis on "following" the possibilities of form resonates with Adorno's argument that experimental innovation emerges not from the intention of the artist, but from the artist's encounter with the unpredictable potentiality of form inherent in the materials of art: "The new is not a subjective category, rather it is a compulsion of the object itself. . . . By exigency, the new must be something willed; as what is other, however, it could not be what was willed. . . . The violence of the new, for which the name 'experimental' was adopted, is not to be attributed to subjective convictions or the psychological character of the artist. . . . productive artists are objectively compelled to experiment" (*AT*, 22–23). Because potential exceeds subjective capacities and emerges from the "objective" possibilities of literary form, which in turn embodies the traces of social relations, the effects of experimental writing are unpredictable and unforeseeable (*AT*, 24). And, conversely, this excess of potentiality in literature manifests itself not only as negativity or privation but as the creation of unprecedented novelty. Experimental writing is neither a "magnificent apparatus for catching life" (*MF*, 630) nor a production of characters or bicycles nor a heroic act of original making (as in Pound's famous slogan "make it new"). Rather the experimental "following" of ever shifting accents and deviations of literary form attempts, through literary making, to convey potential itself. As Woolf asks: "Is it not possible that the accent falls a little differently, that the moment of importance came before or after[?]. . . . Is it not perhaps the chief task of the novelist to convey this incessantly varying spirit with whatever stress or sudden deviation it may display . . . ?" (*MN*, 33). As the unpredictable feminine figure of literary form, Mrs. Brown "changes the shape, shifts the accent, of every scene in which she plays her part" (*MBMB*, 387–388). What following this movement reveals is "something hitherto ignored or unstressed . . . a feeling, a point of view suggesting a different and obscure outline of form. . . . The emphasis is laid upon such unexpected places that at first it seems as if there were no emphasis at all" (*MN*, 35). The shifting accents of the form create, as Lily in *To the Lighthouse* discovers, a "dancing rhythmical movement, as if the pauses where one part of the rhythm and the strokes another, and all were related; and so, lightly and swiftly pausing, striking, she scored her canvas with brown running nervous lines" (*TTL*, 158). In the exchange of "the fluidity of life" for the movement of form, Lily creates and in turn is carried by the rhythm, itself "quiver[ing] with a life," "strong enough to bear her along with it on its current" (*TTL*, 159).

Following "feminine" but nonetheless transpersonal potentiality in the process of writing is what allows for the transformation of female burning rage, melancholia, and loss into art's own "incandescence" (*RO*, 59). Incandescence is a striking metaphor for the metamorphosis of subjective feelings into the aesthetic glow of art's potential—indeed, in the draft version of *A Room of One's Own*, bearing the title "Women and Fiction," Woolf compares the role of the artist to "the lightning conductor," which, as Susan Gubar points out, "has the capacity to feel the shock of electricity and convey it without being consumed by it."[35] Since in its literal meaning incandescence refers to the change of the physical properties of the object, which starts to glow under conditions of extreme heat, this figure underscores first of all the transformation of the material structure of the work of art. But the word *incandescence* also conserves two additional and antithetical meanings: as the *OED* tells us, figuratively, it still refers to the psychological state of being inflamed with anger, while in its generalized sense it means brilliance, glow, or "luminous hallo." Because of its antithetical meanings, incandescence can be read as an aesthetic transformation of loss into art's own shining possibilities. It is through such a transformation of the intensity of anger into the sensibility of form that literature can "resurrect," if you will, lost possibilities and give them a second life. Evocative of the "luminous halo" of life, incandescence is a brilliant figure of art's own possibilities, its luminosity and its intensity.

Following the "feminine" but nonetheless transpersonal potentiality through the experimental practice undermines the classical oppositions between intentionality and sensibility, destruction and innovation, originality and derivation, making and receiving, as well as the gender hierarchy on which these distinctions are based. The aesthetic work of "following" inverts the writer's desire to "capture" life into receptivity and passion. Exceeding subjective initiative, such a passionate determination at the heart of literary experiment undermines the will to power not through its privation, as Agamben suggests, but through receptivity to different passions. Indeed, Woolf suggests that following potentiality through experimental form is like a dance of passion, which, in contrast to the consumption of commodities, reveals an ecstatic relation to the world, language, and others. In its sexual connotations it refers to the transformation of the intensity of female jouissance into the sensible intensity of the work of art. Woolf describes this transformation as writing "as a woman, but as a woman who has forgotten that she is a woman, so that her pages were full of that curious sexual quality which comes only when sex is unconscious of itself" (*RO*, 93).

For theorists as diverse as Kristeva, Irigaray, and Adorno, it is ultimately the relation between passion and aesthetics that reveals a strange potentiality capable not only of its own incapacity but also of revealing the otherness of the world. After all, Agamben himself begins his discussion of potentiality with the Aristotelian discussion of sensibility and sensation that gives the name to aesthetics ("The very word *'aisthesis'* . . . means sensation" [*PCE*, 178]). However, he does not follow through these relations between sensibility, passion, and creation, still resonating in the Greek words *aisthesis* and *poesis*. By contrast, in Woolf's writing the relation between art, potentiality, and passion signifies a welcoming receptivity of novelty and otherness. Understood as passion, potentiality is distinguished from the privation of will suggested by Agamben, since it is intertwined with exstasis, a movement outside oneself into relations with others, language, life, and the world. As Makiko Minow-Pinkney and Julia Briggs suggest in different ways,[36] this passionate dimension of writing is similar to "the self-surrender of sexual consummation."[37] Indeed, as the narrator of *Orlando* reminds us, one of its written manifestations is female "Ecstasy!" (O, 240). Thus the dance of passion in and through writing, the capacity for affecting and of being affected, making and following, is a fundamentally heteronomous and relational movement, transcending the oppositions of potentiality and privation, will and passivity, subjectivity and materiality.

Such an ecstatic, relational possibility disclosed in experimental writing is signified in Woolf's work explicitly or implicitly through lesbian relationships. For Woolf, the lesbian relationship is not merely a subversive/parodic reiteration of heterosexuality, as Judith Butler suggests, but, on the contrary, a passionate movement of female ex-stasis, exceeding the mediation of the male signature and will and, ultimately, exceeding interpersonal relations. At least since the eighties and nineties, Woolf's feminist critics have analyzed the diverse rhetorical strategies, such as allusion, ellipsis, parody, and carnivalesque camp aesthetics, of the different modalities of her encoding of lesbian desire in literary language as well as the ambiguous political stakes of Woolf's "Sapphic" modernism.[38] As Elizabeth Meese points out, "Woolf's texts explored the relation between [the] life, writing, and libidinal energy" of lesbian letters.[39] However, what has not yet been analyzed is the transpersonal, or ontological, dimension of Woolf's erotic passions between women and its contribution to the analysis of the aesthetics of potentiality. Following the trail of Woolf's speculations, we can say that Mrs. Brown—the ontological, or transpersonal, potentiality of freedom—awaits a new generation of women writers and political activists, the arrival of Shakespeare's sisters, who can rescue this "feminine" potentiality from destructive political and literary power arrangements and follow it passionately through the process of political action and artistic creation. In Woolf's essays and novels, experimental writing requires a new relationship between potentiality, the work of art, and femininity—a new alliance between Mrs. Brown and Judith Shakespeare. Reminiscent of Lilly Briscoe and Mrs. Ramsay, or

Olivia and Chloe, or Orlando and his/her partners, Mrs. Brown and Judith Shakespeare form a passionate "lesbian" configuration of potentiality rescued and disclosed through female poetic practice. And, consider-
ing the long history of the figure of the white, heterosexual couple of the
poet and his muse in the history of Western aesthetics, it is hardly surprising that such a configuration of female potentiality in the female
work of art would exceed all "the resources of the English language" in
order to bring this novelty "illegitimately into existence" (RO, 87).

In Woolf's "wild" experiment the invention of a new form of writing is
fundamentally intertwined with relational potentiality, which includes
and exceeds communities of outsiders and passionate relations between
women. One aspect of such a relation is the invitation from the female
audience, another a passionate response to the unpredictable appearance
of phantoms of the past, yet another is ecstatic passion for life, which,
as the brilliant play on life and Vita (both the Latin term for life and the
name of Woolf's lover, Vita Sackville-West, the inspiration for Orlando)
suggests, simultaneously includes and transcends female erotic passions. The interpersonal and transpersonal potentiality disclosed in the
work of art is therefore an unpredictable and passionate encounter with
the delight and the pain of the body, the intensity of luminous moments
of being, the otherness of life, the historical contradictions, and language. As Orlando's narrator reflects, literary experimental practice is
neither a solitary nor an impersonal act, but a passionate transaction
between lovers, the world, life, and language: "Was not writing poetry a
secret transaction, a voice answering a voice? . . . What could have been
more secret, she thought, more slow, and like the intercourse of lovers,
than the stammering answer she had made all these years to the old
crooning song of the woods, and the farms and the brown horses . . . the
kitchen and the fields, so laboriously bearing wheat, turnips, grass, and
the gardens blowing irises and fritillaries?" (O, 238, emphasis added).
Such experimental writing not only questions the fixed boundaries of
the historical world but also discloses through the process of making
what is not a result of making: the unpredictable, almost demonic possibility and otherness suggested through Brown's teasing: "Catch me if
you can."

Poetic work is therefore a "secret transaction" (O, 238, emphasis
added). As the word "secret" suggests, experimental writing also intimates
what cannot appear either in art, work, or politics. Secrecy has often been
interpreted in Woolf's scholarship as the witty evasion of power and

sanction, particularly intense during the obscenity trial of the first explicit lesbian novel, Radclyffe Hall's *The Well of Loneliness,* in October
1928.[40] Woolf's witty evasions of intolerant censorship in *Orlando,* certainly plays the part of this "secret transaction." Yet there is another dimension of the secrecy of writing. It reveals a kind of demonic excess of
potentiality which cannot appear, a dancing phantom of possibility. As
the narrator of *Orlando* describes it, writing attempts to follow "something which . . . is always absent from the present—whence its terror, its
nondescript character—something one trembles to pin through the body
with a name and call beauty, for it has no body, is as a shadow without
substance of quality of its own, yet has the power to change whatever it
adds itself to" (*O,* 236).

As we have seen, Woolf frequently refers to iconoclastic struggles
against the destructive aesthetic conventions, economic production, and
political power; yet, in her refection on feminine potentiality and experimental writing, she also imagines a possibility of reconciliation—the
end of war—between poetic language, feminized nature, and the destroyed body of the female poet. In order to imagine such reconciliation,
Woolf in *Orlando* explores a correlation between two ancient struggles:
one between poetry and the polis and the other between writing and nature. If the first struggle dates back to the expulsion of the poets from the
polis in Plato's *Republic,* the second one is made explicit by Woolf's retelling of the myth of Daphne being transformed into a laurel bush in order
to avoid Apollo's rape (*O,* 14, 11, 171, 317). Evoking the rape of Shakespeare's
sister, Apollo's attempted rape of Daphne—the suppressed background
of the struggle between nature and letters (*O,* 17), body and writing—
draws a correlation between masculine military rivalry (represented by
Apollo's killing of Python) and the erotic conquest of the female body
expelled from culture into nature. Woolf's parodic retelling of this myth
questions the classical reconciliation between power, poetry, and nature
represented by the laurel wreaths made from the Daphne's "renatural-
ized" body. In the mythical heterosexual version, the female body/nature
is a trophy decorating victorious emperors and male poets, who are the
inheritors of Apollo's lyre. For Woolf, however, if there is any chance of
reconciliation between poetry and damaged materiality, destroyed by
military, erotic, and artistic conquests, it will have to come from a female
poet walking "among us in flesh." By exposing the "unrecorded" gendered
contradictions between materiality and spirit, the body and the mind,
things in themselves and art objects, by bearing witness to the damaged

remnants of "feminized" nature and violently "naturalized" female bodies, Woolf's wild experimental writing restores a future possibility for a
nonviolent mediation between nature and politics, or what Luce Irigaray
calls the mediation between flesh and the spirit of freedom. And since
the destruction is intertwined with a heterosexual erotic/imperialist conquest, the possibility of a nonviolent mediation is figured in Woolf's text
as passionate relations between women.

Woolf famously argues that artistic experimentation is intertwined with
"contriv[ing] a means of being free" (MN, 35). Yet, as the tension between
melancholic modernism, bearing witness to the destruction of women's
artistic capacities, and the invention of new possibilities suggests, this is by
no means an easy task. On the contrary, as Woolf reminds us with a great
deal of sobriety, class, gender, and race domination threaten the very possibility of art: in fact, the history of women's literary production begins
with the utter destruction of women's art and their bodies—a destruction internalized by modern writers as madness, melancholia, and resentment. If the collective practice of freedom in the political sphere creates the possibility of overcoming melancholia and the future renaissance
of the female poet, experimental writing, based on passionate and multiple transactions, inaugurates a new feminine aesthetics of potentiality.
The very opposite of the traffic in women, intercourse—or transaction—
between women, the world, history, and the most unpredictable phantom
of all—life itself—manifests relational freedom in the work of art. Exceeding agency and subjective initiative, such passionate freedom implies not
only a negative capacity of literary practice but also an innovation going
beyond the limits of the possible. As the prophetic aspect of Woolf's pronouncements about the new age in literature suggests, literature, despite
its destruction and its tenuous status in modernity, can inaugurate a new
beginning: "the next chapter in the history of literature . . . let us proph-
esize again . . . will be one of the most important, the most illustrious,
the most epoch making of them all" (MBMB, 388). The temporality of
this prophecy, or promise, is not the linear causality of history but a fragile relationship between a poet who is yet to come and the potential that
might disappear from literary practice.

PART II

Female Bodies, Violence, and Form

Introduction *Rethinking the Form/Matter Divide*
in Feminist Politics and Aesthetics

In part 1 I have worked through the opposition between the narratives of female revolutionary and melancholic modernism in order to
propose a feminist aesthetics of potentiality. In part 2 I want to confront
more directly the issue that was already implied in the previous chapters,
namely, the relationship between female embodiment, aesthetic form,
and political violence. At first glance, this heterogeneous constellation of
form, violence, and materiality brings seemingly apolitical, gender neutral aesthetic debates about experimental forms in modernism together
with a gender/race politics of the body. I argue, however, that form and
materiality are both feminist political and aesthetic issues. On the one
hand, as Luce Irigaray and Judith Butler have shown, the form/matter
binary or, as is more often used in feminist theory, the materiality of the
body/discourse—are crucial issues in feminist politics because the philosophical genealogy of these terms is deeply implicated in the history of
racism, sexuality, and power. Associated with passivity and receptivity,
"matter" is a site of the exclusion of the feminine, an exclusion that
"secure[s] a given fantasy of heterosexual intercourse and male autogen-
esis."[1] On the other hand, as Frederic Jameson, one of the most insight-
ful political critics of late capitalism shows, formal experimentations in
modern literature are intertwined with significant political stakes because

they disclose more readily the possibility of revolutionary change that otherwise "is unclear in the reified world" of politics and economics.[2]

My analysis of form/matter/violence replaces the aesthetic form/ political content opposition that structures most debates about aesthetics and politics. I use the term *materiality* not only in the Marxist sense of labor and power relations but also in the feminist sense of gendered, racialized matter and violated bodies. By bringing together these divergent domains and theoretical paradigms, which have usually been discussed separately, I focus on the problem of formal abstraction in political life and its correlative, political and economic violence. At first glance this approach might seem like a contradiction or a categorical mistake, since it is often claimed that the dialectical tradition replaces the older, Aristotelian form/matter distinction with the dynamic, historical notion of material forces of production seeking expression in new social forms. As Jameson argues, the Hegelian and Marxist notions of form are to be "sharply distinguished from the older idea of form which dominates philosophical thinking from Aristotle to Kant and for which the conjugate term is . . . *matter,* inert materials."[3] Following Irigaray, I argue, however, that feminism has to work with both pre-Marxist and dialectical notions of materiality. First of all, as we have seen in Butler's reading of Irigaray, the notion of passive and formless matter, one of the original scenes of the exploitation of the feminine framing the fantasy of heterosexual intercourse, is what is still contested in feminist theories of embodiment and sexuality today.[4] More importantly, what the form/content dialectic cannot account for is the violent schism between abstract forms and damaged materialities inflicted by modern biopolitics. What is nonetheless important in the dialectical tradition for feminist theory is the idea of a new, interactive model of mediation between matter and form. Ultimately I argue that formal experimentation in women's literature has to be considered a critical response to the operations of form and violence inflicted on women's bodies in political life and as an aesthetic invention of a new interaction between form and materiality.

In aesthetics, multiple uses of form are often collapsed under a single term.[5] Dating at least since romanticism, form is regarded as either a generic static structure that is indifferent to a particular work, for example, the form of the novel or the lyric, or, on the contrary, as the manifestation of the singularity of an artwork. Most commonly opposed to the content, that is, meaning, political context, or a theme, of the work, form is defined as the outer sensible shape of the inner signification. But form can also be regarded as an active intelligible principle of the work, articulating the relations between its materials or component parts (different components of plot, language, narrative structures, and so forth). It is in this sense of a dynamic process, similar to and different from other productive activities, that aesthetic "forming" can be most productively compared with political praxis and its impact on collective life.

In discussions of the politics of modern literature of the last sixty years or so, there have been numerous proposals for the overcoming of the experimental form/political content binary advanced by postaesthetic, poststructuralist, and Marxist theories. Most of them rely on the dynamic or active notion of form as the process of shaping meaning and social relations.[6] In the poststructuralist tradition, Derek Attridge, for example, insists on the necessity of overcoming the form/content binary in order to account for the singularity of literature, its difference from other cultural productions. And, instead of the static opposition between form and content, he proposes the performative understanding of literary form as the "staging" of meaning and its otherness.[7] By contrast, Adorno famously claims that political antagonisms themselves, which, in this study, include the antagonisms of race and gender in addition to class conflicts, return as immanent problems of aesthetic form. Yet, as I will argue, political antagonisms are also intertwined with the violence of political forms, and that is why they can be contested or reproduced on the level of form in literature. In his response to Adorno, Jameson, already in the 1970s, proposed that the relationship between literature and politics has to be investigated on the level of form rather than on the level of thematic content.[8] Jameson understands form in two different ways: first, as the form of the work of art and, second, as the historic relationships between art and social reality, between subject and object. For Jameson, however, the primary terms are form and content. As he famously puts it, what Engels learned about French society from the content of French novels, Marxist criticism has to learn from the form of modern literature because formal innovations are indexes of new political content seeking articulation.[9] Thus, in the cultural realm, the terms *form* and *content* "transpose" the oppositions between "subject and object," existence and the world, and individual and the external network of things and institutions.[10]

Yet, despite these divergent proposals, the fixed form/content binary keeps reasserting itself either as the source of embarrassing formalism, as a manifestation of new formalism (a reaction against content-driven political interpretations of literature and art), or as the persistence of content-based psychological, philosophical, or political interpretations of literary works. There are many good reasons why these oppositions of form and content keep recurring as if they were a symptom of the return of the repressed. This recurrence is not only an effect of a faulty methodology but also of the historical persistence of abstract sociopolitical formal relations that are indifferent to the particularity of objects, bodies, and matter. Paradoxically, what the Marxist tradition calls "material relations" of production and exchange are also characterized by the abstract formalism that is a source of damage, domination, and violence. And in fact one of the great contributions of the Marxist tradition in this respect is the analysis of commodity exchange as the question of abstract form. Can we say, then, that political materialism diagnoses a political formalism (by which I mean the constitution of values, political forms, rights, and meaning in total separation from the materiality of the body/matter/ object) of advanced capitalism, a formalism that coexists with the disciplinary regulation and normalization of bodies? By critiquing Marx's numerous references to feminized "bodies" and the prostitution of commodities, Luce Irigaray extends this critique of political formalism to monologic heterosexual intercourse and the ideological split of the so-called natural/social bodies of women. And she argues that the abstraction of social forms from the particularity of bodies, "formless" matter, and desire is evidence that the work of mediation between subjects and objects is performed by the work of death and its correlative, money.

To overcome the static aesthetic binaries of form/political content and literature/politics, I begin with a diagnosis of the violent schism between abstract forms and damaged materialities in political life and then focus on the literary contestations of this divide. This task entails, first, an investigation of the violence inflicted on bodies by political formalism and, second, an analysis of literary responses—ranging from reproduction to transformation—to this formalism. Through the juxtaposition of Irigaray's interpretation of the commodification of women's bodies with Orlando Patterson's discussion of slavery and Agamben's biopolitics of bare life, I show that what the commodity form and biopolitics have in common is the violent severance of collective forms from remnants of materiality, which then become the target of violence. In the case of the commodity form, the split occurs between the abstract exchange of value and use value or "the natural body" of objects. Yet feminized commodity form mirrors not only reified relations of exchange but also the biopolitical fracture in the structure of citizenship, namely, the split between bare life and abstract human rights. In both cases the remnants of materiality excluded from value and common forms of life are targets of violence: the sovereign violence directed at bare life and the violence of commodification directed at bodies and nature. Consequently, the politics of recognition and even the politics of redistribution are insufficient for feminism because they cannot address the violent split between violated materiality and form.[11]

Ultimately, the question that the political diagnosis of violence and formalism poses for feminist aesthetics is whether the composition of the work of art can reveal a different model of mediation between form, bodies, and materiality. In opposition to political formalism, the aesthetic model of mediation that I want to propose stresses the inseparability and interaction between form and materiality in the dynamic structure of the artwork. In this sense the specificity of art and literature stands in an implicit opposition to both the violent production and destruction of bare life in contemporary biopolitics and the increasing commodification of the world. Such interaction between matter, form, and embodiment becomes a source of resistance and creation of new meaning. Thus I propose to read the materiality of aesthetic form, traditionally acknowledged by aesthetics, as an intervention into the violent abstraction of commodity form and the form of citizenship. In opposition to conservative formalism—for instance, T. S. Eliot's abstraction of mythical structure from the disorder of everyday life—the experimental literary works I analyze provide a new model of interconnection, or mediation, between damaged materials, violated bodies, and literary forms.

4 Abstract Commodity Form and Bare Life

In this chapter I diagnose the violence inflicted on women's bodies by the abstract formalism operating in political and social life. I argue that the problem of abstraction in political life (the forms of citizenship and sovereignty) finds its correlative in economic violence in civil society (the relations of production and exchange). I develop this argument through the juxtaposition of different paradigms of power that have not yet been thought together: the commodification of female bodies, the damage of enslavement, and the biopolitics of sovereignty. More specifically, I focus on Irigaray's analysis of the commodification of women's bodies, Hortense Spillers's and Orlando Patterson's discussion of slavery, and Agamben's theory of bare life. Why do we need to think these heterogeneous paradigms of power together? What the commodification of bodies, enslavement, and the biopolitics of bare life have in common is the possibility of violently severing collective forms from the remnants of materiality, which becomes the target of different kinds of violence. On the one hand, the biopolitics of bare life confronts us with the damaged body stripped from its cultural signification, with the abject body separated from symbolic and political forms of life, expelled beyond the realm of the possible, and exposed to violence that does not count as crime. Yet if bare life can be so violently stripped from its form of life—from the protection of rights, cultural genealogy, and values—this means that the modern political forms of citizenship and human rights are separable from life/embodiment. This separation/destitution does not only concern the exceptional case of bare life but all politically invested bodies. It is precisely this total separation of form/value from the materiality of the objectified body that comes into view in another, apparently competing paradigm of modernity, that is, in the production and exchange of commodified bodies. It is the commodity form that reveals the abstract determination of the form of value in total separation from the particularity of the object, that is, its materiality, and shows the erasure of all traces of nonidentity, otherness, and materiality. Consequently, I argue that the feminized commodity form mirrors not only the reified relations of exchange but also the violent division in the structure of citizenship, namely, the split between bare life and abstract human rights.[1] This is especially the case in the instance of enslavement, where the violent commodification of human bodies and their expulsion from political status—what Orlando Patterson calls social death—coincide. Although ignored by Irigaray's discussion of commodification and Agamben's notion of bare life, enslaved bodies reveal a disastrous intertwining of the violence directed at bare life and the violence of commodification directed at bodies and nature.

On the Abstraction of Commodity Form

I begin my diagnosis of the violent schism between abstract forms and damaged materialities in Western modernity by focusing on Irigaray's reading of Marx's theory of commodity in *Capital*. In her classical essay "Women on the Market" in *This Sex Which is Not One*, Irigaray discusses the extreme abstraction and violence of commodity form structuring the conception of gendered bodies in the family and civil society.[2] Irigaray's critique of violence and the formalism of value has been missed by most of her feminist interpreters because she has been read through the lens of the protracted debate in feminist theory between essentialism (false immediacy) and social construction (sociopolitical process of mediation).[3] However, as I have suggested elsewhere, the essentialism/antiessentialism opposition fails to address the violence of political formalism because it itself reproduces the same problem.

By reinterpreting Irigaray's reading of Marx, I argue that the dichotomy of essentialism and social construction arises out of the double and antithetical form of the commodity manifesting itself as exchange value and use value, together with all the oppositions underlying this structure: materiality and form, the natural and the social, the passivity of matter and the activity of production/construction. At stake here is the split between the *abstraction* of the commodity form, which determines the value of commodified objects and bodies in total separation from their specificity and materiality, and the concomitant reduction of the nonsublated remnants of materiality to mere waste or markers of social death. This schism between the abstraction of social values and nonsymbolizable material refuse is itself a source of social injustice that is inscribed in modern conceptions of racial and sexual differences. Thus, in order to contest this injustice, feminist theory has to not only expose and contest the obscured mechanisms of power and the normalization of bodies but also criticize the economic abstraction of *form* as the often invisible source of bodily injury.

Irigaray argues that in Marx's theory of commodity form "the commodity, like the sign, suffers from metaphysical dichotomies. . . . A commodity—a woman—is divided into two irreconcilable 'bodies': her 'natural' body and her socially valued, exchangeable body."[4] Consistently associated with the "physical body,"[5] substance and coarse materiality, "natural" form constitutes the use value of the object, whereas value form, characterized by "total" separation from and indifference to the diverse physical qualities of the product, expresses a homogeneous social substance: undifferentiated social labor. For Marx, "there is nothing mysterious" (CA, 163) about the "plain, homely, natural form" of use value (CA, 138), even though this form is already an effect of the social negation of nature by concrete labor. The mystery of the commodity, like the enigma of femininity, resides in its social form expressing the value of labor, which in turn resonates with the value of "social construction" in feminist theories. This contradiction of the double value of commodified bodies points to the total dissociation of social *form* from the *sensuous body*, which, as a result of this separation, is reduced to passive, coarse *matter*. What Marx's concept of the commodity diagnoses, therefore, is the indifference and separation of social form from the "coarsely sensuous objectivity" (CA, 138) of matter and concrete labor under capitalist conditions of exchange. On the basis of this schism, Irigaray claims that when women are exchanged their bodies are split into *"two things at once: utilitarian objects and bearers of value"* (TS, 175); into "matter-body" and the ungraspable, mysterious "envelope" of value (TS, 176).

What the essentialism/social construction debate fails to analyze is the crucial feature of commodity fetishism, namely, the abstraction of the social form of value. Yet it is precisely this abstraction and the damage it inflicts on materiality that is at stake in Irigaray's and Adorno's critiques of commodification. As Irigaray points out, "money as a means of mediation represents . . . a universal abstracted from the natural without a suitable spiritualization of this natural."[6] In contrast to the concreteness of use value, or the "coarse" materiality of the body, the social form of the commodity is characterized by a triple abstraction. First of all, labor (construction), as the source of the commodity's value, is abstracted from concrete, diverse social activities and reduced to the pure expenditure of homogeneous labor power. This leveling of diverse social activities into homogeneous abstract labor is an effect of capitalist exchange, which conflates the political equality of people with the equality of labor and misrepresents both as abstract economic equivalence. Second, time becomes abstracted from discontinuous and unpredictable becoming by being reduced to mathematical units of measurement.[7] Finally, the social form is abstracted from all the material particularity of the object. That is why Irigaray argues that commodified women's bodies become abstractions without any intrinsic value: "*Woman has value on the market by virtue of one single quality: that of being a product of man's 'labor'*" (*TS*, 175). This utter "indifference" to matter and particularity is especially striking in the case of the relative value of the commodity that is expressed not in its own body but in the body of another commodity serving as its equivalent. As Marx puts it, "the value of the commodity linen is therefore expressed by the physical body of the commodity coat. . . . Thus the linen acquires a value-form different from its natural form. . . . Its sublime objectivity as a value differs from its stiff and starch existence as a body, it says that value has the appearance of a coat" (*CA*, 143–144). Consequently, the "sublime" mediation characteristic of commodity form performs an erasure of all particularity pertaining to the object, temporalization, and concrete labor, and substitutes for it the "phantom-like objectivity" of abstract, homogeneous social labor (*CA*, 128). Furthermore, the language of Marx's analysis suggests that the obverse side of abstraction is an infliction of bodily injury: By "extinguishing" all sensuous characteristics, the value form mortifies and wipes out the physical body and leaves no trace (*CA*, 128).

These three kinds of abstraction performed by the commodity form— abstraction from the heterogeneity of concrete labor, temporalization, and particularity of the object—are mutually interdependent. As Adorno argues, what is at stake in the separation of abstract labor from physical work is the denial of the necessary dependence of concrete labor on its other: on the material, on "nature," on the remainder of the nonidentical, which cannot be appropriated by the spirit of capitalism.[8] According to Adorno, "there is nothing in the world that shall not manifest itself to human beings solely through social labor. . . . But the step by which *labor sets itself up as the metaphysical principle pure and simple* is none other than *the consistent elimination of the 'material'* to which all labor feels itself tied, the material that defines its boundary for it . . . and relativizes its sovereignty" (*H*, 26, emphasis added). By eliminating this "tie" to the material and nonidentical, the abstraction of social form denies that there is any "outside" to the principle of capitalist exchange based on equivalence. In so doing, the abstraction of commodity form turns labor into an ideological principle of sovereignty, which is coextensive with the appropriation of the labor of others and the domination of their bodies. Working in the service of equivalence and domination, this ideology of abstract, sovereign labor dissolves not only every qualitative difference but also every trace of the nonidentical and the incommensurate. We may wonder at this point whether feminist theories of social construction are not vulnerable to a similar critique of the ideology of labor, which sets up production as "absolute."[9] Insofar as these theories consider any "outside" to the abstract mediation of bodies to be the remnant of essentialism, they turn social construction into a "metaphysical principle pure and simple," to use Adorno's term—that is, into a metaphysics of autonomous social production that knows no limits. That is why essentialism/social construction opposition fails to account both for political violence and for form/content binary in modern aesthetics.

This transformation of multiple concrete activities into a metaphysics of production is nowhere more evident than in the so-called spiritualization of bodies. Both Irigaray and Marx associate the abstraction of socioeconomic form with the spiritualization of the commodified body. By endowing the object/body with a soul, commodification bestows social significance upon bodies, while at the same time transforming them, in Irigaray's words, into "value invested idealities" (*TS*, 181). As the culmination of metaphysics, the commodity form discloses the historical truth of the Hegelian spiritualization of matter—that is, the complete transformation of matter into a mere reflection of human values through social praxis or what Hegel and Adorno call spirit. (Let us note in passing that although the term *social spirit* has different meanings in dialectical traditions—for instance, it refers to the progress of knowledge and freedom in Hegel, to the social organization of labor in Marx, or to the movement of concept and the formation of economic/political institutions in Adorno—in all cases it implies different forms of social praxis and the realization of freedom through that praxis). Thus, as Marx points out, the "body" of the commodity, which is consistently compared in *Capital* to the body of the prostitute, is transformed into a "mirror" of value, into a reflection of "abstract human labor" (*CA*, 150). Extending Marx's analysis of this process of reflection, Irigaray, like Virginia Woolf before her, points to the analogous imaginary function of femininity: *"commodities, women, are a mirror of value of and for man.* In order to serve as such [mirrors], they give up their bodies to men as the supporting material of specularization, of speculation" (*TS*, 177). For Irigaray, the spiritualization of matter is intertwined with the specularization of female bodies, that is, with their transformation into narcissistic "mirrors" of masculine value: "participation in society requires that the body submit itself to a specularization, a speculation, that transforms it into a value-bearing object" (*TS*, 180). Or, as Woolf observes in *A Room of One's Own*, the bodies of white women, insofar as they reflect social values, "have served all these centuries as looking glasses possessing the magic and delicious power of reflecting the figure of man at twice its natural size" (*RO*, 35). Furthermore, Woolf draws the connection between the specularization of femininity and political/domestic violence: "mirrors are essential to all violent and heroic action" (*RO*, 35).

What is paradoxical about this process of specularization, which turns bodies into a reflection of abstract social labor, is that it erases its movement of mediation, through which the body/commodity acquires its social value. Thus commodification of objects and subjects presents its speculative result as if it were an inherent property of the object "endowed . . . by nature itself'" (*CA*, 149). As Marx puts it, "the movement through which this process has been mediated vanishes in its own result, leaving no trace behind" (*CA*, 187). It is this vanishing process of mediation that can be most readily associated with essentialism insofar as the most mediated ideality—the abstract soul of the commodity—appears as the concrete immediacy of the body. Let us notice here a striking parallel between the speculative "soul" of the commodity produced through the reiteration of market exchanges and the speculative character of sex constituted by the reiteration of gender norms, as analyzed by Judith Butler.

According to Butler, "'sex' is a regulatory ideal whose materialization is compelled, and this materialization takes place . . . through certain highly regulated practices."[10] By extending Butler's influential argument, we could say that sex, like the soul of the commodity, is the most ideal effect of the economic formation of gender, which nonetheless appears as the most material property of the body. As Marx's famous definition of commodity fetishism similarly suggests, the "phantom" immediacy of value is a speculative effect of capital, which reflects the social relations between men as well as their labor as the "fantastic" properties of things (CA, 165).

The compelling precedent of feminist theoretical debates about the commodification of female bodies and art can be found in women's modern literary texts. For example, Nella Larsen's Quicksand diagnoses the split between the abstract soul of the prostitute and the fantasmatic immediacy of the body attributed to black femininity by the white artist. Helga Crane, the main biracial protagonist in the novel, is the figure of an oppositional black taste, of an aesthetic judgment, which calls for an alternative political community. When she repeatedly fails to find such a community in racist America, she visits her rich white relatives in Europe. Seemingly accepted by the white elites of Copenhagen, Helga, donned by her aunt in all the attributes of exoticism and primitivism, is put on the marriage market in order to attract the interest of the rich and well-established artist Herr Olsen, who might add cultural capital to the financial fortune of her relatives. By "gently" forcing Helga to wear exotic outfits, which make her feel "like a veritable savage" (Q, 69), Helga's aunt "had determined the role that Helga was to play in advancing the social fortunes of the Dahls of Copenhagen" (Q, 68). According to the predictable modernist plot, Helga is to be stripped of her aesthetic judgment and transformed at once into a figure of the prostitute, primitive sexuality, and commodified, passive aesthetic object. By eventually proposing marriage, the white painter proclaims: "'You know, Helga, you are a contradiction. . . . You have the warm impulsive nature of the women of Africa, but, my lovely, you have, I fear, the soul of a prostitute. You sell yourself to the highest buyer. I should of course be happy that it is I" (Q, 87). In his brutal bluntness, the white artist considers his price of marriage to be too high for a black woman, but he is willing to pay it not just for the sake of his sexual desires but for the sake of the priceless "immortality" (Q, 86) of art. The painter unwittingly admits the contradiction in the racist construction of black femininity but fails to understand that the same contradiction per-

tains to his art. Yet, as Larsen ironically points out, the body of white hegemonic art as well as the body of the black woman are caught in the same
dualism of value: violent formalism, on the one hand, and phantom immediacy, or phantom primitivism, on the other hand; the "soul" or the
idealism of artistic value and the prostitution of market transaction. What
enables Helga to reject the racist values ascribed to her for the sake of
economic fortune or for the sake of the aesthetic status of modernist art
is her critical aesthetic and political judgment: Helga not only flatly declares that she is "not for sale. . . . Not to any white man" (Q, 87), but also
rejects the aesthetic value of her portrait. She finds the whole aesthetic
project "disgusting," despite the fact that white "collectors, artists, and
critics had been unanimous in their praise" of Olsen's painting (Q, 89).

To expose the illusory immediacy, the false "naturalness" or primitivism of sexuality, as the most speculative result of social mediation—its
"soul"—is the first step of a feminist critique of the commodification of
white and black female bodies. The second necessary move is to contest
the abstract formalism of social mediation/construction, separated from
materiality and nonidentity. As Adorno's and Hegel's critiques of abstraction show, the abstraction of social form "can never be made absolutely
autonomous vis-à-vis what it is abstracted from. . . . The quality of what it
has been abstracted from is always, in a certain sense, preserved in it at
the same time" (H, 15). To assert the absolute autonomy of social construction, to deny its dependence on the residue of the material and nonidentical, would, paradoxically, lead to another form of free-floating idealism. In the aftermath of Adorno's and Irigaray's work, we could say that
feminist critiques of essentialism likewise have to "acknowledge the in-
solubility of an empirical, nonidentical moment" *within* social mediation,
"a moment that doctrines of the absolute subject, idealist systems of identity, are not permitted to acknowledge as indissoluble" (H, 17).

Ultimately, the reinterpretation of the essentialism/social construction binary in the context of use/exchange value contests the fixity of this
opposition and the abstract character of economic mediation. First of all,
both these terms emerge from, and to a large extent reproduce, the historical process of the commodification of bodies. Furthermore, it is only
through the mutual negation of their untruth that these opposites can
demonstrate their partial insight. Thus the falsity of antiessentialism lies
in the "absolutization" of the autonomy of construction, in the denial of
the persistence of the material and nonidentical even in the most *abstract
form* of mediation. Nonetheless, it reveals the truth of the historical fact

that in capitalism there is nothing, including the bodies of women, that is not mediated by social production and economic exchange. On the other hand, the obvious untruth of essentialism lies in immediacy, as if it were possible to transcend production and mediation and find a positive value in bodies themselves, or, in the context of aesthetics, in the sensibility of artwork. The essentialist argument forgets the fact that the limits of social construction can be indicated only by exposing its internal contradictions and "not through recourse to something transcendent" (*H*, 27). Yet, through this falsity, the recurrent suspicions of essentialism inadvertently bear witness to the remainder of damaged materiality, exteriority, and otherness, which, although reduced to social waste, nonetheless constitute nonsublatable limits of construction/social labor. By misreading this remainder as essentialism and by disregarding the damaging abstraction of social form, the feminist social construction argument remains in complicity with the metaphysics of production, which asserts the "absolute" autonomy of labor and "tolerates nothing outside itself" (*H*, 26). Because of its failure to diagnose abstraction, social construction fails not only to account fully for political violence but also to overcome form/content binary in modernist aesthetics.

The abstract formalism of commodification shows that the domination is perpetuated not only by the concealment of social mediation behind the appearances of immediacy but more importantly by the "total" separation of social values from all remnants of materiality, becoming, concrete labor, and the vulnerability of bodies. Irigaray famously argues that this separation of commodity form from objectified bodies and concrete labor means that mediation is performed by the work of death: "death as the rallying place of sensible desires, the real or symbolic dissolution of the citizen in the community, and enslavement to property or capital" (*ILTY*, 23). Feminist criticism has addressed very well the problem of immediacy by reconstructing again and again the obfuscated process of mediation and by demonstrating that what is posited as an intrinsic signification of the body is in fact produced by social domination. Yet this reconstruction of the social mediation/regulation of embodiment neither diagnoses the full extent of bodily injuries inflicted by the work of death nor poses a sufficient challenge to essentialism, which is why the problem of essentialism keeps reappearing in feminist theory. What also has to be contested is the specific mode of social mediation characteristic of commodity fetishism, namely, the abstraction and autonomy of social form that, reproduced under the rubric of "social construction," disavows the traumatic limits of signification and expels every trace of nonsublatable otherness and matter into social nonexistence.

On the Destruction of Sexual/Racial Differences and Bodily Violence

It is only through the negation of both immediacy and the deadly abstract formalism of value that we can diagnose the injury of racialized, sexed bodies inflicted by the process of commodification. Let us begin such diagnosis with Luce Irigaray's claim that the damage of commodification manifests itself primarily in the mortification of female bodies and the destruction of any possibility of a culture of sexual difference. As she argues, Marx's definition of commodity fetishism as the abstract "social relation among men" reveals the fact that the economic regulation of gender is predicated on sexual indifference—an indifference which constitutes a paradoxical compromise between patriarchy and the dissolving power of capital. Such an erasure of sexual difference in the economic regulation of gender produces a homosocial order of exchange in which women mediate misrecognized, sublimated relations between men, in which any alternative sexualities, such as homosexuality or transgender sexualities, are prohibited, and in which the hegemony of monosexual, white heterosexuality is predicated on the erasure of difference and the mortification of the body: "What is spirit if it forces the body to comply with an abstract model . . . ? That spirit is already dead . . . the capitalization of life in the hands of a few who demand this sacrifice of the majority" (*ILTY*, 25). Because of its reduction of difference into abstract equivalence, the economic formation of gender repeats the subject/object dialectic in which the feminine object is dominated by the (white) subject. In this dialectic, femininity occupies the side of the pseudo-object whose value is produced by a process of exchange based on equivalence and "total" mortification or abstraction from materiality. Consequently, its "objectivity" is merely an illusory effect of the disappearance of the specular process of mediation, which nonetheless completely determines its value or nonvalue. However, as we shall see, the objectification of female bodies assumes different forms of violence across the color line.

Yet, the primacy of the masculine subject in this dialectic can be maintained only at the price of a misrecognition of its dependency on the object and on the presumption of the whiteness of such a subject. Thus

the economic formation of heterosexual white masculinity is characterized not only by a misrecognition of the homosocial relations deposited
in the object but also by the denial of the economic reification of white
masculinity.[11] According to Balibar, this denial takes the form of an introjection of the value objectified in the commodity back into the interiority
of the subject.[12] Through this internalization, the social value of alienated
labor appears as its opposite, namely, the subjective value of free will.
Because it is not accompanied by a change in the relations of production,
such introjection is merely an ideological mechanism that disavows the
alienation and commodification of social relations between white men by
sustaining the fiction of individual free will. Balibar describes this internalization of the objectified social value of labor as "juridical fetishism,"[13]
since the ideology of free will is central to the bourgeois conception of
law. By reinterpreting his analysis in the context of gender, we can say
that commodity exchange produces "juridical fetishism"—or the ideology of free will—on the masculine side and "economic fetishism"—the
phantom immediacy of the object—on the feminine side.

In contrast to the abstract economic equivalence of gender, Irigaray
proposes another labor of mediation based on sexual difference. By
stressing the "disappropriating," "impossible," and "asymmetrical" character of sexual and social relations, such mediation foregrounds the internal limitation of the sexed subject and its exposure to exteriority. It
thus contests both the autonomy of free will and the autonomy of social
production, emphasizing instead the irreducible alterity of the self and
the other: "The *mine* of the subject," Irigaray argues, "is always already
marked by disappropriation. . . . Being a man or a woman means not being the whole of the subject or of the community or of spirit, as well as
not being entirely one's self. I am not the whole [*je ne suis pas tout*]" (*ILTY*,
106).[14] In her *A Politics of Impossible Difference*, Penelope Deutscher has
brilliantly analyzed this impossible status of sexual difference as both a
historically excluded possibility—the pair of empty brackets—and as a
mark of futurity, as that which is yet to come.[15] Yet, in the psychoanalytic
context, the notion of impossible sexual difference also has to be related
to the register of the real as the limit of social mediation. According to
Slavoj Žižek, "the claim that sexual difference is 'real' equals the claim
that it is 'impossible'—impossible to symbolize, to formulate as a symbolic norm."[16] Furthermore, the impossible and disappropriating character of sexual difference not only maintains indeterminacy within social
mediation but also contests its abstraction from all vestiges of material-

ity. As Irigaray's invention of the neologism "sensible transcendental" suggests, "the impossible" of sexual difference is intertwined not only with the excess of signification but also with sensibility, passion, and the traumatic vulnerability of the body.

If Irigaray claims that the damage of commodification produces the erasure of sexual difference, her own analysis reproduces the racial indifference characteristic of so many foundational texts of white feminism. A symptom of widespread historical and textual blindness, Irigaray's failure to take race into account ignores the fact that the economic equation of blackness with property under the regime of slavery, as well as the persisting racist representations of black female sexuality in terms of exoticism and primitivism, constitute, as Hortense J. Spillers, Patricia Williams,[17] and Deborah E. McDowell, among others, point out,[18] the most horrific paradigm of the commodification of human bodies.[19] As Nella Larsen, for example, has shown, the commodification of black female sexuality in terms of exoticism and primitivism represents a striking example of the "phantom" immediacy of unrestrained sexuality produced through highly mediated, abstract systems of cultural, aesthetic, and economic exchanges.

However, Irigaray's reading of Marx betrays not only a historical but also a textual blindness. Although Irigaray is an extremely attentive reader of the persistent rhetorical references to the feminized body in Marx's *Capital,* she ignores the explicit racialized meaning of these references, ranging from the evocations of "tribal religions" to the appropriation of the crucial term *fetishism*. Originating in sixteenth-century European trade with West Africa, the term *fetishism,* as William Pietz has documented, was intertwined in the eighteenth and nineteenth centuries with the colonial, racist representation of the "primitive" mentality of Africans as based on religious superstitions, irrational fear, and institutionalized social delusion.[20] Thus, Hegel, for instance, concludes that the African *Fetich* is but one manifestation of the Africans' lack of any awareness of universality and their *"contempt* for humanity, which . . . is the fundamental characteristic of the race."[21] It is precisely by appropriating and disavowing the racist connotations of *fetishism* that Marx can extend this term to describe the *"contempt* for humanity" and irrationality of commodity exchange in capitalist societies.

Yet what is at stake in the critique of Irigaray's white solipsism is not only a necessary contestation of the exclusion of black femininity from the foundational texts of white feminism. What is also crucial in this critique is the analysis of the damage inflicted on captive black bodies that at once exemplify the process of commodification as such and at the same time constitute an exception to commodified gender regulation. As Hortense J. Spillers's influential essay "Mama's Baby, Papa's Maybe: An American Grammar Book" suggests, the commodification of gender relations cannot take fully into account the traumatic reality of black flesh stripped from values and reduced to social illegitimacy. Spillers's argument that the traumatic legacy of the enslavement of black bodies still threatens to disarticulate the very conception of gender and kinship makes a necessary intervention in both feminist psychoanalysis and Marxist criticism alike. As her analysis of the 1965 Moynihan report, which blames black mothers for the destruction of the black family, shows, the grammar of racialized bodies remains "grounded in the originating metaphors of captivity and mutilation so that it is as if neither time nor history, nor historiography . . . shows movement."[22] One of the deadly contradictions of the "grammar" of slavery is that the commodification of the captive body was in fact synonymous with the destruction of the social significance of gender. Enslaved African persons, Spillers writes, "were the culturally 'unmade.' . . . Under these conditions, one is neither female, nor male, as both subjects are taken into 'account' as *quantities*" (MBPM, 72). In the juridical codes of slavery: "'Slave' appears in the same context with beasts of burden, *all* and *any* animal(s) . . . and a virtually endless profusion of domestic content from the culinary item to the book" (MBPM, 79).

In the grammar of slavery, the "re-gendering" of black flesh occurs only retrospectively, through the conjunction of enforced biological reproduction and the social reproduction of slavery as social illegitimacy (MBPM, 79). The enforced maternal reproduction of the social nonvalue of slavery, passed from the black mother onto a child of either sex, had catastrophic but different consequences for both sexes. It excluded black masculinity from both the symbolic law of the father and from juridical rights. And it degraded black femininity to compulsory maternity robbed of all parental function. In contrast to white femininity, the economic value of enslaved female flesh does not reflect white homosocial relations but reproduces the social nonvalue of slavery. Thus, contrary to Irigaray's claim, enslaved female bodies are not divided into a natural substratum and "bearers of value" but are rather seen as the bearers of nonvalue. In her novels Nella Larsen bears witness to this persisting bitter legacy of white supremacy and the reproduction of the nonvalue of black bodies, even when they are ascribed the racist value of "primitivism," which is consumed by white artists and spectators. In the midst of the Harlem Renaissance, she points out in her novels that for black women motherhood is still the most threatening possibility because of the reproduction of illegitimacy and vulnerability. As Clare, one of the characters in *Passing*, proclaims, "being a mother is the cruelest thing in the world" (*P*, 197). And the ending of *Quicksand*, Larsen's first novel, in which forced motherhood kills the main character, Helga, confirms this diagnosis: "she would have to die. She couldn't endure it. Her suffocation and shrinking loathing were too great" (*Q*, 134).

Through the juxtaposition of Irigaray, Larsen, and Spillers, we can see more precisely the racist division of labor and the damage suffered by white and black female bodies. Whereas white bodies erase their materiality in the reflection of social values, enslaved bodies reproduce the failure of the spiritualization of matter that is associated either with the destruction of social values or with the racist "value" of primitivism. In so doing, they become the bearers of death, illegitimacy, or the exotic unrestrained sexuality. This racist attribution of the failure to specularize matter to black bodies consolidates the white monopoly on the production of social value. Consequently, the difference between the commodified white female body and the black female body is that the economic and aesthetic value of the latter depends on its inability to spiritualize/specularize matter. In Hegel's philosophy of history, the racist attribution of the "failure of spiritualization" is extended to Africa itself,[23] used to justify the enslavement and exclusion of the entire black race from the historical progress of freedom: "What we properly understand by Africa, is the Unhistorical, Undeveloped Spirit, still involved in the conditions of mere nature, and which had to be presented here only as on the threshold of the World's History."[24] By displacing onto black bodies the remnant of materiality that a racist metaphysics of production cannot spiritualize away, white supremacy associates these bodies with enslaving nature and, in so doing, excludes them from the realm of the social spirit, that is, from the historical realization of freedom.

Bare Life, Social Death, and the Biopolitics of Race and Gender

Hortense Spillers's analysis of destroyed black female flesh, stripped of its political significance, language, and genealogy, provides an important insight into another violent separation constitutive of Western politics, namely, the separation of political forms from what Agamben calls bare life. One of the most important contributions of Agamben's work is his claim that the possibility of isolating and expelling bare life from politically constituted ways of being is foundational to the Western conception of sovereignty and politics. The notion of bare life not only allows us to revise the Foucauldian theory of biopower, and the numerous cultural, feminist, queer, and postcolonial studies of the body that take Foucault as their point of departure, but also to analyze another case of a violent political formalism. Although Agamben does not address this issue directly, the violence of implicit political formalism is a consequence not only of the well-known separation of the political status of the citizen from the biological and private existence but, more importantly, of the threat of another severance and destruction: this time, the political severance of subjects from their worthless bodily remainder or what Agamben calls bare life. In other words, if political beings can be stripped of their political significance and reduced to bare life, such severance implies that the institution of the political is characterized by violent and abstract formalism. Thus, if Irigaray and Spillers diagnose the violent production of abstract values that mortify objectified female bodies in so-called civil society, Agamben's theory of sovereignty reveals the violation of the body stripped of its abstract political significance. The double body of the commodity (split between its "natural" use value and abstract exchange value) encounters the double body of a political being, split between political form and bare life.

To develop the violent consequences of political formalism, I want to focus in greater detail on Agamben's theory of bare life and Patterson's analysis of social death. According to Agamben, bare life constitutes the original but "concealed nucleus" of Western biopolitics insofar as its exclusion founds the political realm. Thus, the most fundamental categories of Western politics are not the social contract or the friend and the enemy, as has been claimed in political philosophy, but bare life and the sovereign power that captures and excludes it. Reworking Aristotle's and Hannah Arendt's distinctions between biological existence (*zoē*) and the political life of speech and action (*bios*),[25] between natural life and a good life,[26] in his *Homo Sacer* Agamben introduces a third term—"bare life"— and traces its selective genealogy from antiquity to modernity. As the counterpart and target of sovereign violence, bare life is stripped of its political significance, expelled from the political, and exposed to murderous violence. To avoid misunderstanding, I would like to stress the point that is made sometimes only implicitly in Agamben's work and not always sufficiently stressed by his commentators: namely, the fact that bare life, wounded, expendable, and exposed to violence, is not the same as biological *zoē* but rather the remainder of the destroyed political *bios*.[27] In fact, bare life is captured by the political in a double way: first, by being excluded from the polis—it is included in the political in the form of an exclusion that marks its borders—and, second, by being exposed to unlimited violation that does not count as a crime. To evoke Theodor Adorno, we could say that it is damaged life, life stripped of its political significance, of its specific form of life. Or, as Andrew Benjamin writes, "there could never be 'bare life' except as an aftereffect."[28]

The production of bare life is thus the effect of a twofold political operation: sovereign violence, on the one hand, and the constitution of abstract political forms as potentially separable from denuded life, on the other. In fact, what is implied by bare life is that the political itself is abstract, defined by the threat of the violent separation from the bodily remainder: "There is politics because man is the living being who, in language, separates and opposes himself to his own bare life and, at the same time, maintains himself in relation to that bare life in an inclusive exclusion" (*HS*, 8). The absence of the relation between the abstract, political ways of being and bare life is what enables the sovereign decision on the state of the exception, the referent of which is damaged life. As Thomas Wall argues: "Between bare life and its ways of living, there can be only *decision*. Every sovereign and every state has always confronted this. . . . Bare life is the nonrelational and thus invites decision. It is the very space of decision . . . and, as such, is perpetually *au hasard*."[29] Yet what are the consequences of this claim for the status of the political forms of life? Because political ways of being can be abstracted from damaged flesh, because there is no inherent relation or interaction between political forms and the body, political formalism is the counterpart of sovereign violence.

As Agamben's broad outline of the political genealogy of the West suggests, the position and political function of bare life change historically. For Agamben, this genealogy begins with the most distant memory of bare life expressed in ancient Roman law as the obscure notion of *homo sacer*—that is, the notion of the expelled, banned man, who, stripped of all political and cultural significance, can be killed with impunity by all, but is unworthy of either juridical punishment or religious sacrifice. Neither the condemned criminal nor the sacrificial scapegoat, and thus expelled outside both human and divine law, homo sacer is the target of sovereign violence exceeding the force of law and yet anticipated and authorized by that law. Banished from the political realm, he is the referent of the sovereign decision on the state of exception, which both confirms and suspends the normal operation of the law. In Agamben's genealogy the major shift in the politicization of bare life occurs in modernity. With the mutation of sovereignty into biopower, bare life ceases to be the excluded outside of the political and in fact become its inner hidden norm: bare life "gradually begins to coincide with the political realm" (HS, 9). However, this inclusion and distribution of bare life *within* the political does not mean its integration with political existence; on the contrary, it is the disjunctive inclusion (the inclusion without integration) of the inassimilable remnant that still remains the target of sovereign violence. As Agamben argues, "Western politics has not succeeded in constructing the link between zoē and bios . . . that would have healed the fracture" (HS, 11). Given this failure of the political, we might ask whether feminist aesthetics can construct such a link between zoē and bios—I will return to this question in the next chapter.

In contrast to the ancient ban, or the inclusive *exclusion* from the political, the new form of disjunctive *inclusion* of bare life within citizenship emerges with modern democracies: the "nascent European democracy thereby placed at the center of its battle with absolutism not bios, the qualified life of the citizen, but . . . bare, anonymous life" (HS, 124). In democratic regimes this hidden incorporation of bare life both into the political realm and the structure of citizenship manifests itself, according to Agamben, as the inscription of "birth" within human rights—an inscription that establishes a dangerous doubling between national and biological existence. As the 1789 Declaration of the Rights of Man and of the Citizen proclaims, men do not become equal by virtue of their political association but are "born and remain" equal. Democratic citizens are thus bearers of both bare life and abstract rights. They are, at the same time, the targets of disciplinary power and free democratic subjects. In a political revision of Foucault's formulation of modern subjectivity as an "empirico-transcendental" doublet,[30] Agamben argues that the modern citizen is *"a two-faced being, the bearer both of subjection to sovereign power and of individual liberties* (HS, 125, emphasis added). As this doubling suggests, the democratic subject of rights is characterized by the hidden aporia between political freedom and the subjection of mere life, without mediation or reconciliation between them.

Since, according to Agamben, bare life is included but not integrated within Western democracies and as such cannot mark their borders, modern politics is about the search for new racialized and gendered targets of exclusion, for the new living dead (*HS*, 130). In our own times, such targets, no longer limited to political subjects, multiply with astonishing speed and infiltrate bodies down to the cellular level: from refugees, illegal immigrants, inmates on death row subject nonetheless to suicide watch, comatose patients on life support to organ transplants, sperm banks, frozen eggs, and fetal stem cells. For Agamben, the violence of this disjunction between bare life and abstract forms of life becomes catastrophically apparent with the reversal of the democratic state into the totalitarian regime at the beginning of the twentieth century. As the disasters of fascism and soviet totalitarianism demonstrate, and as the continuous traumatic histories of genocide and ethnic and racial cleansing show, by suspending abstract political rights, totalitarian regimes can reduce whole populations to disposable bare life that could be destroyed with impunity. This genocidal possibility is actualized for the first time, according to Agamben, in the unprecedented horror of Nazi concentration camps where the extreme destitution and degradation of political beings to bare life leads to mass extermination: "Insofar as its inhabitants were stripped of every political status and wholly reduced to bare life, the camp was also the most absolute biopolitical space ever to have been realized, in which power confronts nothing but pure life, without any mediation" (*HS*, 171). If Agamben controversially claims that the concentration camp is not just the extreme aberration of modernity but its "fundamental biopolitical paradigm" (*HS*,181), which shows the "thanatopolitical face" of power (*HS*, 142, 150), it is because concentration camps, for the first time, actualize the danger implicit in Western politics, namely, the total genocide made possible by the reversal of the exception signified by homo sacer into the new thanatopolitical norm. According to Agamben, such collapse of the distinction between exception and norm, the destruction of abstract rights, and the "absolute" and unmediated subjection of life to death constitute "the supreme political principle" of genocide.

The most compelling force of Agamben's work is his diagnosis of the ways the violent separation of bare life from its political distinctions gives rise to new forms of domination and catastrophic turns of Western history culminating in reversals of democracy into the "thanatopolitical" totalitarian politics of fascism. This catastrophic reversal is a consequence not only of sovereign violence but also of the abstraction of political forms from any interaction or dependence on embodiment. Yet, despite its importance, Agamben's theory of bare life does not sufficiently address two questions: first, the role of bare life in the struggle for freedom and, second, the negative differentiation of bare life with respect to the destroyed political, racial, and gender differences that used to characterize a political being. Both these questions contest the absolute severance of anonymous life from political forms and indicate the possibility of an interaction between political relations and the body. It is these questions, I would argue, that are at the center of any critical feminist engagement with the biopolitics of sovereignty and its impact on modern aesthetics.

Thanks to Agamben's revision of biopolitics, it becomes immediately apparent that the task of resistance cannot be limited to contestation of the law or institutionalized power structures; in fact, I would argue that one of the most pressing political questions raised by *Homo Sacer* is whether bare life itself can be mobilized by emancipatory movements. The second issue we need to reconsider is the way bare life is implicated in the gendered, sexist, colonial, and racist configurations of the political and how, because of this implication, it suffers different kinds of violence.[31] I argue that the central paradox bare life presents for political analysis is not only the erasure of political distinctions but also the negative differentiation such erasure produces with respect to racial, gender, ethnic, or class differences that used to characterize a *form* of life that was destroyed. These two questions of resistance and negative differentiation are interrelated because they point to the fact that complete separation and exclusion of bare life from the political is in fact impossible. They reveal a hidden dependence of both sovereign power and constituted political distinctions on damaged flesh.

As several commentators and critics, most notably Ernesto Laclau, argue, what is lacking in Agamben's political theory is the question of the "emancipatory possibilities" of modernity.[32] Laclau claims that the excess of the political vis-à-vis the juridical cannot be limited to the sovereign ban of homo sacer because such excess is also characteristic of the plurality of movements that organize themselves in opposition to the existing law. Through this act of contestation, such movements form an identity that is partially internal and partially external to the existing law. However, in the context of Agamben's work, the question of resistance cannot be limited to the contestation of the law; in fact, I would argue that one of the most pressing political question is whether bare life itself can be mobilized by oppositional movements. By focusing on the way bare life functions exclusively as the referent of the sovereign decision, Agamben, unfortunately, answers this question in the negative and cautions us against a certain naive optimism that sometimes seems to characterize the "politics of the body": "The 'body' is always already a biopolitical body and bare life, and *nothing in it* or the economy of its pleasure seems to allow us to find solid ground on which *to oppose the demands of sovereign power*" (*HS*, 187, emphasis added). Such a claim implicitly repeats the formalism of the political that Agamben himself otherwise wants to contest. And it is because of such an implicit formalism that Agamben ignores the way bare life is implicated in the gendered, sexist, colonial, and racist configurations of biopolitics. If we argue that bare life emerges as the aftereffect of the destruction of the symbolic differences of gender, ethnicity, race, or class—differences that constitute political forms of life—this means bare life is still negatively determined by the destruction of *a historically specific* way of life. This paradox is a simultaneous erasure of the political distinctions of gender, ethnic, and class differences, and the negative differentiation of bare life retrospectively produced by such erasure reveals a hidden dependence of power on flesh and matter even in the instances of their violent destruction.

Let us consider these two issues—the differentiation of bare life and its potential role in emancipatory movements—in turn. Although Agamben's heterogeneous examples of bare life—for instance, the father/son relation in antiquity, the Nazi euthanasia programs for the mentally ill, the extermination of already denationalized Jewish life in the Final Solution, the destruction of the Gypsies, the ethnic rape camps in the former Yugoslavia, the comatose body of Karen Ann Quinlan, and especially the paradigmatic example of the *Muselmann*—are always diversified along racist, gendered, and historical lines, his conceptual analysis runs up against, but does not follow, the implications of such heterogeneity. Consider, for instance, Agamben's brief comment about the difference between the ethnic rape camps and Nazi camps: "If the Nazi never thought of effecting the Final Solution by making Jewish women pregnant, it is because the principle of birth that assured the inscription of life in the order of the nation-state was still—if in a profoundly transformed sense—in operation. This principle has now entered into a process of decay" (*HS*, 176). Needless to say, the sexually and racially marked difference between these two forms of sovereign violence—genocide and rape—cannot be reduced to the principle of birth alone. And if Agamben refrains from further explorations of rape as a political weapon, it is because such analysis would complicate his definition of bare life (let us recall that his paradigmatic definition is always a life that can be killed but not sacrificed). Furthermore, Agamben's comment that it is only "*now*," that is, in the aftermath of WWII, that the principle of birth is made inoperative shows a historical ignorance of the fact that natality had been a target of destruction since antiquity, at least in the case of slavery.

Because Agamben does not consider the hidden dependence of power on bare life, he is unable to formulate either the possibility of resistance or the role of bare life in democratic struggles for freedom. Agamben is right to argue that the possibility of resistance and the praxis of freedom demand a new ontology of potentiality in excess of historically determined actuality. My main point of critique, however, is that Agamben's ontology of potentiality does not consider the role of bare life in acts of resistance. Consequently, the politicization of bare life means that it is the referent of the sovereign decision over the state of exception, but never the object of contestations between different political forces. The sovereign decision over the exception and bare life captured as the target of violence are always two sides of the same political paradigm. By contrast, I stress both the political and ontological ambiguity of bare life, which escapes the very distinction between potentiality and actuality, presence and absence, life and death. Such political ambiguity means that bare life cannot function only as the target of sovereign decision, but that it can also be reclaimed for the sake of political transformation by oppositional democratic movements.

To show the necessity of supplementing Agamben's notion of bare life in the context of the politics of race and gender, I would like to consider briefly its relation to Aristotle's, Hortense Spillers's, and Orlando Patterson's discussions of slavery and its destruction of gender and cultural/political genealogy. In terms of Agamben's history of bare life, slavery is an important case to consider for several reasons: First of all, ancient and modern racialized forms of slavery represent instances of bare life coextensive with both the Greek polis and modern democracy and yet irreducible to the category of either homo sacer or the camp. Thus, on the one hand, the history of slavery, spanning both antiquity and modernity and extending beyond the history of the West, would strengthen Agamben's insistence on the premodern origins of biopolitics; yet, on the other hand, this history forces us to supplement the sovereignty/homo sacer paradigm with master/slave dialectics and commodity exchange. Rather than keeping these paradigms separate or arguing for the relative centrality of one or the other to the politics of Western modernity, we need to consider instead possible substitutions, interactions, and contradictions between them. For instance, how can sovereign violence be transformed into the seemingly "privatized," but also absolute, power of the slave holder? In what sense can the sovereign destruction of bare life be substituted by the "living" death of slavery? What is the relation between the banned life of homo sacer and what Orlando Patterson calls the "liminal incorporation" of enslaved life? And, finally, how could the biopolitics of sovereignty, commodification, and slavery coexist?

In order to explore these questions in a preliminary manner, I begin with the supplementary yet obfuscated relation between mere life and enslaved life in the text that is foundational for Agamben's political theory, Aristotle's *Politics*.[33] As soon as Aristotle introduces the crucial distinctions between *zoē* and *bios*, *oikos* (home) and *polis*, he is confronted with the place and legitimation of enslaved life, which does not seem to fit easily into these distinctions. Thus, it is not only the case that, as Thomas Wall argues, in the Greek polis the bare life of slavery "was abandoned to the home, the *oikos*" or, "tragically trapped" between oikos and polis, but, more fundamentally, Aristotle's defense of slavery creates a conceptual aporia undermining his definition of slavery as an "animate instrument" belonging to the household. Implicated in the whole network of differences fundamental to the differentiation of the public space of the city—such as the differences between body and soul, male and female, human life and animal life, master and statesman, passion and reason—enslaved life, defined by Aristotle as property, does not have a "proper" place. In his apologia Aristotle writes the following: "The soul rules the body with the authority of a master: reason rules the appetite with the authority of a statesman. . . . The same principle is true of the relation of man to other animals. . . . Again, the relation of the male to the female is naturally that of the superior to the inferior. . . . We may thus conclude that all men who differ from others as much as the body differs from the soul, or an animal from a man . . . are by nature slaves."[34] As these multiple levels of analogous reasoning show, the political subjection and exclusion of femininity and slavery is "like" the subjection of the body to reason and animality to the human. Perhaps bearing witness to the threat of enslavement in war, this analogy potentially makes the body of the free Greek citizen "like" the enslaved or inhuman body. And, conversely, the enslaved body both mediates and blurs the distinction between the human and the animal, the household and the city. Because of its in-between position on the "threshold" (to use Agamben's apt term), slavery in Aristotle's text begins to haunt the Greek polis from within and from without, making the Greek citizen, like its modern counterpart, already a double being, subjected to the mastery of reason and a political being among equals. Furthermore, even though Aristotle rigorously distinguishes the political rule of the statesman from the domination of the master, the analogies between the political rule of the statesman, the authority of reason, and the power of the master in the household once again blur these distinctions.

Although subjected to the violence of the master rather than to sovereign banishment, enslaved life in Aristotle's *Politics*, like the obscure figure of homo sacer in Roman law, blurs the boundaries between the inside and the outside of the political. It is Orlando Patterson's influential study of slavery from antiquity to modernity that gives a full account of the liminality of the slave's paradoxical position in the social order. Thus if Agamben in *Homo Sacer* focuses on the paradoxes of sovereignty, Patterson, in his seminal work *Slavery as Social Death*, argues that the enigma of slavery exceeds both the juridical and economic categories of law, production, exchange, and property. What all these categories fail to explicate is both the "total" domination of enslaved life and the liminality of slaves' position. Like the indistinction, or threshold, between the inside and outside marked by homo sacer, the slave's liminality collapses both the political and ontological differences between the human and the inhuman, monstrosity and normality, anomaly and norm, life and death, cosmos and chaos, being and "nonbeing" (*SSD*, 38), and as such a borderline phenomenon, it could never be contained in the Greek *oikos* (household). In one of the most suggestive passages, devoted to an interpretation of the Anglo-Saxon representation of slavery/servitude in *Beowulf*, Patterson writes: "In the role of the slave as guide to the dragon's evil world we find one of the most remarkable statements of the slave's liminal status. . . . It was precisely because he was marginal, neither human nor inhuman, neither man nor beast, neither dead nor alive, the enemy within who was neither member nor true alien, that the slave could lead Beowulf and his men across the deadly margin that separated the social order above from the terror and chaos of the underground" (SSD, 48). Similarly to the state of exception, the institutionalized anomaly of slavery "emphasized what was most important and stable" in the nonslave population (SSD, 464), yet, unlike homo sacer, such liminality could also position an enslaved being as a guide who could cross the borders of the inhabitable world. It is this notion of liminality as subversive trespassing that Larsen will transpose into her aesthetic project.

What is then the relation between these two different expressions of subjugation and liminality represented, on the one hand, by homo sacer and, on the other hand, by enslaved life? If we once again juxtapose Patterson's and Agamben's work, the key concept that links bare life captured in the political sphere of sovereignty with the master slave/dialectic is the substitutability of slavery for death: either for the death of the external enemy seized on the battle field or the death of the internal "fallen" member of the community. According to Patterson, this substitution of enslavement for imminent death is echoed in the "archetypal" meaning of slavery as social death (SSD, 5, 26). It is also registered in Roman terminology (captivus) and the Greek regulations of slavery associated with war. Needless to say, the substitution of enslavement for death does not give pardon but, on the contrary, creates the anomaly of the socially dead but biologically alive and economically exploited being. Because the expropriation of a slave's life constitutes him or her as a nonperson, or a socially dead person, it produces another instance of bare life as violently stripped of genealogy, cultural memory, social distinction, name, and native language, that is, of all the elements that form Aristotle's zoē. Akin to "secular excommunication," slavery, in all its different historical formations from antiquity to modernity, was institutionalized as the extreme destruction of the social and symbolic formation of subjectivity. As a mark of illegitimacy and exclusion from the realm of symbolization, from the polis as well as from the household and kinship, this extreme mode of deracination reconstituted enslaved life as a nameless, invisible nonbeing—as a pro nullo, according to Roman law (SSD, 40).

As we have seen, Hortense Spillers argues that such exclusion of black enslaved bodies from symbolization leads to the destruction of kinship and gender structures. All these social distinctions collapse into what Spillers calls a "lacerated" black flesh as the traumatic zero degree of social and political differences. In order to analyze bodily crimes inflicted by enslavement, Spiller's analysis of the economics of slavery adds the new category of "flesh." By functioning as the traumatic, invisible double

of the socially valued white body, black flesh, as Alexander Weheliye per-
suasively argues,[35] is reminiscent of Agamben's bare life. Spillers writes:
"Before the 'body' there is the 'flesh,' that zero degree of social conceptualization that does not escape concealment under the brush of discourse. . . . Even though the European hegemonies stole bodies—some
of them female—out of West African communities . . . we regard this
human and social irreparability as high crimes against the *flesh*. . . . If we
think of the 'flesh' as a primary narrative, then we mean its seared, divided, ripped-apartness" (MBPM, 67). The "ungendered" flesh suffers a
double damage: not only traumatic physical violations but also a traumatic symbolic destruction of the social significations of kinship, gender,
and name. Spillers's notion of lacerated flesh functions as the linchpin
between Irigaray's and Marx's analysis of "the total mortification" of the
body by economic exchange and Agamben's bare life as target and the
effect of sovereign violence. Emerging in the aftermath of the destruction of the social and symbolic signification of the body, the "hieroglyphics" of wounded flesh (MBPM, 67) nonetheless bear witness to the crimes
of white supremacy and preserve the bloody traces of the forms of life that
have been destroyed. These unbearable "hieroglyphics" of violated black
flesh—"a primary narrative" of its "seared, divided, ripped-apartness"—
contests the total exclusion of bare life from its symbolic meaning and of
commodity form from its mortified bodily remainder. As we shall see,
these hieroglyphics are also a source of the struggle for freedom. Nonetheless, Spillers argues that violated black flesh is excluded from a "cultural seeing" obsessed with the visibility of color, from a white feminist
analysis of "'The Female Body in Western Culture'" (MBPM, 67) and, we
should add, from political philosophy.

The notion of slavery as a substitute for death complicates Agamben's
central thesis that the sovereign decision/bare life constitutes the foundational political paradigm in the West. First of all, although the extreme
delegitimation and nullity of enslaved life makes it another instantiation
of bare life, the very fact that such life undergoes substitutions of one
form of destruction for another undermines from the start any theoretical claims about the centrality of *just one* paradigm of politics. In fact, as
Hortense Spillers, Saidiya Hartman, and Alexander Weheliye, in different ways, argue, the institution of slavery as social death is not merely a
historical phenomenon but rather "engenders the black subject in the
Americas" and constitutes a matrix of Western political modernity.[36] According to Weheliye, "as opposed to being confined to a particular his-

torical period, echoes of new world slavery rest in many contemporary spaces."[37] Slavery raises the question whether the destruction of the human *form* of life is a "condition" of exchangeability as such. As Patterson argues, the destruction of the political forms of life turned human beings into "the ideal of a human tool, an *instrumentum vocal*—perfectly flexible, unattached, and deracinated" (*SSD*, 337). Because of its fungibility, the idea of such a human tool, is also a perfect commodity; and indeed, Patterson notes historical instances where slavery functioned as money (*SSD*, 167–169). On the basis of Spillers's analysis, we can argue, therefore, that the violent production of social death functions as the hidden ground not only of politics but also of exchange, even though it cannot be explained in these terms. Consequently, the substitution of the living social death for biological death indicates the possible transformation of the sovereign ban into ownership, exchange, and use. As Patterson's discussion of the ancient Roman doctrine of *dominium* suggests, here an absolute power over human beings merges with the absolute ownership of *res* (*SSD*, 30–32).

The biopolitics of substitution inscribed in the power relations of slavery changes the character of both death and birth. Deprived of its finitude, the anomaly of social death denotes a spectral duration of nonbeing beyond the categories of absence and presence, potentiality and actuality. On the one hand, the spectrality of social death constitutes a permanent threat of anomaly and aberration; on the other hand, it is continually put to work in order to produce profit and, as such, is the lynchpin of biopolitics and economics. As the ending of Larsen's novel *Quicksand* suggests, this spectral character of social death, which continues to endure in the form of nonbeing, also destroys the principle of natality, understood broadly to include not only biological birth but also the claims of genealogy, the principle of a new beginning. Indeed, for Patterson, even the concept of social death is not sufficient to express the most drastic destruction of being—hence its supplementation by "natal alienation." By signifying the erasure of both biological and social origins, "the term 'natal alienation' . . . goes directly to the heart of what is critical in the slave's forced alienation, the loss of ties of birth . . . a loss of native status, of deracination" (*SSD,* 7). As the destruction of genealogy and history, as exclusion from the past as well as from the future, the lost natality marks the enslaved person not only as socially dead but also as an unborn being. According to Claude Meillassoux's and Michael Izard's apt formulation, as quoted in Patterson, "the slave will remain forever an unborn being (*non-né*)" (*SSD*, 38). The paradox of a being that is not only dead but forever unborn makes indeed "time out of joint"—it destroys the temporal and modal distinctions between finitude and transcendence, presence and absence, inauguration and repetition, and potentiality and actuality.

These institutionalized anomalies of death and birth—the deadly paradox of a life that cannot be born but continues to endure as social death—suggest that slavery, like homo sacer, implies a paradigm of biopolitics intertwined with thanatopolitics. What both slavery and homo sacer have in common is the production of bare life stripped of its human form of life. But, what distinguishes them is the contrast between the sovereign ban and the marginal inclusion of enslaved life. If the sovereign decision on the state of exception captures bare life in order to exclude it, the biopolitics of slavery is confronted with the opposite task, namely, with profitably including the socially dead beings while keeping them in the limbo of nonbeing. Hence, Patterson argues that after the stage of violent depersonalization and "social negation," which most closely corresponds to the sovereign ban, the next stage of enslavement introduces "the slave into the community of his master, but it involves the paradox of introducing him as a nonbeing" (*SSD*, 38). Since, unlike homo sacer, the socially dead being has to be included within and made profitable, this second stage of the biopolitics of slavery poses the dilemma of "liminal incorporation" (*SSD*, 45). The paradox of the liminal incorporation of a life that is already socially dead is the opposite of the sovereign ban, even though it creates similar effects of indistinction. On the one hand, we have an institutionalized containment within the law of a permanent anomaly that confounds the differences between life and death, destruction and profit. Yet, on the other hand, the enslaved, exploited beings mirror the hidden, potential threat that biopolitics presents for so-called free citizens: the destruction of their way of life and violent reduction to bare life that can be killed with impunity.

As we can see, the notion of "bare life" can open new interpretations of the biopolitics of race and gender for contemporary political philosophy, feminist thought, and critical race studies. Yet, as my discussion also shows, such a reconsideration of "bare life" in the context of racial and sexual politics calls for some fundamental revisions of that concept. First of all, bare life cannot be regarded as completely separate from all cultural/political characteristics. If bare life emerges as the remnant of a destroyed human form of life, then its formulation has to refer, in the negative way, to the racial/sexual/ethnic/class differences that used to characterize this *form* of life. In other words, bare life has to be defined as the remnant of a specific form of life that it not yet or no longer, is. To repeat Spillers's haunting formulation, these destroyed symbolic remnants are inscribed as a bloody hieroglyphics on wounded flesh. Furthermore, bare life cannot always be considered as the exclusive referent of sovereign decision, but has to be reconceptualized as a more complex, contested terrain where new forms of domination, dependence, and emancipatory struggle can emerge.

***

By juxtaposing the commodification of female bodies, the brutality of enslavement, and the biopolitics of bare life, I have diagnosed the violent effects of abstract formalism in political life and their correlative, damaged materialities. What this juxtaposition reveals is the possibility of the violent severance of collective forms from the remnants of materiality, which becomes the target of violence. The destruction of bare life threatening so-called free citizens is catastrophically realized in the two other paradigms of Western modernity: the social death of enslavement haunting the history of democracy from within and the reversals of democracy into totalitarianism. The separation of social form from materiality is also at stake in another, apparently unrelated formation of modernity, namely, the production and exchange of commodified bodies, labor, and objects. Characterized by the abstract determination of value in total separation from the particularity and materiality of the object, the commodity form mirrors the schism in the structure of citizenship, the split between bare life and abstract human rights. Such disastrous intertwining of the violence directed at bare life and the violence of commodification is what produces the social death of captive bodies. Yet what is at stake in the configuration of political violence, abstract forms, and damaged materialities is not only a new diagnosis of the brutal oppression and destruction of gendered and racialized bodies but also a new formulation of emancipatory political struggles and aesthetic inventions. As I will show in the next chapter, political and aesthetic contestations cannot be limited to either the symbolic politics of recognition or even the politics of redistribution because they also have to oppose the violent split between materiality and form.[38] Evocative of the severance between the signifier and affect in melancholia, this violent schism calls for new modes of mediation, or interaction, between abstract forms and damaged materialities to be invented in political and aesthetic practices.

In fact, despite the different trajectories and philosophical genealogies I reconstructed in this chapter, all the thinkers I have discussed implicitly or explicitly call for a rethinking of embodiment and materiality outside the violent and abstract regulation of bodies in modernity: outside exchangeability and abstract commodity form (Irigaray), outside sovereign decision on the state of exception (Agamben), and outside the violence of white supremacy (Spillers and Patterson). Contesting both sovereign decision on bare life and abstract forms of exchange, this different form of mediation between bodies and forms of living cannot be confused either with a dialectical reconciliation, social construction, or especially with a naive celebration of prepolitical life. On the contrary, as Agamben suggests at the end of *Homo Sacer*, such a task would involve thinking the inseparability of form and life beyond the binaries of Western metaphysics:

> This biopolitical body that is bare life must itself instead be transformed into the site for the constitution and installation of a form of life that is wholly exhausted in bare life and a *bios* that is only its own *zoē*. . . . Yet how can a *bios* be only its own *zoē*, how can a form of life seize hold of the very *haplos* [bare being] that constitutes both the task and the enigma of Western metaphysics? If we give the name form-of-life to this being that is only its own bare existence and to this life that, being its own form, remains inseparable from it, we will witness the emergence of a field of research beyond the terrain defined by the intersection of politics and philosophy, medico-biological sciences and jurisprudence.
>
> (*HS*, 188)

In this difficult passage Agamben only hints at what this new interconnection between form and life might look like.[39] By making their separation and unification equally impossible, the conflicting inseparability of bare life and political form—*bios* and *zoē*—takes us beyond the three alternatives that govern the discussion of the body in politics: the paradigm of biopolitics, the nostalgic return to the remains of the natural body, and the equally naive social construction of a new technological body.

5   Damaged Materialities in Political
Struggles and Aesthetic Innovations

The diagnosis of the violent severance between destroyed materialities and abstract political forms discussed in chapter 4 reveals a new
task for feminist, antiracist political struggles and new stakes for aesthetic innovations. The task is to contest not only racist and gendered injustice but also the severance of symbolic political forms from bare life
because such severance itself is the source of violence. In chapter 1 I
showed that the suffragettes' militant struggles for inclusion in citizenship and political rights redefine the politics of recognition as a revolt
aiming to create a new organization of political life. In the context of our
analysis of the biopolitics of sovereignty, it becomes clear, however, that
at stake in such struggles is not only intersubjective freedom but also the
transformation of the violent split between materiality, bodies, and political forms. In other words, women's revolutionary struggles acquire a
bodily and materialist turn that goes beyond both symbolic recognition
and the materialist politics of redistribution because it addresses not only
capitalist relations of production but also calls for a new model of reciprocal interaction between damaged materialities and abstract forms of life.[1]
As we have seen, the absence of such interconnection and the expulsion
of gendered and radicalized bodies from the polis are two sides of the
same political operation.

Such severance between form and materiality is also opposed by experimental aesthetics. Thus I propose to read the materiality of aesthetic form, traditionally acknowledged by aesthetics, not merely as a source of enjoyment or apolitical formalism but as a necessary intervention into the violent abstraction of commodity form and citizenship. In contrast to conservative formalism, such as T. S. Eliot's abstraction of mythical structure from the disorder of everyday life, the experimental literary works I analyze provide a new model of interconnection between damaged materials, violated bodies, and literary forms.

Let me begin with facts that tend to be all too easily taken for granted: at the turn of the twentieth century racialized and gendered subjectivities were still marginalized in Western democracies and, as such, associated with the occluded proximity to bare life. As Falguni A. Sheth argues, the political effectiveness of racism depends in large measure on the danger of being abandoned by the law.[2] And yet these marginalized subjectivities were also the "bearers" and creators of a very different legacy of modernity—the legacy of multiple liberation movements, from international suffrage struggles to labor protests and decolonization movements. By analyzing bare life as the target of sovereign violence, Agamben allows us to diagnose new forms of domination and political danger in modernity. Although any praxis of freedom is dependent on such a diagnosis, such praxis at the same time requires reflection on the often occluded role of bare life in another paradigm of democratic modernity— that of revolutionary traditions. The first section of this chapter looks at the two important examples of insurgency in which bare life itself is at stake: the hunger strike of British suffragettes at the beginning of the twentieth century and struggles against antiblack racism. Why bring together such diverse historical cases on the two sides of the Atlantic? As I have argued in the previous chapter, what these two cases reveal is, first of all, the paradoxical racial and gender differentiation of the violated bodies stripped of all meaning and their subjection to different kinds of violence. Second, despite their differences, the hunger strike and the struggle against anti-black violence reveal the sovereign power's dependence on life deprived of its political status. It is precisely because of such dependence that bare life can be a contested terrain, that it can mobilized by political movements.

The Feminine Invention of the Hunger Strike

The British suffragettes' use of the hunger strike in the struggle for women's voting rights at the beginning of the twentieth century, one of the most dramatic turns of the suffrage movement, reveals new possibilities of the mobilization of bare life in the struggle for freedom. In fact, suffragettes' hunger strike can be regarded as an invention of a new mode of political contestation that mobilizes bare life for emancipatory struggle. What is at stake in the hunger strike is the struggle to endow the female body—understood in the political imaginary as a remnant of bare life, subservient to the reproduction of the species and exposed to sexual violence—with new, embodied political forms of public speech and collective action. The hunger strike can become such an important method of political intervention for the subjugated groups of the twentieth century and in our own times because life itself has become the object of political violence and disciplinary regulations. Yet suffragettes' hunger strike shows that mere life, although always already the object and aftereffect of biopower, can nonetheless be usurped as a weapon by oppositional groups. In a crucial supplement to Agamben's theory, the suffragettes' hunger strike not only reveals the hidden gendering of the split between bare life and abstract human rights but also shows how this severance can enable revolutionary transformation. By willing to destroy their bodies for political freedom, hunger striking suffragettes put bare life at the center of the struggle for human rights. In so doing, they not only refuse the status of bare life deprived of a political *bios* but turn it into a weapon against the sovereign power of the state. And yet, if bare life can be used in the struggle for political freedom, this means that such struggle invents a new reciprocal interaction between bodies and citizenship.

In the British militant suffrage struggle for the vote, the deployment of the hunger strike, followed by governmental retaliation through forcible feedings, is one of the most paradoxical and dramatic episodes. According to Jane Marcus, the hunger strike and the reprisals of forcible feedings are "perhaps the primary image in the public imagination regarding the 'meaning' of the suffrage movement."[3] What does this "primary" political scene tell us about the white feminine body, its function in oppositional democratic movements, and the "biopolitical" paradigm of sovereignty?[4] In what sense can the weapon of self-starvation be mobilized by women as a rebellious response to the government's punishment of women for their public demand for the constitutional rights of which they were deprived despite the long history of suffrage agitation? The performative and political effects of the hunger strike expose the modern relations between bare life, revolt, human rights, and the violence of sovereignty. As Kyria Landzelius puts it, the hunger strike is a "corporeal challenge" to "the discursive practices of power,"[5] a bodily intervention in the complex network of relations between politics, power, discourse, and the ritual of self-sacrifice.

Although one of the most dramatic episodes in the struggle for women's suffrage, hunger striking and the political reprisals of forcible feeding are, like the hunger strike in general, still undertheorized means of democratic protest. In his monumental study of nonviolent political action, Sharp classifies the hunger strike as a means of political intervention that demands a transformation of power relations and a redress for injustice. Although, as Kyria Landzelius argues, the historical origin of the hunger strike is unclear, the hunger strike was practiced in ancient Rome, medieval Ireland, and India as a means of protest, usually to force the debtor to return his debt or to exert moral pressure.[6] After the Easter Rising of 1916 in Ireland, the hunger strike tactic was adopted by the Irish struggle for independence in 1917[7] and, most famously, by Mohandas Gandhi, who fasted at least fourteen times in British occupied India.[8] Nonetheless, it was British militant suffragettes who in 1909 revived and redefined the hunger strike as the modern political weapon of an organized social movement by linking it for the first time with the discourse of human rights. The political practice of hunger striking in the suffrage agitation was initiated in 1909 by suffrage artist Marion Wallace Dunlop, who was arrested and sentenced to one month's imprisonment for having written on the wall of Parliament an extract from the Bill of Rights guaranteeing the right of petition to all British subjects.[9] Suffragettes appealed to and tested the modern usage of this right when they organized deputations to the prime minister, the representative of the king, who refused to receive them. While in prison, Dunlop began hunger striking to protest her having been denied the status of "political offender." After ninety-one hours of fasting, she was released from prison because prison officials, ignorant about the effects of a hunger strike, were afraid to create a martyr for the suffrage cause. When other prisoners were also released before the expiration of their sentences, the hunger strike was adopted by the suffrage movement as an effective political weapon both to terminate prison sentences and to create new possibilities of revolt within the disciplinary apparatus of the prison. In response to this unprecedented act of protest, after King Edward VII's personal intervention in August 1909, the home secretary, Herbert Gladstone, ordered forcible feedings of the hunger striking suffragettes—a brutal punitive retaliation that, up to this point, had been practiced primarily in insane asylums.[10]

How can we understand this configuration of the hunger strike as a weapon of resistance and the sadistic brutality of forcible feedings, which have often been compared to rape? Why, in the struggle for the vote, which classical liberal theory defines as an abstract contractual possession, did women's bodies have to undergo such violence in order to challenge the law? We may say that the hunger strike is a continuation of revolutionary struggle by the summoning of the starving body in place of banned political speech and action. Consequently, at the beginning of the twentieth century, the starved bodies of the hunger striking suffragettes subjected to the state machinery of "forcible feeding" staged a new political conflict in which bare life was both the target of sovereign violence and a weapon in the struggle for political rights. Suffragettes reverted to the hunger strike not merely to reduce their prison sentences but to reverse the position of femininity in relation to the political: they risked the destruction or injury of the body for the sake of political freedom, speech, and action.

Consider, for example, the letter of another leading militant suffragette, Lady Constance Lytton, written to the *Times* on her own behalf and that of eleven other hunger striking suffragettes on October 10, 1909. As this letter suggests, the hunger strike is both a protest and a demand for new freedoms, an appeal articulated through the double medium of the publicly circulating press and the starving body secluded in prison and barred from public appearance. Lytton claims that subjugated groups resort to violence against their bodies when rational arguments based on law fail—that is, when instituted political speech is deprived of its performative power: "We want to make it known that we shall carry on our protest in our prison cells. We shall put before the Government by means of the hunger-strike four alternatives: to release us in a few days; to inflict violence on our bodies; to add death to the champions of our cause by leaving us to starve; or, and this is the best and only wise alternative, to give women the vote. We appeal to the Government to yield, not to the violence of our protest, but to the reasonableness of our demand."[11]

Lytton's emphasis on the "violence" of the hunger strike seems paradoxical: such violence, inflicted on the self as a substitute target for political power, acts by refusing to act; it collapses clear distinctions between passivity and activity, victim and enemy. On the one hand, the hunger strike repeats, mimics, and exposes in public the hidden irrational violence of the sovereign state against women's bodies. On the other hand, by usurping the state's power over bare life, self-starvation calls for the transformation of citizenship.

The liberal government's response to the "four alternatives" posed by the suffragettes was the physical and moral torture of forcible feeding—a failed attempt to degrade femininity to a life stripped of all political meaning and reduced merely to physical survival. In the context of Agamben's definition of bare life as the referent of sovereign decision and violence, the torture of forcible feeding is also paradoxical. What Agamben's theory allows us to clarify is that the violence of forcible feedings does not represent a juridical punishment but rather a case of the sovereign decision to restore the normal situation of the law's operation. Although all the trappings and the representation of forcible feedings as a "medical treatment" administered by the prison doctor were meant to mask this sovereign violence by relegating it to medical science, the medicalization of torture most clearly reveals the biopolitical character of sovereignty. However, forcible feedings compel us again to expand and supplement Agamben's notion of sovereign violence. First of all, this case reveals not only a negative gendered and class differentiation of bare life but also the sexualized character of sadistic violence to which it is exposed. The objective of forcible feeding is neither murderous violence nor the production of social death but a camouflaged sexualized violence of bodily penetration that reenacts rape. Forcible feedings reveal, therefore, not only the fact that the rational authority of the law is haunted by archaic sovereign violence but also that this violence manifests itself in different ways in relation to gender and racial differences: as the power to kill without committing homicide or the power to inflict torture and rape with impunity. The double character of sovereign violence has been obfuscated in modern democracies by women's unequal access to the political, so that rape appears as a private act of violence, still difficult to prove as a crime, rather than as a remnant of sovereign biopower. At the beginning of the twentieth century women were not only excluded from the rights and aporias of citizenship but were subjected to a different form of sovereign violence—to the seemingly "apolitical" violence of rape masquerading as "medical" treatment. Second, as the "reactive" attempt to reestablish the normal frame of reference of the law disturbed by the suffragettes' hunger strike, forcible feedings reveal the government's struggle to regain power over bare life. Yet, if the torture of forcible feedings is an attempt to recapture bare life as the referent of sovereign power, this means that sovereign power over bare life is tenuous and open to contestation. The consequence of this state of affairs is that in modernity mere life is the contested object of diverse political struggles and thus can no longer be taken for granted as the exclusive referent of sovereignty.

Although not analyzed by Agamben, the emphasis on the collective political struggles over resignification of bare life is an important element in Lady Constance Lytton's January 31, 1910 speech, which, as Jorgensen-Earp suggests, offers the first "political theory" of the hunger strike.[12] Lytton defines the hunger strike as a weapon providing an alternative to physically violent struggle against the political enemy:

> People say, what does this hunger-strike mean? Surely it is all folly. If it is not hysteria, at least it is unreasonable. They will not realize that we are like an army, that we are deputed to fight for a cause, . . . and in any struggle or any fight, weapons must be used. The weapons for which we ask are simple, a fair hearing, but that is refused us. . . . Then we must have other weapons. What do other people choose when they are driven to the last extremity? . . . They have recourse to violence . . . These women have chosen the weapon of self-hurt to make their protest, and this hunger-strike brings great pressure upon the Government [but] . . . does not physically injure their enemies.[13]

In response to antisuffrage propaganda, Lytton argues that hunger strikes are not unreasonable attacks of hysteria but a political strategy of the last resort by an "army" of the dispossessed. As acts of "warfare" by the paradoxical means of self-injury, hunger strikes allow suffragettes to continue revolutionary struggle without a direct engagement in war. Furthermore, by extending possibilities of militancy from the street and the public sphere to prison itself, the hunger strike reverses imprisonment into new means of "fighting for a cause," transforms punishment into rebellion, and turns subjection into the ambiguous political agency of "self-hurt." It puts physical health and biological life at risk in order to regain political life and to terminate women's exclusion from citizenship.

The most suggestive way Lytton's speech evokes the notion of bare life as a new weapon of oppositional movements is through the figurative juxtaposition of feminine, animal, and divine bodies. Her speech begins with an analogy between the degraded female body, deprived of rights, and a deformed animal body, humiliated and abused on its way to the slaughterhouse, and ends with the contrast between the tortured and despised body of imprisoned suffragettes, condemned by the prison priest, and Christ's sacrificed body. Unlike the sacrificial lamb with which Christ is frequently compared, the deformed sheep, a powerless "creature" mistreated by the crowd, is the very opposite of either a human or a divine sacrifice. Designating the passage between the animal and the human, "the old and misshapen" sheep is the figure of damaged life, deprived of political or religious significance, a life whose biological survival is at risk.[14] When, in a sudden insight, Lytton discovers this hidden relation between white aristocratic femininity, sheltered by class privilege, and deformed, abused animal life, she decides to join the suffrage militant movement—a decision that transformed her *life* and gave it a political and collective meaning. We can glimpse the depth of this transformation from the contrast between the frightened isolated animal, powerless to protest its abuse, and the "army" of women forming a revolutionary collective movement in order to fight for access to the political.

Suffragettes' usurping of the sovereign decision over mere life in the struggle for political rights suspends the unjust law, at least on the symbolic level. Yet this act does not constitute a state of exception, which, through an act of exclusion, establishes the normal frame of reference or, as in the case of fascism and totalitarian regimes, turns exception into a new norm. Rather, suffrage militancy represents a revolutionary call for a new law yet to come. As Landzelius argues, the hunger strike stages a political trial of the existing law and political authority. In this "meta-juridical" trial, the private act of starvation reverses the guilty verdict imposed on the militant suffragettes into a public condemnation of the government. Thus the starving female bodies "pervert" juridical punishment into a means of interrogation of the law itself and a contestation of government's authority. By reversing the roles of the defendants and the accusers, the drama of the hunger strike publicly condemns the government, delegitimates the authority of the existing law, and calls for its transformation. In opposition to sovereign violence, hunger-striking suffragettes "seize hold" of their bare life, wrestle it away from the hold of sovereign violence, and transform it into an inseparable component of embodied political forms of citizenship. Thus suffragettes' public re-definition of the female body, so that it no longer bears the repressed signification of bare life and acquires instead a political form, not only challenges the sovereign decision over bare life, but calls for a new interrelation between life and form outside the parameters of that decision. In contrast to the absence of the relationship between abstract rights and bare life in democratic citizenship, the hunger strike performs a double inter-action between bare life and the law: on the one hand, it transforms the private act of bodily starvation into a condemnation of the existing law; on the other hand, it summons and legitimates the as yet nonexistent authority of law by risking the physical life of the body. In a catachrestic movement, the struggle over bare life anticipates what is unpredictable and beyond anticipation: a new embodied law and a future resignification of female bodies. In so doing, the hunger strike reveals modes of inseparability between life and political form outside the purview of sovereign decision.

White "Parasitism," "the Scream" of Commodities, and the Black Struggle for Freedom

Let us now move to the other side of the Atlantic and consider a much earlier paradigm of the mobilization of bare life in liberation movements, namely, black struggles for freedom. In contrast to the self-inflicted bodily violence of the hunger strike as a means of protest against the law, black subjectivities were brutalized by sovereign power, and such violation was authorized by law. This contrast between self-inflicted bodily hurt and the brutal violation of bodies, as well as the legacy of different forms of struggles, is one of the pivotal racial differences between white and black femininities. Nonetheless, despite the very different positions and valorizations of black and white bodies, both the hunger strike and the struggle against antiblack racism show that bare life, deprived of its political status and meaning, can be the object of political contestation.

What black feminists and theorists of slavery like Hortense Spillers, Alexander Weheliye, and Orlando Patterson show is the obfuscated and

disavowed dependence of sovereign power on black bodies. Such dependence provides a new ground for struggles against racism and the devastating effects of slavery. In a very significant move, Patterson stresses the
reversal of the slaveholder's absolute domination into its dependence on
black bodies. In so doing, he rewrites the Hegelian master-slave dialectic—
which explains such dependence in terms of the desire for recognition by
the other—as "human parasitism" (SSD, 336). The consequences of
adopting the biological "framework of parasitism" far exceed Patterson's
claim that it merely clarifies and amplifies the Hegelian discovery of the
slaveholder's dependence (SSD, 336). More than ten years before the publication of Homo Sacer, Patterson's turn to social biology implicitly replaces both the philosophical and political analyses of power and recognition with a biopolitical paradigm. It is not only the last chapter, "Slavery
as Human Parasitism," that makes the biopolitical framework of Patterson's study apparent; the implied biopolitics of slavery is equally at work
in his discussions of social death and natality. How does "the parasitism
of slavery" supplement both Agamben's and Hegel's philosophies? What
it adds to Agamben's theory of sovereignty is the parasitical and unstable
dependence of power on bare life; the novelty it introduces to the Hegelian struggle for recognition is the "biopolitics" of the body—the "consumption" of bare life by the parasitical master (SSD, 46, 336). Indeed, as
Patterson points out, social parasitism is meant to reveal the instability of
the master's dependence on his subjugated other: "The dominator, in the
process of dominating and making another individual dependent, also
makes himself (the dominator) dependent. . . . On this intersubjective
level the slaveholder *fed* on the slave to gain the very direct satisfaction of
power over another" (SSD, 336–337). As the other side of mastery, the
parasitical dependence of power on bare life is precisely what escapes
both Agamben's biopolitical paradigm of sovereign will and Hegel's paradigm of recognition. Like a reversed figure of the vampire sucking the
blood of the living, the parasitical side of absolute power suggests that
perhaps sovereignty is one of the most powerful political fantasies, mask-
ing power's dependence on bare life, which, although socially "dead,"
continues to threaten and provide sexual satisfaction.[15]

    The parasitical dependence that Patterson detects in relations of abso-
lute exploitation has another important consequence that is downplayed
in Agamben's theory of sovereignty: such dependence provides a new
ground for the possibility of resistance and rebellion. Sometimes such
resistance took the form of a direct rebellion and the practice of what

Houston A. Baker Jr. calls "radical marronage" or the creation of inde-pendent communities among the fugitives;[16] in other cases, even fleeting acts of resistance refused dehumanization and cultivated among subju-gated people a desire for respect, community, and freedom. As Saidiya Hartman writes, such every day acts of resistance "encompassed an array of tactics such as work slowdowns, feigned illness, unlicensed travel, the destruction of property, theft, self-mutilation, dissimulation, physical confrontation with owners and overseers. . . . What unites these varied tactics is the effort to redress the condition of the enslaved, restore the disrupted affiliations of the socially dead, challenge the authority . . . of the slaveholder, and alleviate the pained state of the captive body."[17] The emphasis on resistance culminates in Patterson's claim that the fundamental discovery of enslaved peoples is freedom, enshrined as one of the most cherished values of Western democracies: "The first men and women to struggle for freedom, the first to think of them-selves as free . . . were freedmen. . . . Without slavery there would have been no freedmen" (*SSD*, 342). Freedom, for Patterson, emerges from the negation of social death and human parasitism as well as from the yearn-ing for the creation of new forms of political life. Although Patterson is uneasy about making enslavement even a contingent condition of free-dom, nonetheless his insistence on the ongoing struggle for liberation by dominated peoples points to another legacy of modernity that Agam-ben sidesteps in his analysis: the legacy of revolutionary and emancipa-tory movements.[18]

If, for Patterson, the possibility of freedom and liberation lies in the manipulation and contestation of the parasitical dependence of power on bare life, for Hortense Spillers resistance is more directly intertwined with the invention of a new, embodied grammar of race and gender. In her emphasis on crimes against the wounded flesh, Spillers also recog-nizes the biopolitics of power and its sadistic dependence on captive bod-ies. Building on Spillers's analysis, Robyn Wiegman has demonstrated how identification with the masculine gender—which constitutes one form of the politics of symbolic recognition—has been for black male writers an important rhetorical strategy in the struggle for political en-franchisement and the subversion of white supremacy.[19] In Spillers's ar-gument, however, such a symbolic politics of recognition of the existing gender formations, though essential, is insufficient. What she calls for is a formation of new embodied masculinities that would reclaim, rather than reject, proximity to the maternal body, a proximity negated by the normative kinship structure: "The African-American male has been touched . . . by the *mother*" in ways he cannot escape through paternal identification the way the white American male can (MBPM, 79–80). Rather than being a threat, or a mark of illegitimacy imposed by white supremacy, the black maternal touch is, on the contrary, a condition of resistance. According to Spillers, the African American masculinities must reclaim the "power" of "yes" to the "female" within (MBPM, 80). In response to Spillers's analysis, Fred Moten argues that the resistance to enslavement, "being *maternal* . . . is indistinguishable from it being *material*."[20]

By contrast, since black femininity was historically associated with the maternal reproduction of illegitimacy (the memory of which still haunts racist American culture blaming the "destructive" power of black mothers for the economic and social injustices suffered by African Americans), reclaiming the female gender as a route of resistance has been more difficult: "This problematizing of gender places her, in my view, *out* of the traditional symbolics of female gender, and it is our task to make a place for this different social subject" (MBPM, 80). To create a new significance for black femininity and to reclaim their power of insurgency amounts, according to Spillers, to "*claiming* the monstrosity (of a female with the potential to 'name'), which her culture imposes in blindness" (MBPM, 80). This provocative reappropriation and redefinition of monstrosity as an alternative means of black women's struggle for freedom implies a double strategy. First of all, the monstrous power to name, which racist ideology has associated with the power of the black mother, jams the reproduction of social illegitimacy and rewrites the function of the maternal body: rather than reproducing social nonvalue, it contests the white/paternal monopoly on value and the expulsion of wounded flesh from political life. Second, such monstrosity inscribes the hieroglyphics of flesh within the new symbolic language and, in so doing, contests the violent separation between empty symbolic forms and damaged bodies.

As Spillers argues, this double strategy of usurpation of symbolic power and inscription of the wounded flesh within language is intertwined with the radicalization of the negative, which "'overreaches' the given discursive conditions" rather than producing identifications with racial and gender norms.[21] In the context of Adorno's work, the monstrous radicalization of the negative implies a certain spiritualization of black bodies since the movement of spirit, understood in the dialectical

tradition not only as conceptual work but also as the struggle for freedom, depends on the contestation of oppression. By repositioning black
female bodies as the bearers of embodied freedom rather than social
illegitimacy, such monstrous spiritualization of the "female with the
potential to name" (MBPM, 80) does not repress materiality and nonidentity but, on the contrary, reclaims what sovereign power and the
commodified gender and racist systems of exchange disavow: sexual and
racial differences, traumatized stolen flesh, and the damaged remnants
of materiality. By negating these disavowals, monstrosity transforms
the failure of specularization, associated by racism with social death and
the proximity to the maternal body, into a vital source of resistance to the
"total mortification" of bodies by the economic values of racist homoso-
ciality. Consequently, Spillers's reappropriation of monstrosity also implies a different model of social relations. Through the negation of the
autonomy of production and the abstraction of social values, such collectivity preserves the "hieroglyphics" of wounded flesh as a source of resistance and thus as a necessary moment of the materialization of the
"spirit" of freedom.

If, following Spillers and Patterson, we can theorize possibilities of
resistance within the biopolitics of power, Fred Moten, like Luce Irigaray,
locates such possibilities by disarticulating the paradigm of commodification. For Moten, the impossible figure of such resistance is Marx's "counterfactual" (inscribed only as "as if"), improper metaphor of the speaking
commodity. By juxtaposing Marx with Frederick Douglass, Moten hears
in the impossible speech of the commodity the scream of the violated
body of Douglass's Aunt Hester. Because Marx fails to see the relationship between the intercourse of commodities and the traffic in slaves, he
"underestimate[s] the commodity's powers, for instance, the power to
speak and to break speech" (ITB, 17). This improper figure of speaking
and breaking speech performs a passionate protest against subjugation;
it constitutes a material disruption, or a "cut," of the abstract commodity
exchange. According to Moten, the black performance of freedom and
free citizenship both inaugurates and repeats the performative transvaluation of values: It transforms "material degradations" and exclusions
into a creation of new embodied values (ITB, 14). The passionate transvaluation of values is the effect of "the freedom drive that animates black
performances" (ITB, 12). By contesting abstract exchange values, such a
performance preserves both the trace of the maternal body and the trace
of the materiality of the object in its passionate production: "We must be

attuned," Moten argues, "to the transmission of the very materiality that is being described while noting the relay between material phonography and material substitution" (*ITB*, 15). In contrast to essentialism, the element of materiality in the black performance of freedom is but a trace that marks loss as well as the materiality of inscription. Such material transmission of the commodity's scream in the black performance of freedom is both a testament to the past and an anticipation of a more capacious freedom to come: It "takes place on the bridge of lost matter, lost maternity, lost mechanics that joins bondage and freedom" (*ITB*, 18).

The struggle for liberation from gendered and racist oppression implicitly or explicitly points to the often occluded role of bare life in the revolutionary traditions of modernity. Exceeding the logic of recognition, such a materialist reformulation of revolutionary struggles also goes beyond the materialist politics of redistribution (to use Nancy Fraser's well-known formulation) because, in addition to contesting capitalist relations of production, it addresses damaged materialities stripped of their value. This inscription of damaged materialities in political praxis not only contests the violent severance of abstract political forms from their bodily remainder but also calls for a new interrelation between form and materiality outside the paradigms of commodification, citizenship, and sovereign violence. By stressing the inseparable interaction between form and materiality, such mediation does not reify racial and gender differences— on the contrary, it marks openness to what is yet to come: a possibility of political transformation, a creation of new, embodied forms of life, and an arrival of a more expansive conception of freedom and speech.

Materiality and Form in Aeasthetic Innovation

In the first half of this chapter I have argued that the contested role of bare life in political praxis calls for a new interaction between political forms and materiality. Now I want to explore the possibilities of such a transformative interconnection between aesthetic form, artistic materials, and bodies in the context of a feminist aesthetics. At first glance, aesthetics seems to be a more promising domain for these explorations than politics because sensible experience and the body are its central concerns. According to Adorno, for example, the inseparability of materiality and form can be more readily achieved in artistic production than in the degraded political practices available in late capitalism. Indeed, in contrast to the abstraction of political forms, the Western philosophical tradition of aesthetics emphasizes the embodied aspect of aesthetic experience and the sensibility of form as the basis of its self-definition. From the definition of aesthetics as sensible experience in Aristotle,[22] the definition of art in Hegel as the work of the sensible spirit speaking through and to the senses,[23] to the *partage* of the sensible in Rancière,[24] the materiality of form and sensibility are fundamental parameters of Western philosophical aesthetics. The transformative role of sensibility and the body is also at stake in different articulations of feminist aesthetics. Despite ambivalence and the numerous critiques of the appropriation of female bodies in Western art, sensibility and the body have played an essential role in diverse feminist approaches to aesthetics, from Woolf's materialist, erotic conception of poetry in *A Room of One's Own*; Irigaray's poesis of sexual difference; Kristeva's conception of the sensible "revolutionary" poetic language and a feminine alphabet of sensibility;[25] the language of black female desire theorized by Tate and Henderson;[26] to the Deleuzian aesthetics of sensible intensities elaborated by Grosz.[27]

Yet, feminist engagements with the sensible and the material aspects of aesthetics are also fraught with ambivalence and impasses. As Irigaray has already noted, the association of the feminine and sensibility in Western aesthetics and philosophy has been the invisible place of the exploitation of the feminine (*TS*, 76). In fact, the crisis of melancholia, explored in chapter 2, is one of the manifestations of such exploitation. In philosophical aesthetics the subordinate role of the feminine and racialized hierarchies in the structure of aesthetic categories marks the exclusion of marginalized subjectivities from the artistic tradition. This is especially the case with black femininity, which, despite the modernist fascination with primitivism and black sexuality, has been excluded even from models of feminine beauty. Thus, despite the promise of a central role of sensibility in philosophical aesthetics, the feminist project is confronted with gender and racial exclusions inscribed in the conceptual apparatus of aesthetics, including the opposition of matter and form.[28] Not surprisingly, historically, the first task of feminist criticism, to put it in Irigaray's words, has been to make this invisible place of the exploitation of the feminine visible. However, once we move beyond the critique of aesthetic terminology to a feminist reformulation of relations between sensibility, matter, and form, we encounter a different aporia, namely, suspicions of essentialism.[29] Consider, for instance, Rita Felski's argument that any connections between innovative form and embodiment/sexuality either tacitly rely on the gendered content of literature or on the essentialist evocation of feminine bodies.[30] Despite different orientations, feminist analyses of materiality and form still seem to be suspended between either a critique of the exclusions of the feminine from the history of aesthetics, on the one hand, or suspect references to sexuality and women's bodies without "proper" political mediation, on the other.

One way to move beyond the impasses that mark these encounters between feminism and aesthetics is to recover and transvaluate the suppressed "feminine," "racialized" possibilities of mutual interaction between matter and form that lie within the tradition of aesthetics in order to open up new possibilities beyond its boundaries. At stake in my approach is not only the negative critique of aesthetic categories but, more fundamentally, an interrogation of the seemingly apolitical aesthetic matter/form binary in the context of the political violence inflicted on women's bodies and materiality. In other words, through interrogating the relationship between aesthetic form, political violence, and female embodiment, I argue that the form/materiality interrelationship is a crucial feminist concern in political and literary practices. In the concluding chapter of this study I will examine in greater detail the relation between the materiality of literary form and political violence by focusing on the work of Nella Larsen and the debates about art and politics in the Harlem Renaissance. The task of this chapter, however, is to elaborate a new feminist theoretical approach to the transformative *interaction* between aesthetic form, bodies, and materiality in the structure of the work of art. I begin this transvaluation of aesthetic values with the dialectical tradition of aesthetics, in particular, with the work of Adorno and Hegel. In what sense can a feminist engagement with Adorno's and Hegel's philosophies help us to articulate such a transformative aesthetic model of mediation between form, bodies, and materiality in women's modern literature? What I find productive in this "body" of work is the emphasis on the historical and social role of aesthetic practice without disregarding the specificity of the artistic process itself. It thus answers, most emphatically, feminist worries about essentialism without subordinating aesthetics either to apolitical experience or to instrumental political ends.

The importance of Adorno for my project lies in the fact that, although he works within the dialectical tradition, he finds the Marxist replacement of the form/matter opposition by the aesthetic form/social content dialectic insufficient. As we have seen, according to Fredric Jameson, the Hegelian/Marxist notion of form is "sharply distinguished from that older idea of form which dominates philosophical thinking from Aristotle to Kant and for which the conjugate term is . . . *matter,* inert materials, filling, the passive."[31] To be sure, Adorno eloquently demonstrates the interaction and the contradiction between form and content, construction and expression, in the work of art: Aesthetic form is always already a sedimentation of an older political content, whereas new content seeks its articulation in experimental form. Yet the form/political content dialectic is only one side of Adorno's aesthetic theory; another important task is to work out a dynamic exchange between form and matter so that we depart from the static opposition of passive receptive matter and active but abstract form. As we have seen, this opposition is a source of political exploitation. Indeed, as Irigaray's and Butler's readings of Plato and Aristotle suggest, the notion of passive, formless matter is one of the scenes of the exploitation of the feminine, providing ideological support for the fantasy of heterosexual intercourse and political violence in the Western philosophical imaginary.[32] Consequently, Adorno's question of how the process of artistic making can contest the sociopolitical domination of materiality, bodies, and nature is a critical issue for feminist aesthetics, even if Adorno disregards the gendering and racialization of aesthetic categories. To diagnose the contradictory manner in which gender and race are inscribed within the matter/form dialectic, I return to Hegel's aesthetic theory, where such gendering and racialization are still visible. Thus this return to Hegel is a feminist transvaluation of values, a mobilization of the devalued possibilities of aesthetics associated with femininity and blackness against hegemonic trends of the Western dialectical tradition.

If there is one shortcoming of the dialectical tradition, it lies in the fact that even its emphasis on the practical, material, and historical aspects of artistic practice remains open to the charge of privileging truth over sensibility. It is precisely at this point that feminist theory provides intervention. Indeed, my critical engagements with Adorno and Hegel are framed by feminist concerns, especially by Hortense Spillers's critical deployment of the "monstrous" black female body with the power to name (MBPM, 80) and Luce Irigaray's notion of the "sensible transcendental" (a neologism invented to contest the opposition between immanence, associated with sensibility/matter, and transcendence, ascribed to productive form).[33] Although I approach bodies as always already regulated by discursive mechanisms, political decision, and economic exchange, the aesthetic paradigm of mediation that I propose preserves the remnants of nonsublatable materiality as a source of resistance and nonconceptual expressivity. Elaborated on the basis of aesthetic praxis, the interrelation between materialities and form not only testifies to the damage and domination inflicted on bodies, feminized matter, and nature but also contests the abstraction of the political/economic forms that are one of the sources of this damage.

Let us begin with the most important point in Adorno's aesthetic theory for my project, namely, his emphasis on the revolt of modern experimental literature against the sociopolitical domination of materiality, body, and nature. Modern literature and art can expose what is erased by abstract commodity exchange and testify to the damaged remnants of materiality, which, as I have argued, include feminized and racialized bare life. For example, Larsen's novel *Passing* opens with a detailed description of the outer appearance of the seductive and dangerous letter of black experimental writing, which stresses its materiality, foreignness, and illegibility—"its almost illegible scrawl" (*P*, 143). Nonetheless, modern literature's protest against the social destruction of materiality is ambiguous: on the one hand, literary experimentation exposes and negates the social domination of matter, sensibility, and bodies. As we have seen, such domination culminates in the abstract equivalence of commodity form and the sovereign violence expelling bare life from the political realm. On the other hand, however, this contestation risks collapsing art into "crude" physicality or, to recall frequent feminist arguments, into essentialism and primitivism, both of which are in complicity with reification. If women's literature is to avoid this crude physicality, it has, first of all, to foreground in its own process of making the fact that the materials entering art—paint, color, sound, or literary language—are always already socially formed and exploited. As we shall see in chapter 6, for Larsen the most emblematic example of such material devastation of language is the biblical curse of slavery and the transmission of its racist and sexual violence in destroyed female writing and the suffocating tongue—the bodily instrument of voice. Second, modern literature and art not only expose the history of violence and the exploitation condensed in its materials, but gather those materials that have been eliminated from the social constitution of meaning and reduced to nonsignifying refuse: "Art is related to its other as is a magnet to a field of iron fillings.... Work's gravitational force ... gathers around itself its *membra disjecta*, traces of the existing" (*AT*, 7). In Larsen's novels the petrified female tongue, the destroyed writing, the destitution of the world, are exposed as the effects of the violence of white supremacy and heteronorma-tivity. At the limit of signification, the speaking tongue turns into a paralyzing, nauseating "thing" that, in its suffocating materiality, bears the traces of tortured and sexually violated bodies. Similarly, in *A Room of One's Own* the violent tearing and "pulling asunder" (*RO*, 50–51) of both the artwork and the female poet manifests a history of violence against women's bodies, matter, and nature (*RO*, 48). For Adorno, as for Larsen and Woolf, the materials entering the artistic composition bear scars and "traces of damage" (*AT*, 107) of political, economic, and aesthetic violence.

We should pause and think about the status of the damaged material-ity bearing scars inflicted by political domination and capitalist produc-tion—the status of materiality as *membra disjecta* (*AT*, 7) of the historical world. This is certainly one of the most important points in Adorno's aesthetics for feminist theory. What Adorno allows us to diagnose is not only the historicity of the material world and female bodies but, more importantly, their destitution and injury as effects of sociopolitical praxis. Furthermore, this concept of damage is not limited to bodies and organic life, because, as we have seen in Larsen's novels, political and economic violence also "ruins" language and the world itself. Prefiguring the de-struction of the body of the writer, Clare, the fragments of the destroyed black female modernism are scattered on a barren landscape (*P*, 178). Thus, despite different genealogies of power in Adorno, Woolf, and Larsen, I argue that the terms of material damage, scars, and ruin resonate with Agamben's notion of bare life and Spiller's violated flesh but expand the notion of injury and destitution beyond the human, beyond the very dis-tinction between political/biological life, to the scorched landscape of the world.

The first task of the literary work is to recover the material remnants obliterated by the history of political violence and capitalist production: art "seeks to salvage what the active spirit . . . reduced to its materials" (*AT*, 107). Yet this act of recovery is contradictory because it can occur only through the artistic process of making, which is also implicated in unjust social relations, white supremacy, heteronormativity, and sexual violence. For Adorno, this is the central dilemma of modernism: "How can making bring into appearance what is not the result of making," the other as such? (*AT*, 107). Nonetheless, by negating the unmediated mate-riality as illusory and by maintaining the protest against historical domi-nation, artistic praxis can initiate a different process of "forming" in which damaged materials themselves play an active role. Consequently, artistic process not only makes explicit the contested role of bare life and wounded flesh in political struggles, analyzed in the first half of this chapter, but, more importantly, shows the coimplication of matter and form in the creation of meaning. By preserving rather than obliterating the otherness of materiality, aesthetic form foregrounds the conflicting but inseparable interrelation between the intelligible and the material, the conceptual and the sensible in the creation of meaning. Adorno calls such an inseparable interrelation a "synthesis from below," which means that a sensible form of the work of art emerges from a relation between divergent elements: "The art work is to be organized from below. There is nothing, however, that guarantees in advance that the art work, once its immanent movement has blasted away the overarching form, will in any way cohere, that its *membra disjecta* will somehow unify" (*AT*, 108). The synthesis from below is what is at stake in the familiar modernist rejection of established literary forms. As Virginia Woolf famously declares, in the work of art "nothing—no 'method,' no experiment, even of the wildest—is forbidden, but only falsity and pretense" (MN, 36). What is however less frequently noted is that experimental search for meaningful relations among heterogeneous "membra disjecta" is an act of noncoercion opposed to political violence.

Such an interaction between matter and form is predicated on the assumption of a certain expressivity of the material elements that artwork brings to the fore. As Adorno puts it, the composition from below seeks to uncover "eloquent relations" among material elements: "The synthesis achieved by means of the artwork is not simply forced on its elements" (*AT*, 7), as is the case in commodity form or sovereign power. On the contrary, literary form is inseparable from materiality because it "recapitulates that in which *these elements communicate with one another*; thus the synthesis is itself a product of otherness. Indeed, the synthesis has its foundation in . . . material dimension of works. . . . This unites the aesthetic element of form with noncoercion" (*AT*, 7). The noncoercion in the work of art is intertwined with a strange mode of communication removed from the exclusive domain of the subject and extended to material elements of language and the world. Although deformed by traces of violence and mediated by the subject, material elements are endowed in artistic praxis with a certain degree of expressivity of their own, expressivity irreducible to subjective intention, conceptual language, or sociopolitical determination. Consequently, the aesthetic noncoercion stands in stark contrast to the violence of biopolitics and commodity production.

Because material communication exceeds subjective intentions and remains opaque to comprehension, the artwork can preserve nonidentity and otherness on the level of form and resist the compulsion to identity imposed by truth, capital, globalization, and heteronormativity: "Aesthetic identity seeks to aid the non-identical which . . . is repressed by reality's compulsion to identity" (*AT*, 4). Such aesthetic eloquence, which exceeds subjective expression and emerges from a relation among diverse material elements, is inseparable from antagonism, discord, and heterogeneity: "in artworks, the criterion of success is twofold: whether they succeed in integrating thematic strata and details into their immanent law of form and in this integration at the same time maintain what resists it and the fissures that occur in the process of integration" (*AT*, 7). By preserving scars, fissures, and nonidentity on the level of aesthetic form, which nonetheless aims for aesthetic coherence, the work of art expresses the tension between heterogeneous material fragments in its formal composition. Such multiple tensions express in an immanent way, on the level of literary form, political struggles in which bare life, damaged materiality, and commodification are at stake. As Adorno famously puts it, "the unsolved antagonisms of reality return in artworks as immanent problems of form" (*AT*, 6). In Larsen's novels such political struggle manifests itself in the episodic structure and the abrupt tragic endings of her texts, which expose the irreconcilable historical contradictions between aesthetic harmony, on the one hand, and mutilated black female flesh, on the other hand. For Larsen, such contradictions not only bear witness to black suffering but also reclaim the foreclosed possibilities of inauguration: the "revolutionary" possibilities of renaming, desire, and community.

By gathering rejected social refuse and preserving the expressivity, otherness, and nonidentity of materiality in the process of composition, modern literature speaks in a way that is denied subjects potentially reducible to bare life or commodified objects. It is perhaps only in the material eloquence of art that we can hear what Fred Moten has called the "counterfactual speech" (*ITB*, 13) of commodities and what Irigaray describes as "commodities talking among themselves" (*TS*, 192–197). By critiquing Marx's inability to anticipate the speech of commodities, Moten detects in the aesthetics of black performance the trace of commodities' speech, which exists as if "before" exchange value (*ITB*, 10) and anticipates a new kind of sociality without domination. Moten stresses the sensual, embodied aspect of black artistic improvisations, which both

testify to the violation of flesh and preserve "objections" of the commodified object: "The revolutionary force of the sensuality that emerges from
the sonic event" of commodities' speech is "itself broken by the irreducible materiality . . . of the commodity's scream" (*ITB*, 12). Animated by
black artistic performance, such a counterfactual sensual speech of commodities, interrupted by the scream of violated flesh, has nonetheless the
capacity to break and remake the abstract process of exchange, the values
of property, spirit, and form. As the last chapter of Larsen's *Passing* suggests, the damaged materialities stripped of value—brutalized bodies,
torn letters, and destroyed things—are retrieved from the circuit of commodities and the cycle of violence and returned into the common "pool of
talk" (*P*, 237). In the shortest imaginable parenthesis between recurring
racist and gender violence, damaged materialities are transformed into
collective objects of enjoyment and improvisation, freely drawn from the
collective reservoir of language, which belongs to everybody and yet cannot be owned.

Such material expressivity and "eloquence" of modern literature contests the dialectical relation between matter and spirit as well as the implicit gendering and racialization of these concepts. In philosophical
aesthetics, the activity of the spirit, in contrast to feminized and racialized sensibilities and passive matter, has been associated with the self-
determination of the subject and the constitution of meaning. Although
feminist aesthetics cannot entirely dispense with the notion of the sprit
because it has also been historically intertwined with the critical potential of art to contest domination, the self-determining spirit of both idealism and materialism is illusory and violent. When separated from the
sensuous, the spirit of freedom reverses into the domination of materiality and otherness, which includes but is not limited to "othered" subjectivities. As Adorno, Moten, and Irigaray point out in different ways, if we
call art's expressivity an "aesthetic spirit," then such spirit is a "carnal
spirit" (*AT*, 88), inseparable from materiality and "the concretion of the
aesthetic structure" (*AT*, 92). It is only by making spirit sensible that art
can preserve its truth as the labor of the negative and the struggle for
freedom on which both the critical potential of modern literature and
political contestation depend.

By contesting the violent schism between abstract forms and damaged materialities, between activity and passivity, the work of art performs *both* the incarnation of the spirit *and*, to use Adorno's apt formula-

tion, the "radical spiritualization" (AT, 92–93) of damaged materialities otherwise stripped of their meaning, form, and expressive capacities. Like Irigaray's notion of the "sensible transcendental," contesting the opposition between the immanence of feminized matter and the transcendence of productive spirit,[34] Adorno's "radical spiritualization" implies a nonabstract mediation in which damaged materials play an active role in the constitution of meaning. Thus, in contrast to the subjugating abstraction of commodity form and political forms violently separated from bare life/wounded flesh, aesthetic mediation establishes a dynamic, conflicting, and mutually constitutive relation between matter and form, the sensuous and the spiritual. Although the spiritual and sensible are not reconciled or unified, they are inseparable because through their multiple tensions they constitute each other as well as the form of the work of art: "Spirit forms [sensible] appearance just as appearance forms spirit" (AT, 87). For Adorno, "nothing counts in artworks that does not originate in the configuration of their sensual elements;" yet "the sensual in artwork is artistic only if in itself mediated by the spirit" (AT, 87). On the one hand, this dynamic and conflicting exchange between matter and form, sensibility and spirit, preserves the traces of expressive capacities in the remnants of materiality reduced to social waste. On the other hand, such dynamic interaction particularizes and materializes the abstraction of social relations, breaks down their violent autonomy, and reveals their dependence on and struggle with disavowed others: flesh, sexuality, and remnants of matter. In so doing, modern literature and art embrace the affective, the impure, and the hybrid. Inseparable from the aesthetic configuration of material elements, the incarnate and impure spirit nonetheless points toward the possibility of becoming and embodied freedom.

Although developed in the context of Adorno's aesthetic theory as well as feminism, the reciprocal exchange between form and matter is not limited to art alone but reveals a blueprint for progressive politics and thought. It contests the static opposition of passive receptive matter and active but abstract form, which, as feminist critics have shown, is one of the original philosophical tropes of the exploitation of the feminine in providing ideological support for the fantasy of heterosexual intercourse. In the context of feminist political theory, such a model could not only enable a better diagnosis of the damage inflicted on gendered, racialized bodies by the schism between abstract exchange value and the nonvalue of material waste, between political forms and bare life, but also contest the domination of materiality, bodies, and nature. It is therefore rather ironic that neither Adorno nor his feminist critics follow through the political implications of his aesthetics for a feminist rethinking of embodiment, sexuality, and racial differences.

Given the paucity of explicit references to sexuality or antiblack racism in Adorno's work, I would like to develop further gendered and racialized dimensions of the form/matter interaction by turning to Hegel's aesthetic theory where such gendering and racialization are still visible. This return to Hegel is not a historical regression but a feminist transvaluation of aesthetic values—values associated with the devalued feminine, blackness, and materiality—against the dominant trends of the Western dialectical tradition. In particular, I want to focus on Hegel's racialized and sexualized symbol of the monstrous figure of the Sphinx. In Hegel's aesthetics, let us recall, the Sphinx is the discredited symbol of symbolic Egyptian art, which, in predictable Eurocentric fashion, like the enslaved body analyzed by Spillers, represents the least spiritualized, and therefore least liberated, art form—the very antithesis of Christian art. Yet, as Paul de Man suggests, we can contest this devaluation of the symbolic on the ground of Hegel's own philosophy: "In a dialectical system such as Hegel's, what appears to be inferior and enslaved may well turn out to be the master."[35] For de Man, Hegel's aesthetics as a whole "is a discourse of the slave" and, "as a result, it is also politically legitimate and effective as the undoer of usurped authority" (AI, 118). If the whole of Hegelian aesthetics is a discourse of the slave, then Egypt, a slave of a slave, might claim most legitimately the role of political contestation. It is the possibility of such a dialectical reversal leading to the overthrow of white supremacy that has constituted the grounds for the rereading of the master/slave dialectic by black intellectuals, from Du Bois to Gilroy, and Hortense Spillers's reclaiming of the transformative potential of enslaved black female flesh can be read as a black feminist intervention in this tradition.

Another important aspect of Hegel's aesthetics for my argument is his emphasis on the sensible and collective significance of art. In fact, it is the sensibility of form that gives art its specificity by distinguishing it from philosophy, religion, and, we can add, the commodity form: art "represents even the highest ideas *in sensuous forms*, thereby bringing them near to the character of natural phenomena, to the senses, and to feeling" (*ILA*, 9). Furthermore, the Hegelian aesthetic underscores the struggle between form and content—a conflict that preserves the alterity of the material, despite the fact that the labor of spiritualization already attempts to "strip the outer world of its stubborn foreignness" (*ILA*, 36) and to transform objects into a mere reflection of the hegemonic subject. Thus, even though Hegel defines the perfection of classical art as a harmony of form and content (*ILA*, 44), in fact all art is characterized by different modalities of the contradiction between the spiritual and the sensible, the interior and the exterior.

This contradiction is nonetheless most striking in symbolic art, associated with Egypt and the figure of the Sphinx's riddle. Thus, even in terms of Hegel's own aesthetic theory, some critics, like de Man (*AI*, 93), have claimed that the most characteristic features of Hegel's concept of art are embodied by Egypt rather than the classical art of Greece or the art of Christian Europe. Symbolic art represents a diametrical opposite to Christian art in the sense that it does not yet reach "that perfect unity of inner meaning and external shape" that modern art already "*transcends in its superior spirituality*" (*A*, 143). In other words, if in European art the spirit transcends its material form, then in symbolic art the material resists the domination of sprit. It is precisely because of such resistance to spiritual transcendence that the Hegelian notion of symbolic art prefigures some of the most characteristic features I would like to reclaim for a feminist aesthetics of modernism, such as the sensibility of form, the primacy of the object, antagonism, and, most importantly, the enigma of art, associated with the otherness of sexual and racial differences. For instance, the most important feature of symbolic art—the foreignness and divergence of its external shape from its internal idea—anticipates in an uncanny way Adorno's definition of the form/materials interaction as "the nonviolent synthesis of the diffuse that nevertheless preserves it as what it is in its divergences and contradictions" (*AT*, 143). In both symbolic and modernist art, the interaction between matter and form "interrupts itself through its other just as the essence of its coherence is that it does not cohere. In its relation to its other—whose foreignness it mollifies and yet maintains—form is what is anti-barbaric in art" (*AT*, 143).

For Hegel, symbolic art represents the first step toward liberation from immediate sensuous existence through the double negation of labor and death. Rather than representing sensuous immediacy or unifying the spiritual and the material aspects of aesthetic production, Egyptian art represents unconscious artisanal labor similar to "the building of a honeycomb by bees."[36] For Hegel, this artisanal labor corresponds to the immediate negation of natural existence by death, which becomes the first determination of spirit's content. By contesting this association of artisanal labor with death, Adorno reinterprets it as a testimony to the concreteness of social labor and its dependence on the material, which is not yet negated by the abstraction of the commodity form. In his discussion of Egypt, "Hegel," Adorno argues, "includes human labor in its concrete material form among the essential characteristics of spirit as the absolute. Only a little more would be needed—remembrance of the simultaneously mediated and irrevocably natural moment in labor" (H, 25).

Yet perhaps something else needs to be remembered in the context of Hegelian aesthetics in addition to the testimony of symbolic art to the concreteness of labor and its irreducible dependence on materiality. What also has to be recalled is Spillers's claim that the persistence of materiality is a condition of resistance. In the context of her work, the failure of spiritualization in Egyptian art, like the failure of spiritualization ascribed to black female bodies, can be reinterpreted as an act of resistance to the Western spirit's hegemony and domination. We can see traces of such resistance in Hegel's emphasis on the unreconciled conflict between the material and the collective spirit, which in turn corresponds to the contradiction between form and content, the sensible and the intelligible. Thus, in contrast to the complete mortification of sensuous materiality by the abstract commodity form or sovereign power, the symbolic artwork becomes a veritable battleground between materiality and intelligibility, exteriority and interiority: "In so far as symbolic art just struggles towards true meanings and their corresponding mode of configuration, it is in general a battle between the content which still resists true art and the form which is not homogeneous with that content either. . . . In this respect the whole of symbolic art may be understood as a continuing struggle for compatibility of meaning and shape" (A, 317). Because it preserves the traces of foreign matter, Egyptian art is an aporetic and antagonistic art that refuses to disguise domination as a reconciliation between social spirit and its subjugated others: "This wrestling [of Spirit] with itself before perception by means of art . . . is characteristic of Egypt" (A, 354). For Hegel, the antagonistic, symbolic art, in which materiality resists the domination of spirit, is a sign of failure; yet it is precisely this failure that feminist aesthetics can transvaluate as a paradoxical achievement of modern art and literature. The antagonistic and aporetic character of the form/matter relation points to political conflicts and struggles in which ruined materiality, damaged bodies, and objects are at stake. It is these conflicts that, to recall Adorno's formulation, "return in artworks

as immanent problems of form" (*AT*, 6). The return of political antagonisms in the structure of modern art and literature not only renders abstract spirit more sensible, but associates formal experimentation with
struggle and resistance.

The preservation of antagonism in the artistic process not only refuses
the false reconciliation offered by commodity culture but voices the "protest against the mastery over material itself" (*AT*, 212). Ultimately, what
Hegel views as defect—and I regard as a unique accomplishment of the
work of art—is art's relation to traces of materiality and alterity, to what
remains nonidentical: remnants of nonsymbolizable matter, flesh, sex,
and the scars of bodily injury. For Hegel, Egyptian art presents an affin-
ity between both "meaning and shape" and their "mutual externality,
foreignness, and incompatibility" (*A*, 300). Unwittingly, in his notion of
symbolic art, Hegel gives us a theory of the work of art that testifies to the
resistance of matter/flesh to the violence of spiritualization and abstract
formalism. Unlike the specular character of the commodity form, or the
sovereignty of biopolitics, here the foreignness of matter exceeds and resists political and aesthetic forms. This last point is important because
any unmediated relation to the body or alterity would collapse into another version of the reification, essentialism, or ideology of primitivism.
Consequently, the remainder of materiality cannot be confused with immediacy. Rather than representing the unmediated truth essentialism
ascribes to bodies, such a remainder contests the absolute autonomy of
social production and political sovereignty and their erasure of all traces
of otherness and nonidentity.

This active and resisting role of materiality in the production of the
work of art is most striking in Hegel's concept of enigma, which resonates with Irigaray's notion of wonder, Spiller's monstrosity, and Adorno's enigmaticalness.[37] Consequently, the excess of materiality cannot be
confused with essentialism because it constitutes the cipher of art rather
than a disclosure of the immanent truth of the body. Such rupture is
what is at stake in Irigaray's definition of the wonder of sexuality as that
which cannot be anticipated or known.[38] According to Irigaray, wonder is
often regarded as monstrosity because the conceptual categorization cannot tolerate the surprise of enigmatic sexuality and its resistance to
power/knowledge.[39] This is precisely why Hegel interprets the enigma of
Egyptian art as monstrous. Resisting the autonomy of production, the
monstrous symbolic form veils its significance not because the process of
mediation "vanishes without a trace," as is the case with commodity

form, but because the remainder of alterity obstructs the progress of spiritualization and turns the work of art into "the objective riddle par excellence" (*A*, 360).

In contrast to Hegel, however, feminist aesthetics reclaims enigma as a crucial feature of modernist art and literature. The enigmatic figures of women's modernism represent neither an immanent truth of the body nor a deficiency of aesthetic mediation. On the contrary, enigma is a paradoxical achievement of women's modernism, which preserves the foreignness of materiality within literary form. In Larsen's *Passing*, for example, the enigma of writing and the female body, of sexuality and race is both a constitutive feature of aesthetic beauty and a source of fear in the world of white supremacy. Consider, for instance, this dangerous intertwining of enigma, beauty, and nonnormative female sexuality in the figure of Clare, who is also a writer of the illegible script of black modernism:

> Dark, sometimes absolutely black, always luminous. . . . They were Negro eyes! Mysterious and concealing. . . . Yes, Clare Kendry's loveliness was absolute, beyond challenge, thanks to those eyes which her grandmother and later her mother and father had given her.
>
> (*P*, 161)

> Puzzling again over that look on Clare's incredibly beautiful face. . . . It was unfathomable, utterly beyond any experience or comprehension of hers.
>
> (*P*, 176)

What the juxtaposition of these passages shows is the constellation of "absolute" female beauty, "absolute" blackness, and the enigmas of desire and art exceeding comprehension. Can we read this repetition of the adjective *absolute* as the ironic reinscription of the Hegelian absolute onto black female aesthetics? If so, the enigma associated with the feminine, blackness, and illegible script exceeds the limitations of Hegelian aesthetics. Oscillating between attraction and fear, such enigma poses a challenge for the hegemonic values of aesthetics in complicity with white supremacy and heteronormativity.

In Hegel's aesthetics the breakdown of abstract equivalence that reveals the racialized and gendered struggle with the body, sexuality, and the enigma of art is of course most evident in the symbol of symbolic art, that is, in the monstrous figure of the Sphinx. Mediating two extremes of symbolic art—the preserved human corpse in the externality of the pyramid and the live animal body revealing a "higher," though still "repugnant," intimation of the living spirit (A, 357)—the Sphinx is the heterogeneous figure par excellence. Yet what Hegel regards as the monstrosity of art, which ruins the principle of identity and negates the reconciliation of binary oppositions, feminist aesthetics reclaims as another crucial feature of women's modernism. Like the insurgent, monstrous female figure of resistance that Spillers imagined, the Sphinx's refusal to reflect the immortality of the white soul, the sovereignty of the spirit, or the abstract values of commodified labor presents aesthetic process as the site of struggle, as the turbulent, reversible passage between the human and the animal, spirit and body, form and matter, the subject and the other, labor and its objects, the West and Africa. In contrast to the self-determination of the Hegelian spirit, the autonomy of production, political sovereignty, or the utter indifference of the abstract commodity form, the impure figure of the Sphinx bears witness to spirit's parasitical dependence on and entwinement with its disavowed others: "Out of the dull strength and power of the animal the human spirit tries to push itself forward, without coming to a perfect portrayal of its own freedom and animated shape, because it must still remain confused and associated with what is other than itself" (A, 361). What Hegel calls here intermingling and confusion of spirit with its other—flesh, animality, matter, femininity—constitutes the necessary moment of the materialization, sexualization, and racialization of artistic form.

But ultimately what is most interesting about the aporetic figure of the Sphinx in Hegel's text is the fact that this alternative model of aesthetic "intermingling" of matter and form bears an implicit testimony to the not-yet-forgotten, not-yet-erased enigma of sexual and racial differences *at the very moment* of its erasure. Although Hegel fails to analyze this enigma, his text produces it as the very riddle of aesthetics. In his work, the body that struggles but fails to extricate itself completely from materiality and nature, the body that marks the irreducible obscurity and estrangement of spirit from itself, is presented as a feminine, non-European body. And even though the feminization of the Sphinx is more readily apparent, its racialization is produced through the denial of any connection between Egypt and black Africa in order to subordinate symbolic art to what de Man calls an "ideologically loaded genealogy of the modern as derived from the classical, Hellenic past" (AI, 108). Associated with animalistic "wild" and "natural" sensuality, Hegel's construction of "Africa *proper*" (emphasis added) bears no connection to civilization, history, or art: Africa "has remained—for all purposes of connection with the rest of the World— . . . the land of childhood, which lying beyond the day of self-conscious history, is enveloped in the dark mantle of Night."[40] Even African "Fetich" has no religious or aesthetic value.[41] As if in response to Hegel, Du Bois, in his celebrated essay "The Criteria of Negro Art," argues that it is precisely the racist propaganda of Western aesthetics that presents "The Cathedral at Cologne" as an example of beauty but fails to see aesthetic value in an African village (CNA, 319).

Yet, although Hegel claims that Egypt can be regarded as a "center of independent civilization" only insofar as it may be separated from the rest of Africa,[42] the very possibility of such separation is negated by the hybrid, *improper* figure of the Sphinx. By making the erasures of racial and sexual differences legible, the impure body of the Sphinx poses an enigma of sexual difference and black flesh, an enigma inscribed in the aesthetic mediation between spirit and matter, form and meaning. This enigma is repeated in the very form of the Sphinx's riddle, which vacillates between abstract spiritual essence ("what is") and the process of temporalization and materialization of spirit ("what in the morning goes on four legs, at mid-day on two, and in the evening on three?" A, 361). Despite Hegel's emphasis on the immobility of symbolic art, the Sphinx's "conundrum" is split between fixed identity and bodily becoming, between abstract universality and the movement of differentiation, between specularization and materialization. By contrast, Western oedipal masculinity is associated in Hegel's text with a self-conscious, autonomous spirituality that determines its meaning from within. The imperative of self-knowledge obliterates the aesthetic enigma of the flesh and sex and presents this obliteration as the condition of the self-production of the hegemonic subject. In response to the riddle of the Sphinx, the oedipal abstract and universal answer—"a man"—remains blind both to the split form of the question and the impure locus of its enunciation. Anticipating the course of Western philosophy, Oedipus wrongly assumes that the beginning of the question, namely, "What is it?" can sublate flesh, temporality, and disavowed sexual and racial differences into the principle of identity. By substituting universal subjectivity, which is nonetheless associated with whiteness and masculinity, for the antagonistic relation between the temporality of differences and the universality of the concept, the oedipal answer in Hegel's text culminates in a double erasure: in a disregard of sexual and black flesh, on the one hand, and in the denial of finitude, temporality, and alterity, on the other. The oedipal answer in Hegel's text constitutes, therefore, the beginning of the damaging specularization/abstraction of the body that Irigaray detects in the commodity form.

Yet the condensation of sexual differences, black flesh, and the symbol in the body of the Sphinx resists the philosophical solution to the enigma. This solution would not only reduce the significance of the work of art to the imperative of self-knowledge but also present the practice of mediation as the abstract work of the concept, which disavows the traumatic limits of flesh, finitude, and sexuality without at the same time materializing and particularizing the universal. Persisting beyond the oedipal answer, the interconnected enigma of art, sexuality, and black flesh troubles and disorients European modernity, its ideological genealogy, and its equation of the labor of mediation with the spiritualization of matter culminating in the abstract commodity form. For Hegel, this preservation of enigma, antagonism, and nonidentity is what constitutes the monstrosity of symbolic mediation. For feminist aesthetics, however, monstrosity, as the other side of wonder, contests the abstract equivalence of the commodity form and the violence inflicted on bare life. In so doing, it refers to a reciprocal and conflicting exchange between matter and form. As Spillers suggests, the critical reappropriation of the monstrous transforms the failure of specularization, associated with the social death displaced onto black bodies and black Africa, into a vital source of resistance to the monopoly of white values. It is precisely the oedipal answer to the insolvable enigma of aesthetics, race, and sexuality that is contested in Larsen's and Woolf's novels.

In this chapter I have juxtaposed the problem of form in two seemingly unrelated social phenomena: the hunger strike of British suffragettes and the struggle against antiblack racism, on the one hand, and the formal experimentation of modern literature, on the other hand. What this juxtaposition of political insurgencies and aesthetic innovation reveals is that the seemingly neutral form/matter opposition is at stake in both feminist political struggles and aesthetic interventions, and, therefore, that matter and form are both aesthetic and political categories. The consideration of form/matter in politics shows that what is contested in feminist,

antiracist struggles is not only racist and gendered injustice but also, implicitly, the violent severance of abstract forms from bare life, insofar as
such severance is the source of political violence. Consequently, political
forms and damaged materialities—bare life, injured bodies, commodified
objects—are themselves contested terrains, mobilized by political struggles. And such contestation implies inseparable interconnection between
form, matter, and antagonism.

If feminist politics implicates the form/matter distinction in violence,
bodily damage, and the struggle for liberation, the task of feminist aesthetics is to elaborate a new model of interaction between damaged materialities and aesthetic form. Although the sensible qualities of art and
literature have been traditionally acknowledged, the notion of a feminist
aesthetics I have proposed in this chapter not only contests the gendering
and racialization of the matter/form distinction but also stresses a new
understanding of the materiality of aesthetic form. In opposition to formalisms of various stripes, or worries about essentialism, an aesthetic
invention of a reciprocal and often conflicting interaction between literary forms, damaged artistic materials, and violated bodies in experimental literature has to be considered a critical response to the violent abstraction of commodity form and citizenship. Through my explorations
of the feminist and dialectical traditions of aesthetics, I have proposed
different formulations of such interaction, ranging from monstrosity and
enigma to the "sensible transcendental." Although damaged bodies are
always already regulated by political and economic mechanisms of power,
the dynamic, interactive exchange between form and matter I have elaborated preserves remnants of nonsublatable materiality as a source of
nonconceptual expressivity and resistance to the absolute autonomy of
production, sovereign power, and oedipal heteronormative desire.

Contestation of the violent, gendered, racialized schism between passive matter and abstract political/aesthetic forms shows that the "new
formalism" is the other side of the new materialism and vice versa. On
the one hand, the new materialism not only embraces the Marxist notion
of labor and power relations but also the feminist analysis of gendered,
racialized matter and critique of violated bodies. Yet, on the other hand,
the new formalism cannot be limited to innovation alone, as has been recently proposed in modernist studies, because it contests the violent split
between damaged materialities and political/aesthetic forms. The interconnection between formalism and materialism stems from the dynamic
interaction between form and matter in the production of meaning and

reveals a conflicting but inseparable relation between the universal and the particular, the intelligible and the sensible. Such interaction between materialities and forms does not reify racial and gender differences—on the contrary, it marks an openness to what is yet to come: the possibility of political transformation, the creation of new, embodied forms of life, and the arrival of a more expansive conception of freedom and speech.

PART III

Toward a Feminine Aesthetics of Renaissance

6 The Enigma of Nella Larsen

Letters, Curse, and Black Laughter

Recovered in the 1980s, thanks to the labor of the numerous black feminist theorists and literary critics, as a major writer of the Harlem Renaissance, modernism, and the "feminist literary canon,"[1] Nella Larsen has been praised for her exploration of racial, class, sexual, and linguistic dangers and ambiguities.[2] However, despite her prominence in literary, cultural, gender, and race studies, Larsen has not yet entered into the canon of philosophical aesthetics, which predictably tends to reproduce mostly male and mostly white writers as its exemplary figures. And yet the structure of Larsen's novel interrogates the crucial philosophical questions of art's autonomy and its vexed relationship to race and gender politics, a relation termed "art and propaganda" in the mid and late 1920s by the Harlem Renaissance's most important critics and artists. As Thadious Davis argues, Larsen took the art side of this battle and announced that choice publicly in her reviews, interviews, and letters. The choice of art over propaganda does not mean, however, that Larsen relinquished the task of exploring art's vexed relation to politics, female desire, and racial/sexual violence; rather, it means that such exploration exceeds the available means of language and thus cannot propagate explicit political or philosophical ends. By taking us to the limits of linguistic expression and bodily injury, Larsen exposes the mythical legitimation of white supremacy through a misappropriation of the biblical curse of Ham. What Larsen's experimental modernism transforms is the originary, violent division within language itself between malediction and benediction, curse and promise, the founding exclusion and inclusion, bodily damage and abstract racist laws. It is these binaries that establish the borders of the racist polis and its excluded outside. By opposing the curse of racism, Larsen's experimental black modernism transforms the performative violence of discourse in order to reclaim the foreclosed possibilities of inauguration—the conditions of a black female renaissance as such. Such an aesthetic transformation of the entire register of racialized, gendered language not only contests racist law but also enables the emergence of female desire and a utopian black community in the midst of the disaster perpetuated by racist violence. Thus the question Larsen's experimental modernism poses is how the destruction inflicted by racist violence upon bodies, language, and communities can be transformed into conditions of inauguration. What kind of risks does this task of aesthetics involve? What kinds of interconnection between damaged speech and bodies does it have to invent?

Art or Propaganda; or, On the Aesthetic and Sexual Dimensions of Racial Politics

Larsen's recovery in the 1980s echoes the complex debates about aesthetics, race, and politics in the Harlem Renaissance in the late 1920s and the conflicting relation between modernist and realist aesthetics in trans-Atlantic modernism more generally. Emphasizing the aesthetic side of this divide, Claudia Tate in her seminal essay of 1980, "Nella Larsen's *Passing*: A Problem of Interpretation,"[3] argues that Larsen's texts have been ignored because of their narrative complexity and figurative ambiguity. Tate was one of the first critics to praise the enigma of Larsen's novels, which defy not only the conventions of realism and the narrative structures of the "tragic mulatto" but also the possibility of interpretation.[4] According to Tate, another marginalized aspect of black textuality is sexual desire: "the racial protocol for African American canon formation has marginalized desire as a critical category of black textuality by demanding manifest stories about racial politics."[5] Significantly, Tate proposes the term *textual enigma* to designate the "enigmatic surplus" of desire and language over collective black "master narratives" of social protest.[6] Interrogating the relation between aesthetics and gender/racial politics in Larsen's novels, Hazel Carby underscores unresolved contradictions that mock clarity and legibility. Reflective of the contradictions between freedom and racial, gender, and class domination, Larsen's refusal of textual resolution, most evident in destructive, "abrupt," or "unearned" endings so often criticized by her interpreters, is, according to Carby, a hallmark of her texts' political complexity and artistic achievement.[7]

This conflicting relation between political struggle and artistic innovation is at the core of the intense debates on art and racial politics in the mid and late 1920s among the Harlem Renaissance's intellectuals and artists. As Davis argues, "although the Art versus Propaganda battle had been waged in the pages of *Crisis* in 1926, the debate about the portrayal of African Americans in literature was ongoing as the Renaissance progressed."[8] While W. E. B. Du Bois or Claude McKay underscored complex relations between art and propaganda based on aspirations to freedom, others, like James Weldon Johnson or Alain Locke, advocated artistic experimentation.[9] For instance, in his essay on the revolutionary impact of African masks on experimental European painting, "The Legacy of the Ancestral Arts," Locke concludes that "any vital artistic expression of the Negro theme and subject in art must break through the stereotypes to a new style, a distinctive fresh technique, and some sort of characteristic idiom."[10]

Discussions of art, racial politics, and propaganda in the mid and late 1920s among Harlem Renaissance intellectuals show complex affinities with and differences from the debates on modernism and capital between Brecht and Lukács in the 1930s and their subsequent elaboration by Adorno and the Frankfurt school. Nonetheless, these two modernists' articulations of aesthetic theory have rarely been discussed together, despite the new emphasis on trans-Atlantic studies of modernity. The juxtaposition of Harlem Renaissance aesthetic theories with those of their European counterparts not only brings together critiques of racism and class exploitation but also enables different articulations of the political functions of aesthetic autonomy—or what Theodor Adorno calls the contradictory status of modern art as "the social antithesis of society" (*AT*, 8). In a significant departure from Adorno's pessimism about the possibilities of political praxis, W. E. B. Du Bois rejects Booker T. Washington's program of accommodation and articulates instead the political strategy of the black struggle for freedom and racial justice. Consequently, the subversive function of black art and literature is closely intertwined with the collective, organized struggle against the crimes of white supremacy. As Du Bois puts it in his 1926 "Criteria of Negro Art," "how is it that an organization like this, a group of radicals trying to bring new things into the world, a fighting organization which has come up out of the blood and dust of battle . . . can turn aside to talk about Art?" (CNA, 317). One needs to appreciate the political and the theoretical novelty of Du Bois's analysis of the relation between aesthetics and politics. For Du Bois, the question is not whether art can preserve the possibility of praxis unavailable in society; but rather why the militant movement needs art in the first place. Despite the controversial claim that all art is propaganda, Du Bois does not imply an instrumental subordination of art to politics, but turns to art in order to emphasize a creative, noninstrumental dimension of politics itself. For Du Bois, the group of radicals has to consider art in the midst of the political urgency of "the blood and dust of battle" in order to preserve a noninstrumental dimension of politics itself beyond its commodification.

Du Bois articulates two different senses of art as propaganda: the first one unmasks the racist ideology of seemingly apolitical Western art, the second articulates the innovative dimension of political struggle. First, Du Bois unmasks the destructive racist propaganda of supposedly autonomous Western art and key concepts of aesthetic theory such as taste, beauty, or genius. It is such racist propaganda that, for example, excludes "a village of the Veys in West Africa" from the category of beauty, which is embodied in Western monuments such as the cathedral at Cologne (CNA, 319). In *Quicksand* Nella Larsen interrogates the tragic consequences of the ideological perversion of aesthetic categories like taste and beauty. The main character of the novel, Helga Crane, is a person of "rare and intensely personal" aesthetic taste, which helps her to create "a small oasis in a desert of darkness" (Q, 1). This aesthetic taste is consistently undermined and assaulted by the world of white racism. For instance, in the demeaning and patronizing sermon to the black Southern college, the white preacher "praises" the students for their "good taste." Having nothing to do with the appreciation of art, such "good taste" is supposed to show future black intelligentsia their proper "place" as "hewers of wood and drawers of water" (Q, 3). For Du Bois, such overt or implicit ideology means that supposedly disinterested aesthetic judgments of taste are in fact pronounced by "a white jury" (CNA, 325). That is why, prior to "aesthetic taste," Du Bois advocates a judgment of "distaste" for the "ugly" (CNA, 319) world of racism, poverty, and sexism. Second, the racist and sexist ideology of art excludes dominated peoples from the possibility of artistic production. Like Virginia Woolf, Du Bois claims that recognized black artists represent merely "the remnants of that ability and genius among us whom the accidents of education and opportunity have raised on the tidal waves of chance" (CNA, 323). In an implicit argument with Kant, Du Bois points out that genius is therefore not the free expression of the greatest abilities of an individual artist or the people, but a matter of historical accident or political privilege. Consequently, the racist propaganda of Western art restricts and destroys the "endless" possibility of the perception and creation of beauty in the world (CNA, 319). By contesting the racism of Western art, by expanding the notion of beauty, and by calling for "free and unfettered judgment," black art is always already a counterpropaganda. Its political function, which it shares with "radical" black politics, is to contest the racist oppression and exclusion of African Americans from full human rights.

Yet, for Du Bois, art as propaganda is not limited to a contestation of the racist ideology of Western aesthetics; it also has the positive function of revealing and safeguarding the creative function of freedom. Paradoxically, art as "propaganda" reveals an aesthetic dimension of politics. It opens the utopian possibility of a free, beautiful world, for the sake of which the political battle is waged in the first place: "pushed aside as we have been in America, there has come to us not only a certain *distaste* for the tawdry and flamboyant but a vision of what the world could be if it were really a beautiful world; if we had the true spirit; if we had the Seeing Eye, the Cunning Hand, the Feeling Heart; if we . . . lived in a world where men know, where men create, where they realize themselves and where they enjoy life" (CNA, 319, emphasis added). Beyond the contestation of the ugly world, politics needs a utopian category of the beautiful in order to protect political freedom from the instrumental values of the "free market" and consumption. The "infinite" variety and "endless" possibility of beauty (CNA, 319) reveals the transformative role of freedom, which is not only different from modern consumerism but ultimately more capacious than the struggle against the color line. It is precisely this creative function of freedom that compels the political organization, that is, the "group of radicals trying to bring new things into the world . . . to talk about Art" (CNA, 317).

Du Bois's emphasis on the aesthetic dimension of political practice recalls and reworks in a black idiom Marx's use of aesthetics to articulate the difference between transformative praxis and its degradation into commodity production. As we have seen in chapter 2, Marx similarly argues in *Economic and Philosophic Manuscripts of 1844* that practice in a liberated society would not be limited to production, but would encompass the entire process of self-transformation and the realization of freedom in a community. Thus, despite the critique of aesthetic ideology, both writers presuppose a certain autonomy of art from the market in order to set up beauty and sensibility—"the Seeing Eye, the Cunning Hand, the Feeling Heart" (CNA, 319)—rather than profit as the aspiration of political struggle. As we have seen, Adorno also shares this critique of the commodification of the political, and that is one of the reasons why he so strongly opposes the integration of Western autonomous art into "a profit-driven industry" (*AT*, 18). Yet Adorno and Du Bois draw radically different conclusions regarding the autonomy of art: for Adorno, such autonomy separates art from the commodified field of politics *tout court*, for Du Bois, it reveals the most creative aspect of politics, not yet colonized by consumption. Thus if art for Adorno preserves the utopian possibility of a better praxis still impossible in reality, art for Du Bois reveals the most innovative aspect of the political battle for freedom.

While the most original contribution of Du Bois to modern aesthetic theory lies in his analysis of the aesthetic aspect of freedom and political action, his main limitation consists in his choice of romance to exemplify such a creative dimension of politics. As Hazel Carby argues, romance promises an imaginary reconciliation of economic, class, racial, and sexual contradictions, often by evoking the romantic figure of the folk.[11] By citing Scott's "Lady of the Lake" as an example of romance, Du Bois claims that "the romance of the world did not die and lie forgotten in the Middle Age" (CNA, 320). Romance posits an idealized heroic black masculinity at the center of the political striving for the creation of a beautiful world. For instance, Du Bois sums up the military achievements of black soldiers fighting in a heroic battle in German Africa with the comment that "such is the true and stirring stuff of which Romance is born" (CNA, 321). According to Tate, romance allows Du Bois "to idealize the members of the NAACP as dusty, blood-stained crusaders. . . . Fighting in this crusade on the behalf of an ideal, traditionally figured as feminine."[12] By promising an imaginary reconciliation of contradictions in the ugly world, this black romance also counters the racist rhetoric of the primitivism and exoticism associated with black female sexuality and provides a chivalric idealization of black femininity. As Tate argues, such a reappropriation of the chivalric codes of romance performs two functions: first, it posits feminized black beauty as both the sexual object and aesthetic ideal of reconciliation of political conflicts. Second, it counters the chivalric rhetoric of white honor symbolized by idealized white femininity in the supremacist propaganda of the Ku Klux Klan. Thus, paradoxically, the "chivalric idealization of female sexuality was the means for inciting and representing both the Klan's racist propaganda for white supremacy and Du Bois's counterpropaganda for racial equality in *The Crisis*. . . . Du Bois retaliates by using *The Crisis* to (re)appropriate chivalric imagery so as to idealize himself and others fighting for racial equality."[13]

This brief discussion of Du Bois's definition of propaganda as the aesthetic dimension of politics illuminates the stakes of Larsen's choice of experimental modernism. Her rejection of propaganda was deeply influenced by the critique of heterosexual romance and its racial, sexual, and textual politics of beauty. As Carby puts it, Larsen stressed the "unresolvable" and "contradictory nature of the search for a female self by refusing the romance."[14] Larsen first of all refused the heterosexual male model of romance and freedom. Rather than providing an antidote to the capitalist confusion of freedom with consumption, romance is an aesthetic manifestation of the commodification of female bodies. As *Quicksand* shows, the entanglement of romance, commodity, and beauty has tragic rather than liberating consequences for black women. By replacing heterosexual romance with explorations of female bisexuality and lesbian eroticism in *Passing*, Larsen not only eroticizes beauty but questions its role of reconciliation.

By rejecting romance, Larsen's experimental modernism explores what cannot appear in the free, beautiful world disclosed by propaganda. The aesthetic function of propaganda is insufficient because it does not interrogate the violent racialized and sexualized exclusions that establish the boundaries of the polis, the world, and language. Thus what cannot appear in the beautiful world are not only unresolved political contradictions but also founding acts of exclusion and their ritualized, brutal articulation in flesh and language. Often the threatening disturbance of such nonappearance is signified in Larsen's fiction through the tropes of enigma, danger, and ghostly shudder. In the previous chapters I have interrogated the political boundaries established through the violent oppositions between homo sacer and the citizen, bare life and political forms, and social death and viable forms of living. Larsen moves this discussion in a new direction by diagnosing and contesting the political and discursive borders of white supremacy, in particular, the oppositions between the curse and the promise, the suffocating horror of racist violence and the torn letters of experimental black modernism. Larsen's aesthetic acts of trespassing not only contest the tragic entanglements of the color line, gender, sexuality, and commodification but also subvert the boundaries of the world *in which such violent entanglements operate*. By taking us to the edge of the world and the limits of language, Larsen's black modernism explores alternative possibilities of a poetic disclosure of the world apart from the violent mechanisms of exclusion and inclusion, curse and benediction. In so doing, she attempts to reclaim the foreclosed possibilities of the inauguration of the world, literature, and language. Yet, how can the destruction inflicted by racist and sexist violence be transformed into inauguration, that is, into the very possibility of renaissance? What kind of mediation does it perform between bodily injury and viable forms of living?

Torn Letters, Racist Violence, and the Commodification of Female Bodies, or, The Politics of Larsen's Experimental Aesthetics

Larsen has not left us a sustained manifesto of a black feminist aesthetics that would be equivalent to Du Bois's, Locke's, or Woolf's essays. Perhaps this is one of the reasons why the question of aesthetics is still a marginalized topic in Larsen's fast-growing body of criticism. For instance, in her introduction to the Norton critical edition of *Passing*, "Nella Larsen's Erotics of Race," Carla Kaplan writes that Larsen is "hailed for helping create modernist psychological interiority, expanding our uses of irony. . . . Most importantly, Larsen's work is now prized for its portrayal of black, female subjectivity and for its depiction of the social and psychological vertigo caused when identity categories break down."[15] In Kaplan's long list of Larsen's artistic achievements, there is little reference to aesthetics other than irony or revision of the familiar tropes, such as the tragic mulatta or passing narrative conventions. And, while Kaplan herself provides a brilliant analysis of the way Larsen shifts focus from the ethics to the erotics of race,[16] she omits from this discussion the question of the aesthetics and interpretive judgments that Larsen's earlier critics, such as Claudia Tate, have raised. The only essay on aesthetics included in the Norton critical edition, Thadious Davis's "Nella Larsen's Harlem Aesthetic," focuses less on Larsen's own artistic practice and more on the "somewhat inexplicable area of motivation and intention," that is, on Larsen's desire for social recognition, which ultimately produced a destructive "split between her work as a creative process and her work as a source of public recognition."[17]

Nonetheless, the question of aesthetics is crucial to an understanding of Larsen's project, even if this question is resistant to conceptual pronouncements or manifestos. In place of a conceptual articulation of a female black aesthetics, Larsen gives us an immanent vision of literature—that is, embedded in the self-reflexive moments of the texts themselves—and its vexed relation to desire, freedom, commodification, and racist/sexual violence. And one of the most significant tropes through which Larsen articulates her sense of aesthetic form is the figure of the letter, deployed in a double sense: first, as the enigmatic trope of nonsignifiable violence, freedom, and desire and, second, as an intimation of a literary praxis exceeding the existing conditions of reception and interpretation.

It is perhaps not an accident that Larsen's most sustained discussion of black aesthetics begins with her own polemical letter written in defense of black experimental texts, just as her last published novel, *Passing*, begins with the arrival of an equally disturbing letter. Solicited by *Opportunity* editor Charles S. Johnson, and written in response to a negative review of her friend Walter White's 1926 novel *Flight*,[18] Larsen's letter is an articulation of her own aesthetic vision, which sides with African American and transnational experimental modernisms rather than with realism or propaganda. Larsen critiques the realist assumptions of the negative review of *Flight* by critic Frank Horne and argues that it is experimental rather than realist literature, which promises the most daring expression of racial and sexual freedom.[19] Larsen's letter opens with her "violent" objection to the aesthetic "blindness" of the reviewer, who lacks the "ability or the range of reading to understand the book which he attacked with so much assurance":[20] "It is the blindness, not the abuse which annoys me" (LCJ, 159). First, Larsen attacks the reviewer's political limitations, which blind him to the sexual and racial complexity of the struggle for freedom of White's female character, "the rebellious, modern Mimi" (LCJ, 159). Similarly to Du Bois's critique of commercialized whiteness, Larsen argues that the reviewer fails to understand that "it is the white race which is lost, doomed to destruction by its own mechanical gods" (LCJ, 159) because it confuses political freedom with material possessions.

This narrow political vision of freedom comes from the equally limited view of aesthetics based on anachronistic realist standards of legibility and identity of character. Adopting the realist criteria provided by "Mrs. Wharton" rather than the criteria of the experimental fiction of Conrad, Proust, or Mann, the reviewer "grumbles about 'lack of clarity'" and "faulty sentence structure" (LCJ, 160). To show that the reviewer completely misses the linguistic complexity of the modern novel, Larsen reminds her readers that even Galsworthy "opens his latest novel with a sentence of some thirty-odd words" (LCJ, 160), not to mention the syntactic complexity of Conrad or Proust. Larsen's most "violent objection" concerns the reviewer's expectations of an aesthetic resolution to political conflicts. According to Larsen, the ending of *Flight* is "perfect" precisely because it leaves the protagonist suspended on the verge of the promise of new freedom without providing narrative reconciliation of political and psychological contradictions (LCJ, 160). Eluding direct representation, narrative completion, and the existing parameters of interpretation, such an act of inauguration can only offer an inconclusive disclosure of an unknown trajectory, which nonetheless calls for freedom of the imagination: "Authors do not supply imaginations, they expect their readers to have their own" (LCJ, 159).

Larsen's juxtaposition of the rebellious side of the Harlem Renaissance, here represented by Walter White, with the European modernism of Galsworthy, Conrad, Proust, or Mann, and her comparison of the reviewer's aesthetic standards with American realism, represented by Edith Wharton, situates her future work in trans-Atlantic, experimental modernism and modernity. The epigrams from Harlem Renaissance poets, from Langston Hughes in *Quicksand* and from Countee Cullen in *Passing*, complicate this transnational trajectory by underscoring the role of the African Diaspora both in the Harlem Renaissance and in European modernism.[21] In *Quicksand* Larsen foregrounds different modes of these conflicting trans-Atlantic exchanges in modern aesthetics. On the one hand, her main character, Helga, is revolted by the demeaning representation of black femininity by an aspiring European painter according to the stereotypes of exoticism, primitivism, and commodification (Q, 69, 70, 74). On the other hand, she is inspired to return to Harlem after recognizing the familiar motifs of African American spirituals in Antonín Dvořák's *Symphony No. 9*, entitled *From the New World*: "Her definite decision to go was arrived at with almost bewildering suddenness. It was after a concert at which Dvořák's 'New World Symphony' had been wonderfully rendered. Those wailing undertones of 'Swing Low, Sweet Chariot' were too poignantly familiar" (Q, 92).

Larsen's critique of realism and the heterosexual propaganda of romance is also at work in the self-reflective moments of her early stories written under the male pseudonym "Allen Semi"—the anagrammatical reversal of Larsen's married name (Nella Imes). From her early texts to her mature novels, Larsen consistently associates the aesthetics and politics of heterosexual romance with racism and the commodification of women. As Thadious Davis observes, Larsen's masculine pseudonym of Allen Semi implies a partial or misleading meaning.[22] Larsen's anagrammatic play on her husband's last name Imes/Semi ruins property and the paternal signifier as well as interrupts a kinship structure based on the exchange of women. A prefix rather than a complete word in its own right, *semi*, or *quasi*, assumes a feminized function as it cannot signify on its own but only in relation to some other proper name. In contrast to the exchange of commodities, the modifying proximity of *semi* turns everything to which it relates into something partial, imperfect, similar, but not quite so, as, for instance, *semiautobiographical, semifictional, semitransparent*. Larsen's pen name, Semi Allen, performs her first act of gender/sexual trespassing, which ruins and mocks the dominant identity of what it passes for. As the ironic interplay between the title of the story and the pseudonym suggests, a woman passing for a "Semi"-male turns masculinity into "The Wrong Man," just as a black woman passing for semiwhite ruins the signifier of whiteness and its pretension to mastery and universality.

The title "The Wrong Man," and the fictitious name of the author, "Allen Semi," anticipate the dangerous trajectory of the letter, which disturbs gender and generic conventions of romance and political propaganda. Unlike the circulation of women and commodities, letters in the early stories never arrive at their intended destinations—they either reach a "wrong" reader ("The Wrong Man") or, like the dead letters in Melville's short story, "Bartleby, the Scrivener," arrive belatedly when the addressee is already dead ("Freedom"). By undercutting the aesthetic criteria of clarity and by ruining heterosexual plots, the trajectory of letters is also at odds with Du Bois's notion of romance. Instead of the free world the politics of racial liberation is fighting for, Larsen's letters threaten to disclose the secret of romance: romance does not provide an alternative to commodification but is, in fact, the very "soul" of the commodity. The main protagonist of "The Wrong Man," Julia Hammon, a successful artist, fears the revelation of a secret about her past: in her youth Julia was discovered and "rescued" from homelessness and poverty by a famous explorer, Ralph Tyler, who paid for her art education in exchange for sexual favors. Similarly to Helga and Clare in Larsen's novels, Julia circulates among men: her former lover, her wealthy husband, and an unknown third party, the "wrong" man, who receives her letter. Yet she has to conceal this trajectory in order to maintain her value as a successful female artist and respectable married woman. Her artistic success depends on her capacity to hide the shameful history of racial, sexual, and class exploitation, of which she herself has been a victim. By contrast, her former lover is well versed in the art and danger of bringing the buried secrets of the glorious past back into the light of "civilization." Considered dead, he returns from a dangerous journey to the underground and brings with him the revelation of a "buried city" and lost Oriental treasure.[23] Ralph's triumphant return from the dead is juxtaposed with Julia's dread of sinking into social death, a situation reinforced by Larsen's recurrent use of the proverbial saying "someone walking over my grave" (WM, 5).

As a figure of black female aesthetics, the letter of the story is at odds with the gendered conventions of the political romance, in particular, with the masculine disclosure of achievements of civilization and the feminine concealment of its barbarism. The ending of Larsen's story neither discloses the past nor keeps it secret but rather preserves a threatening enigma associated with danger and death. Neither buried nor disclosed, a traumatic past haunts the narrative. At odds with the logic of concealment or disclosure, Larsen's letters leave us in a dangerous suspension between the "menacing shadows" of the past and the uncertainty of the future. They neither reveal the secrets of the dead nor guard their silence, but take us to "the edge of nowhere," to an encounter with the *impossible*—a word that recurs repeatedly in the story (WM, 5–6). As is the case in *Passing*, sexuality, racism, and the impossible enigma of writing are intertwined with dread and danger. On the one hand, such a dangerous enigma points to foreclosed catastrophes, traumas, and violent contradictions, which cannot appear either in the beautiful utopian world or in the glory of the past. On the other hand, the *impossible* is a signifier for the alternative possibilities of the aesthetic disclosure of the world, of the unrestrained blaze of color and musical improvisation—

"wild and impressionistic . . . primitive staccato understrain of jazz" (WM, 4)—which accompanies the scene of writing.

The debate between art and propaganda continues to be waged in Larsen's novels, especially in *Passing*, but the stakes of these debates change: if, in the early stories, the opacity of the letter exposes and opposes the deadly secret of commodified female beauty, in the novel, illegible letters bear witness to the traumatic past of slavery, bodily injury, and linguistic dispossession. As Hortense Spillers, Saidiya Hartman, and Alexander Weheliye argue in different ways, the trauma and devastation of slavery are not only historical phenomena but also the continuous unfolding of the suffering and dispossession that "engenders the black subject in the Americas."[24] According to Weheliye, "as opposed to being confined to a particular historical period, echoes of new world slavery rest in many contemporary spaces."[25] In Larsen's novels, the more muted these echoes are the more powerful and destructive their effects. More explicit in Larsen's first novel, *Quicksand*, references to the violence of antiblack racism function more like a palimpsest—a hidden subtext—that disarticulates the letters and narrative structure of *Passing*. Consider, for example, a bitter condemnation of America for the horrors of antiblack racist violence in *Quicksand* by the main protagonist, Helga:

> Never could she recall the shames and often the absolute horrors of the black man's existence in America without the quickening of her heart's beating and a sensation of disturbing nausea. . . . The sense of dread of it was almost a tangible thing in her throat.
>
> (Q, 82)

> The existence of ignominy which the New World of opportunity and promise forced upon Negroes . . . more black folk to suffer indignities. More dark bodies for mobs to lynch.
>
> (Q, 75)

Helga's outrage is echoed in *Passing* by Irene's husband, Brian, who views racist America as "the hellish place" that he wants to leave (P, 232). It is this horrific reality that Irene, in her structural function as the main character and as the unreliable narrator, tries to suppress. She forbids Brian from talking to her sons about lynching, which she calls, euphemistically "the race problem," because she wants to maintain the illusion of family happiness and safety (P, 232). Nonetheless, the repressed fears of lynching and racial trauma reappear in a displaced and distorted form as Irene's "primitive paralyzing dread" over Brian's imaginary affair: "Her hands were numb, her feet like ice, her heart like a stone weight. Even her tongue was like a heavy dying thing" (P, 233). Echoing Helga's dread of the terror of antiblack violence, Irene's frozen body is a symptom of the unspeakable horror of black bodies brutalized by white mobs.

These passionate expressions and suppressions of the brutality of antiblack racism are crucial for the interpretation of Passing. The narrative of Larsen's second novel centers on the ambivalent relationship between two black female characters: Irene, the unreliable narrator who is a self-proclaimed race woman but who occasionally passes for white "for the sake of convenience" (P, 227), and her orphaned childhood friend, Clare, who, when she loses kinship ties to the black community, passes for white. Their accidental encounter as married adult women passing for white in the Drake Hotel in Chicago leads to an unpredictable and eventually tragic circulation of nonnormative female desire and letters. The narrative abruptly terminates with the death of Clare, the novel's enigmatic subject of eroticism, beauty, and writing, at the very moment when she plans to return to Harlem.

As even this brief summery implies, the aesthetic composition of Passing foregrounds the violent split between the "promise" of the New World and "the absolute horrors" of black existence, between the world of opportunity and the threat of bodily dismemberment, between the affirmation of a new beginning and the destruction of possibilities. Such a split reveals the material devastation of language itself and the transmission of racist and sexual violence in the torn letters of female experimental writing and in the suffocating tongue—the bodily instrument of voice. Consequently, the form of the novel oscillates between ostensible surface legibility and its subterranean nauseating paralysis, between ordinary letters and the alien suffocating object. In particular, the figure of the tongue "like a heavy dying thing" evokes Helga's dread of lynching like "a tangible thing in her throat" (Q, 82). At the most extreme, the proximity of horror obliterates the distinction between the signifier and suffocation, between the symbolic realm, which includes politics, and what psychoanalysis calls the realm of the real (or what is foreclosed from signification). At the limit of signification, the speaking tongue turns into a paralyzing, nauseating "thing" that, in its suffocating materiality, bears the traces of tortured and sexually violated bodies reduced to bare life. The depth of this painful inexpressibility is unavailable to the idealized language of propaganda. Thus what is most at odds with the romance of propaganda is the disjointed, experimental structure of *Passing*, which conveys and contests the political violence inflicted on black bodies and languages in its narrative form, its main figures, and its abrupt tragic ending.

In *Passing* the painful enigma of damaged materiality is announced by the figure of the torn letter. The novel begins with the arrival of the dangerous but seductive letter, which signals Larsen's own arrival as an African American novelist—a woman of letters—and evokes her first polemical letter, which launched her artistic career in 1926. From the outset the narrative stages the conflict between realism—the ordinary "clearly directed letters" (*P*, 181)—and the experimental "illegible" script of black modernism, provoking fear and desire. A detailed description of the letter stresses its materiality, foreignness, and illegibility: "thin Italian paper with its almost illegible scrawl" (*P*, 143). Only belatedly attributed to Clare, the anonymous letter repeats in fictional form the struggle against the aesthetics of propaganda that Larsen already waged in the pages of *Opportunity*. Reproduced in narrative structure as the ambivalent and conflicting relation between two main characters, Clare and Irene, this struggle between "clearly directed" letters and the "almost illegible scrawl" (*P*, 143) exposes the violent, racialized, and gendered exclusions on which legibility and the promise of freedom in the New World depend.

Ironically, Larsen names her most enigmatic character "Clare," as if to suggest that both the trauma of social death and the inaugural possibilities of freedom are inaccessible to the expectations of legibility. From the Latin *clarus*, "Clare" means not only "clarity" but also "brightness" (we might recall here Woolf's incandescence), a light that can be blinding. In a dialectical opposition to her name, Clare's bodily expression at moments of narrative crises is "so dark and deep and unfathomable that she had for a short moment the sensation of gazing into the eyes of some creature utterly strange and apart" (*P*, 172). This juxtaposition of Clare's name with her "illegible scrawl" and her "unfathomable," dangerous bodily expression stages the tragic conflict between the aesthetic propaganda of the beautiful world and that which cannot appear in such a world: the unpredictability of female desires, the injured bodies reduced to bare life, and the suffocating horror of racist violence. In a further twist, Irene, the figure of the reader in the text, shares the expectation of legibility that the letter refuses to fulfill. Irene claims to know contents and the identity of the writer without opening the envelope: "Not that she hadn't immediately known who its sender was" (*P*, 143). In her "knowing" without reading, Irene suppresses any contradiction, or any "break," as Fred Motten suggests, between the traumatic "scream" of the commodified flesh and the promise of freedom—any contradiction between expression and a dying tongue.[26] However, Irene's insistence on the immediacy of meaning is undermined by the belated and only partial disclosure of the dangerous contents of Clare's last letter—of its numerous pages there are just a few fragments, which Irene tries to "puzzle out" (*P*,145). What delays even this partial reading is Irene's involuntary recollection of Clare's painful past: her poverty-stricken childhood, her rebellious defiance, and the death of her father. These initial narrative acts—the arrival of the dangerous letter, the recollection of death, and Clare's disappearance—set the narrative in motion and call for a connection between an expressive voice and a dying tongue.

Although Irene's claim to immediacy of knowledge is denied by a rather classical dialectical form of the negation of the negation—"not that she hadn't immediately known who its sender was" (*P*, 143)—the aesthetic mediation in *Passing* does not work according to a dialectical model, but rather assumes an aesthetic movement of trespassing. In its subversive aesthetic function, trespassing cannot be limited to the "passing plot," which, as many commentators note, simultaneously undermines and preserves class, heterosexuality, and white supremacy. Trespassing also differs from the political contestation of racist and gender domination, although such a struggle is the important first step "on the edge of danger" (*P*, 143). Moving further on the edge of intelligibility, trespassing crosses the boundaries of the inhabitable world to contest the violent founding exclusions of the racist, patriarchal polis. Through transgression and transformation, the traversal of the limits of signification aims to reestablish the severed link between expressive voice and a dying tongue. In so doing, Larsen's experimental aesthetics not only bears witness to black suffering but also reclaims the foreclosed possibilities of inauguration: the "revolutionary" possibilities of renaming, desire, and community.

By opposing such a dangerous aesthetic and political movement of trespassing, Irene repeatedly suppresses any contradiction that calls into question her insistence on imaginary knowledge and security, which are based on the denial of the danger of racism, the material opacity of writing, and nonnormative desires. Irene's violent destruction is directed at any text that presents a threat to her "safe" middle-class world of respectability. One of the most haunting scenes of obliteration—which, according to David Marriott, is a figure of failed mourning[27]—occurs on the train when Irene, having witnessed the humiliation to which Clare and her friends are subjected by her racist husband, tears to pieces Clare's letter, which expresses love and asks Irene for forgiveness. Instead of forgiveness, Irene "tore the offending letter into tiny ragged squares that fluttered down and made a small heap in her black *crêpe de Chine* lap. The destruction completed . . . she dropped them over the railing and watched them scatter, on tracks, on cinders, on forlorn grass, in rills of dirty water" (*P*, 178). What is striking in this passage is the emphasis on the fragmentation and scattering of the text beyond any possibility of its recovery. The same fate meets the second letter, the last letter, which, in violation of chronology, appears in the novel first: "Tearing the letter across, she had flung it into the scrap-basket. . . . The basket for all letters, silence for their answers" (*P*, 191–192). If Virginia Woolf's *Orlando* has been called the longest love letter in literature, Nella Larsen's *Passing* is the shortest one, shredded to pieces, and scattered over the ashes.

Beyond the psychology of the characters, the destruction of letters is Larsen's version of the death of art, bearing witness to the horrors of social death, the brutality of racism, and the commodification of female bodies. By recalling the epigram from Countee Cullen's poem, "Heritage," that opens the novel: "One three centuries removed / From the scenes his fathers loved, / Spicy grove, cinnamon tree. / What is Africa to me?" (*P*, 140), the destruction of writing on the train journey between the two centers of African American Renaissance, Chicago and New York City, is haunted by the trauma of the middle passage. This is especially the case since the work of destruction is not limited to literature but extends to the world itself. The world, receiving the fragments of the letter, becomes an ugly, abject, and scorched wasteland; even the beauty of nature is destroyed by the scars of destitution and violence. By expelling beauty into dirt and waste, the work of art, instead of opening the world, tears apart its false, beautiful facade. The incorporation of the recurrent destruction of letters and waste into the composition of *Passing* makes visible the death of art repressed by the dominant American literary and political traditions, that is, the destruction of freedom and black female creativity by white supremacy.

By making the suppressed violence visible, Larsen moves beyond the single artwork toward an interrogation of the role of this destruction in the formation of literary history: she reconfigures the significance of the tear and disaster at the heart of American letters. The tear in the text resonates with the ghostly echoes of the African origins of languages and cultures on American soil. Through acts of burial and mourning of which the characters are not capable, the return of the remnants of writing, in a negative evocation of diaspora, is an act of the sowing of seeds. Although diasporic sensibility is refused by Irene, who defensively proclaims herself as an American (*P*, 235) and vehemently opposes her husband's desire to emigrate to Brazil, the act of scattering the letter, the scattering of language and cultures, incorporates traces of diasporic memory into the composition of the text. Bearing witness to such dispersed traces, the destruction of this particular letter of African American female writing also points to an impossible future that might arise from the scene of its destruction. If Clare's last letter stands in a metonymic relation to the novel as a whole, then it implies that the death of art always already haunts the beginning of African American female writing and, conversely, that a new beginning can emerge from such destruction. Since proliferating refuse, waste, and ugliness are presented as essential elements of the work of art yet to come, they also raise a question about the status of the novel as a dispersed gathering of the material traces of racist violence, waste, and destruction: how can such a gathering be transformed into the possibility of a female renaissance?

"On The Edge of Danger": Trespassing the Curse/Benediction Divide

In order to see how potentiality—the tour de force of *Passing*—can emerge, like the Phoenix from ashes, from destruction and ruin, we need to reread the trajectory of the destroyed letter as a response to the catastrophe of slavery and the legacy of the black struggle for freedom. The main figure through which the notion of America as a "hellish place" is inscribed in the novel is Noah's mythical curse of slavery. The curse points to the transmission of racist and sexual violence and to the expulsion of cursed bodies from the realm of signification. By choosing this particular signifier of slavery, Larsen recalls not only the long barbaric history of religious/cultural legitimations of the enslavement of Africans and African Americans but further develops her idea of aesthetic "trespassing" as well. Larsen's struggle with the bodily and linguistic violence of the curse reveals the main political function of her experimental black aesthetics: such aesthetics attempts to contest and transform the linguistic and bodily force of devastation into new modes of signification. Yet the difficulty of such a transformation lies in the fact that the mythic act of cursing cuts language itself into the suffocating tongue and the "cursed" signifier of whiteness. The traversal and transformation of the cursing/cursed language is the task of the countermovement of trespassing, motivated by a desire to subvert the persisting effects of death, linguistic dispossession, and racist violence. It is one of the reasons why the narrative structure of *Passing* is organized around the recurrence of the curse and different modalities of tres-pass, from defiance to mockery, from laughter to writing, all of which transform the curse into a feminine "cursive" scrawl. Thus, from the opposition between propaganda and the experimental script of black aesthetics, we move to a far more dangerous disjunction between the circulation of the torn letter and the transmission of the curse—a chasm that the numerous acts of literary trespassing attempt to bridge and eventually transform into new possibilities of signification.

According to Houston Baker Jr., the task of transforming cursed language is shared by most black writers of the Harlem Renaissance. In his revaluation of the legacy of the Harlem Renaissance, Baker discusses the relevance of the curse in the context of the discursive strategies of black modernism, which he defines in terms of multiple tensions between the mastery of form and the deformation of mastery. In his rereading of Shakespeare's *The Tempest*, Baker views Caliban's curse as always already a metacurse, deforming the nonsense of white mastery and speaking of the dispossession of indigenous speech. African American writers, according to Baker, share the task of Caliban, since they also "must transform an obscene situation, a cursed and tripled metastatus, into a signal self/cultural expression. The birth of such a self is never simply a coming into being, but always, also, a release from a BEING POSSESSED."[28] Although Larsen also disarticulates the cursed language of white mastery, for her the paradigmatic case of the curse is not *The Tempest* of the British Renaissance, but the more primordial curse of Noah in the biblical book of Genesis—that is, the role of the curse in the Western genesis of the world. By traversing the origins of the world, Larsen does not produce a "metacurse" but develops further the transformative possibilities of aesthetic trespass.

Evoked in the novel as the origin of slavery and patriarchal domination, the curse of Noah, also called the curse of Ham, refers to the long history of racist misappropriations of the biblical text. The paternal curse makes its first appearance in the first chapter of the novel immediately after the arrival of Clare's letter and is pronounced by Clare's own drunken father. In the second chapter, however, the curse assumes a religious and mythical status by becoming explicitly associated with the biblical story of Noah cursing the future generations of his youngest son, Ham, into the eternal damnation of slavery (Genesis 9). The racist appropriation of Noah's curse occurs when Clare, after the death of her father, is removed from the black community and sent to live with her white aunts. To justify the racist abuse of their niece and the domestic exploitation of her labor, the aunts evoke Noah's curse: "The good God . . . intended the sons and daughters of Ham to sweat because he had poked fun at old man Noah once when he had taken a drop too much. I remember the aunts telling me that old drunkard had cursed Ham and his sons for all time" (*P*, 159). What Clare's white relatives are referring to is the biblical text of Genesis 9: "When the Noah awoke from his stupor he learned what his youngest son had done to him, and said: 'Accursed be Canaan, / he shall be / his brothers' meanest slave.' / He added: 'Blessed be Yahweh, God of Shem, / let Canaan be his slave!'" (Genesis 9:24–27).

In her ironic retelling of the racist reappropriation of biblical text, Clare mocks Noah as the drunken "old man" who violates the divine promise of peace and life and introduces instead the curse of eternal slavery into the world. In so doing, she "pokes fun" at the mythical curse of the white father while, at the same time, bearing the brunt of the curse. The biblical curse is also internalized by Irene, who, at the moment of the psychological crisis in the "Finale" part of *Passing*, acknowledges for the first time the brutality of racism: "It was a brutality, and undeserved. Surely, no other people so cursed as Ham's dark children" (*P*, 225).

Like the torn letter, the figure of Ham's cursed "dark children" frames the narrative structure of *Passing*. By tearing the narrative screen of legibility at the beginning and end of the text, the curse refers to the long history of racist misappropriations of the biblical text of Genesis 9 to justify slavery in America. The relation between Noah's curse and the justification of slavery is well known to both biblical scholars and historians of slavery; it is surprising, therefore, that Noah's curse has not played a more significant role in the numerous interpretations of Larsen's text. As David Davis argues in *Inhuman Bondage*, the story of Noah's curse in Genesis 9 is "absolutely central in the history of antiblack racism. No other passage in the Bible has had such a disastrous influence through human history as *Genesis* 9:18–27."[29] Similarly, David Goldenberg, a biblical scholar, writes that the story of Genesis "has been the single greatest justification for black slavery for more than a thousand years."[30] Focusing primarily on the American legacy of Noah's curse, Stephen Haynes demonstrates that "the scriptural defense of slavery had evolved" by 1830 "into the 'most elaborate and systematic statement' of proslavery theory."[31]

The racist interpretations of Genesis 9 stressed the dual—political and bodily—effects of the linguistic curse, which "generated both slavery and blackness,"[32] despite the absence of any references to skin color in the Bible. Confronting this tradition, Larsen examines both the performative and the "epidermal" force of the curse. The curse fuses into the same utterance the linguistic violence, bodily injury, and religious/juridical justification of that violence. Signifying, according to the OED, *male-diction*, excommunication, or symbolic death, the performative violence of the term *curse* is the opposite of "blessing," or *bene-diction*, and, as we have seen, of the promise of the New World. As the opposite of bene-diction, the curse can be read as the exemplary and originary performative act of male-diction. Prior to any signification, the curse is an act of violence expelling bodies from the political realm and reducing them to bare life. Such an expulsion instantiates the borders of communal life and social death, speech (bene-diction) and dying tongue (male-diction), being-in-common and the destruction of community. Because the curse inscribes the limits of politics and speech on bodies, Larsen's black female writing not only trespasses the color and gender line but also redraws the borders of the political beyond the male-/bene-diction divide. Such an art gathers material remainders that have been violently expelled from the social constitution of meaning and reduced to nonsignifying waste—the torn letters, the dying tongue, the scorched landscape, the broken cup from the Underground Railroad (*P*, 221–222)—and treats them as sources of resistance, remembrance, and nonconceptual expressivity.

Racist appropriations of Noah's curse recall Patterson's interpretation of enslavement as excommunication and Agamben's interpretation of banishment as the original political act, both of which establish the caesura between inclusion and exclusion in the political community, discussed at greater length in chapter 4. American readings of Noah's curse also underscore the substitution of slavery for "immediate death" and interpret skin color as the bodily effect of this substitution—as the mark of degradation and punishment. As Stephen Haynes argues, in the

American context the curse of slavery—"the antithesis of honor"—was a "substitute for death."[33] Consequently, Noah's curse signifies in American cultural imaginary "the absolute horror" of what Orlando Patterson calls social death, Agamben terms "bare life," and Hortense Spillers discusses as the hieroglyphics of wounded flesh exposed to unlimited violence.

Since Noah's curse performs and transmits "social death" through generations, it also destroys what Arendt calls the principle of natality, understood in the broadest terms as the principle of a new beginning in political life. As the destruction of genealogy and history, as an exclusion from the past as well as from the future, the loss of natality marks the cursed person not only as socially dead but also, to recall Patterson's analysis of natal alienation, as an unborn being (SSD, 38). Consequently, the malediction of the curse annuls the claims of birth, the symbolic meaning of the name, and the future for the children of Ham. This cruel inversion of natality to social death in Larsen's novels turns the scene of birth, the moment of a new beginning, into a moment of death for mother and child. In Quicksand Helga "saw, suddenly, the giving birth to little, helpless, unprotesting Negro children as a sin, an unforgivable outrage. More black folk to suffer indignities. More dark bodies for mobs to lynch" (Q, 75). This indictment of birth as "an unforgivable outrage," which resonates with Clare's own sense of the cruelty of motherhood, stands in sharp contrast to the affirmative signification of Winold Reiss's painting of The Brown Madonna, which was used as a frontispiece for the first edition of Alain Locke's The New Negro anthology in 1925. As Baker suggests, the choice of this particular painting of "the energized portrait of a Madonna who gives life to succeeding generations" emphasizes the relationship between the family and the foundation of a new nation of African Americans.[34] By contrast, Larsen's representation of the "outrage" and trauma of black motherhood not only points to the fragility of such national foundations but also exposes the disavowed, destructive legacy of natal alienation.

The use of Noah's curse as a religious justification for and legitimation of the slave law points to what Agamben calls an "archaic link" between law, religion, and magic. According to Agamben, law itself grounds its efficacy not in rationality but in a "prejuridical sphere in which magic, religion, and law are absolutely indiscernible from one another" (TR, 114). For Agamben, the paradigmatic expression of this archaic link is the act of oath. As exemplary benediction, oath creates contractual bonds and obligations. Yet, if the exemplary benediction belongs to the most archaic areas of prelaw, then its opposite is curse, which annihilates all communal links. In contrast to oath, the curse of Ham performs a radical act of expulsion that instantiates the borders of communal life, speech, and being-in-common. Through expulsion from the realm of symbolization, from the polis as well as from kinship, this "archaic" act of malediction institutes the border between collective life and speech, on the one hand, and utter illegitimacy, death, and suffocating tongue, on the other hand.

The liminality of Noah's curse resonates with Orlando Patterson's discussion of the slave's marginal position. However, in contrast to the biblical expulsion, Patterson points to another function of liminality, namely, to the transgressive possibility of trespassing the deadly border between human order and inhuman chaos. Because the enslaved being "was marginal, neither human nor inhuman . . . neither dead nor alive," she could traverse "the deadly margin that separated the social order above from the terror and between chaos of the underground" (SSD, 48). It was one of the contradictions of slavery that the most powerless position enabled the most dangerous mediation between the human and the divine, cosmos and chaos. Since such crossing of limits cannot be controlled, the act of passing turns in Larsen's novel into a transgressive trespassing. The possibility of trespass is also inscribed in the biblical story, but it is limited to the opaque sexual transgression of the son, who, by witnessing his drunken father's exposed genitals, puts paternal mastery in question. The son's transgression, therefore, is what precedes the male-/benediction divide, whereas the reactive reinstatement of paternal, sovereign authority is based on that divide.

Associating these dangerous possibilities of trespassing with the daughter's rather than the son's act, Larsen transforms the force of exclusion enacted through Noah's curse into an inaugural possibility of new signification, community, and desire. Understood as a traversal or a transgression of the borders of intelligibility separating the habitable world from its excluded outside, the act of trespassing does not lead to a reconciliation but perverts and corrupts the existing boundaries and, in so doing, destabilizes their structure, exposing their arbitrary violence as well as their impermanence. This dangerous crossing of the border between the living and the dead is consistently figured as "walking on one's grave" or becoming "the second grave digger" (P, 219). However, the corroding effects of transgression point not only to danger but also to the possibility of redrawing the crumbling boundaries of the common world from the position of those who have been excluded or marginalized. By inscribing gender as well as the "race problem" within the biblical curse, Larsen assigns this dangerous task to the impossible, unlivable position of the "daughter of Ham," who contests the vitiated structure of racialized paternity in its mythical (the real in Lacan's terminology), symbolic, and imaginary functions.[35] As Clare confesses to Irene in their first encounter, she "was determined get away, to be a person and not a charity or a problem, or even a daughter of the indiscreet Ham" (P, 159). The determination not to be "a problem" evokes Du Bois's problem of the color line, symbolized by double consciousness,[36] and Alain Locke's proclamation in *The New Negro* that one of the tasks of the Harlem Renaissance is to transform the old "Negro problem" created by racist white culture into the "artistic self-expression of the Negro today."[37] Yet, for Larsen, what stands between "being a problem" and "being a person" is a triple disaster: the mythic curse, bodily injury, and damaged language. The dangerous task of black female aesthetics is to transform all three of these traumatic impasses into possibilities of a new "genesis."

The mutually exclusive relation between being "a person" and a "daughter of Ham" situates the ambiguous struggle with racialized fatherhood at the center of the narrative structure of the novel. Already, in the opening chapter, Clare's mulatto father is presented as a defective, but still violent, replica of the drunken biblical father: "Her drunken father, a tall, powerfully built man, raged threateningly up and down the shabby room, *bellowing curses and making spasmodic lunges at her* which were not the less frightening because they were, for the most part, ineffectual" (P, 143–144, emphasis added). The implicit reenactment of Noah's curse splits Clare's father into the untenable and unlivable contradiction between a pathetic replica of the white mythical father and the humiliated black son who, despite his university education, works as a poverty-stricken janitor, deprived of symbolic authority and mocked even by black children. Both of these positions—the humiliated imaginary father and the faulty semblance of the mythical father—fall short of the symbolic function of (white) fatherhood, which usurps signification and writing.

The association of Clare's father with a defective, but nonetheless threatening, semblance of the cursing Noah shows how the violence of the curse situates the biracial child always already on the "edge" of danger, on the "farthermost" border of home, kinship, subjectivity, and the world. Even as a child, Clare refuses "allegiance" to the mythical father, staring down at the mythical facet of fatherhood "with a sort of disdain" and greeting the news of its death with "an outpouring of pent-up fury" (*P*, 144). In this first childhood act of open defiance, Clare already fights for artistic expression, symbolized by the transgressive act of making her own dress, despite the danger "to herself and her work" (*P*, 144), and struggles, later, for freedom, writing, and desire in the public and private spheres. If Clare contests the mythical violence of fatherhood, she simultaneously defends her own biracial father, who is humiliated by the same curse: "she would fight with a ferocity and impetuousness that disregarded or forgot any danger; superior strength, numbers. . . . How savagely she had clawed those boys the day they had hooted her parent and sung a derisive rhyme, of their own composing, which pointed out certain eccentricities in his careening gait!" (*P*, 145). Clare's revolt against the paternal curse and paternal ridicule are the first acts of the daughter's struggle, not yet supported by linguistic transformation.

When the narrative of Clare's "passing" moves away from the black community, the struggle against Noah's curse becomes more explicit. In a distant echo of the plantation house, Clare's white female relatives pronounce the biblical curse of Noah to justify their exploitation of Clare's domestic labor. In a twist of the passing plot, they force Clare to pass for "white" in public, forbidding her to visit the black community or to speak about "Negroes to the neighbors" (*P*, 159). Mythical white fatherhood is thus intertwined with a perversion of kinship and a further bracketing of symbolic possibilities. In a vicious circle of the passing plot, Clare, passing for white, ends up marrying another version of the cursing Noah. Associated with the violence of antiblack racism and patriarchy, the act of *bellowing* curses, first performed by Clare's own father, is inscribed in Clare's married name, *Bellew*. This lack of distinction between the violence of the curse and the symbolic value of the (im)proper name splits Clare's linguistic and bodily being. Furthermore, the dubious escape from economic exploitation and the loss of family occur at the exorbitant price of living with racist humiliation in married life. By marrying a racist international banking agent, a specialist in symbolic and financial capital, Clare, instead of becoming a person, becomes the incestuous daughter/wife/commodity of obscene Noah.

As these impasses suggest, contestation of the destructive legacy of social death cannot be limited to a struggle with mythical, symbolic, and imaginary fatherhood within the convention of the "passing plot." That is why the struggle in Larsen's work against deadly effects of the paternal curse is intertwined with the transformation of language itself:

in opposition to the paternal curse, the cursive letter of black aesthetics traverses linguistic liminality, suspending the borders of the racist patriarchal order from without and from within so as to expose and oppose the racist patriarchal terror upholding the structures of exploitation. Each self-authorizing act of crossing the "edge" of danger and the edge of language suspends the boundaries of the racist patriarchal order and shows their permeability, despite the racist terror upholding their structures. Such a linguistic traversal of the limits of being, signification, and the world not only bears witness to black dispossession but also creates alternative "revolutionary" possibilities of renaming, desire, and resignification. Despite the tearing apart and scattering of Clare's letter and the mutilation of her beautiful body, the novel, through witnessing, recording, and incorporating "scraps" of language and traces of bodily injury into its own composition, opens the possibility of interpreting the scene of dispersion as the sowing of the new seeds of an alternative, utopian black community and female desires. By initiating an insurgent movement, *Passing* restores the destroyed conditions of renaissance, the possibility of rebirth. Yet, as Irene's erotic nickname, Rene (evocative of the French *re-née*), signifies, such a possibility of genesis no longer occurs under the auspices of the name of the father but emerges from erotic relations among women.[38]

Such a traversal of the borders of intelligibility separating the habitable world from its excluded outside renders the division between bene-/male-diction, and its correlatives—bare life/polis, dying tongue/expressive voice, violated flesh/commodity form—inoperative. What is then the dimension of language that is revealed through the subversion of the performative violence of benediction and malediction? What the benediction/curse doublet obscures is, according to Agamben, the primordial event of language, which exceeds not only the performative power of law but also the sovereign decision on the state of exception that suspends and confirms juridical status (*TR*, 136–137). In the context of Agamben's analysis, we could say that the binary of Noah's curse and blessing both points to and conceals a more originary dimension of linguistic performativity, namely, a primordial event of language that precedes any determined signification (*TR*, 134–135). According to Agamben, there are two opposed ways of approaching the event dimension of language: the first operates according to the oath paradigm to "ground contract and obligation" (*TR*, 135). The second moves beyond the paradigm of the oath toward "a pure and common potentiality of saying . . . open to a free and gratuitous use of time and the world" (*TR*, 136). By rendering the opposition between malediction and benediction inoperative, the movement of trespassing in Larsen's novel follows the second path in order to disclose a communal, open and free, possibility of embodied speech. What in *Passing* keeps the event of language open is the intertwining of female enigmatic writing with mocking laughter, which turns the authority of the cursing father into a joke.

Laughter, Jokes, and Common "Things"

To transform cursed language into the common event of speech, the "scrawl" of female letters repeatedly provokes insurgent laughter. Although in the biblical text the "transgression" of laughter justifies the curse of servitude and slavery, in Larsen's text this relation is reversed: laughter not only undermines mastery and the oppositions between bare life/political forms that support it, but, more importantly, annuls the performative power of malediction. Indeed, jokes, mockery, derisive laughter, and irony are frequent insurgent responses to false authority and to racist violence. The black artist, Dave Freeland, and his wife, Felice, are known for their irony, witticism, and mockery. Yet it is Clare, the figure of aesthetic and erotic beauty, enigma, and writing, who is most often associated with both seductive and mocking laughter: "Clare laughed for a long time, little musical trills following one another in sequence after sequence" (*P*, 199). That is why she admires the defiant writing of Dave Freeland, "the author of . . . devastating irony" (*P*, 221). Clare's laughter is mixed with "poignant rebellion" (*P*, 196), seduction, and disdain. More enigmatically and more threateningly, Clare also seems to be laughing "at some secret joke of her own" (*P*, 210), a joke that cannot yet be disclosed but awaits its public dissemination in the black community and, in so doing, calls for a utopian "Freeland."

To approach the insurgent force of Clare's laughter I would like to juxtapose the white fears of rebellious black laughter in racist American interpretations of Noah's curse with Freud's discussion of jokes' subversive, political, and sexual function. According to Haynes, mockery and laughter at the father were a prominent theme in American proslavery interpretations of Genesis 9: Ham's derisive laughter was often viewed as sufficient justification for the curse. What makes Ham's transgression intolerable is his contempt and mocking laughter at his father's exposed/

emasculated body. Such a transgression is also intolerable for Irene, who is horrified by the possibility that Clare's deadly disdain for her father can reenact the symbolic murder of her racist husband: "She saw again the vision of Clare Kendry staring disdainfully down at the face of her father, and thought that it would be like that that she would look at her husband if he lay dead before her" (P, 196). Haynes argues that mocking laughter occupied this prominent position in the interpretation of the biblical text in the American antebellum South because it signified white fears of black insurrection and rebellion. In fact, laughter was regarded as the first sign of resistance and revolt.[39] As such fears imply, laughter, rather than being the cause of the curse, signifies insurrection against paternal authority and white supremacy. Ham's laughter implies, therefore, that the curse of eternal slavery is not an originary sovereign ban, but rather a response to the opaque and enigmatic transgression of the son, who, by gazing at his drunken father's exposed genitals, puts paternal sovereignty and honor in question. It is thus the transgression associated with laughter and sexuality that seems to be an originary act, whereas the reinstatement of the paternal and sovereign authority through the curse is reactive and secondary. Reclaiming such transgression, Larsen explores not only the rebellious aspects of black laughter but also its power to reshape language, sensibility and community.

White fears of black insurgent laughter resonate with Freud's discussion of the subversive function of political jokes that undermine and disparage political authority, unjust institutions, and power structures. In Freud's words, the political jokes of subjugated groups represent a conscious and, more significantly, unconscious "rebellion against that authority, a liberation from its pressure."[40] Although they incite pleasure, political and hostile jokes stem from the experience of bitterness, which through such jokes, is transformed into a sense of liberation and libidinal enjoyment: "By making our enemy small, inferior, despicable or comic, we achieve in a roundabout way the enjoyment of overcoming him—to which the third person . . . bears witness by his laughter" (JTRU, 122). That is why Freud suggests that jokes are related to the struggle for freedom: "freedom produces jokes and jokes produce freedom" (JTRU, 7).

What black political jokes make possible is an attack on racist white power, an attack that might otherwise be impossible. At first glance, jokes seem harmless since they make a transfer from explicit political struggle to the libidinal enjoyment of "nonsense." Yet, thanks to their verbal wit, jokes liberate not only foreclosed and suppressed libidinal possibilities of enjoyment but also new linguistic and political means of struggle. This conversion of impossibility into new opportunities of subversion and libidinal pleasure occurs thanks to the verbal nonsense, duplicity, and ambiguity in the structure of the joke. The linguistic play with nonsense conceals another target of the joke: the nonsense and the injustice of ruthless power.[41] As Freud puts it, "thanks to their façade they [jokes] are in position to conceal not only what they have to say but also the fact that they have something—forbidden—to say" (*JTRU*, 126). Thus what is most subversive politically in the case of black laughter is an exposure of the nonsense and stupidity of the political power of whiteness. Evocative of the enigma of Clare's letter, the verbal play and duplicity in the structure of the joke allow those who are humiliated by ruthless authority to "avenge the insult" by turning "it back against the aggressor" (*JTRU*, 124). Freud illustrates the verbal ambiguity and political subversion of jokes by referring to the famous verbal play of "translator-traitor" (*JTRU*, 36). Like an illegible scrawl of black female modernism, cynical jokes, which attack the ruthless authority of the rich and powerful, are not only most treacherous politically but also most duplicitous linguistically. If the targets of the joke's attack are political authorities, then such a revolt "can only be made under *the mask of a joke* and indeed of a joke concealed by its façade" (*JTRU*, 129, emphasis added). Duplicity and the facade of verbal nonsense allow those who tell and laugh at the jokes to expose "another piece of nonsense" (*JTRU*, 66)—the nonsense of political authority. In *Passing* the joke transforms the curse itself into a piece of nonsense. Opposed to the curse, the nonsense liberated and disseminated through laughter is thus the counterfigure of linguistic and libidinal liminality, a figure that suspends the borders of the racist patriarchal order from without and from within. Thus, by rereading Freud with Larsen, we can say that subversive jokes, thanks to their exposure of the nonsense of political authority, linguistic wit, and shared laughter, open alternative possibilities of collective resistance, sensibility, and enjoyment.

In *Passing* the most cynical, treacherous, and duplicitous joke is ironically called a "priceless joke" (*P*, 171). During the scene of the worst humiliation inflicted on Clare and her friends by her racist husband, such a cynical joke subverts the cruelty of the racist joke within which it is concealed. When Clare asks her husband to explain to her guests why he calls her "Nig," Bellew jokingly declares that Clare, who used to be white, is now "gettin' darker and darker" and that one day she might turn completely black (*P*,171). It is only as a joke that Jack can betray his unconscious

attraction to Clare's blackness. Bellew unwittingly speaks the unconscious truth of his and Clare's own desires for blackness, but only by
laughing at it as "nonsense." The novel's priceless joke takes as its target
the racist and obscene joke of Clare's husband, another figure of cursing
Noah, and treacherously subverts its cruelty by exploiting Bellew's ambivalent desire for Clare's "darkness." In this scene the joke works as both
traitor (betraying white supremacy) and translator moving between different codes of power, language, and desire. Irene assumes that the joke
is on Clare, as it reveals the concealed humiliating truth of her marriage.
But the joke is also on Irene, who, in her function as the unreliable narrator and witness, fails to comprehend that Clare's becoming darker entails
a "dangerous" desire for Irene and for the black community of Harlem—
a desire incompatible with Irene's need for safety. Clare's counter-re-
sponse to her husband's roaring laughter with "ringing the bell-like
laugh" of her own, followed by Irene's uncontrolled explosion of "gales of
laughter," make Bellew's aggression and ignorance the butt of his own
joke. As Ralph Ellison suggests in his "Change the Joke and Slip the Yoke,"
the joke stages here the complex, unconscious confrontation between
black and white Americans and changes the terms of that confrontation:
"It is across [the] joke that Negro and white Americans regard one another."[42] With each turn, "the priceless joke" starts to acquire a different,
more cynical, more hostile, and more erotic significance (*P*, 171)—and the
full menace of the joke is delayed until the end of the novel when the
"dark" Clare confesses that she could kill her husband should he block
her desire for Irene and accepts her own death as the price of that desire.
Thus, masked within the envelope of a racist joke, the novel's "priceless
joke" "translates" the biblical curse into a piece of white patriarchal nonsense and subverts its cruelty through laughter. By turning Noah's racist
curse against itself, the "priceless" joke liberates new possibilities of insurgent signification and libidinal jouissance.

Like the enigma of Clare's writing and bodily expression, the nonsense liberated through the plural modalities of laughter circulating in
Passing—irony, mockery, jokes, witticisms, play—not only annuls the
performative violence of the racist curse but also enacts alternative social
relations within the black community. The subversion of the maledic-
tion/benediction divide and its correlatives—exclusion/inclusion, bare
life/citizenship, social death/political life—initiates a new, insurgent
movement toward a utopian black community, feminine desire, and a

free, common event of language. In wanting to be with Irene and to live in Harlem, Clare, like Dave Freeland, wants to participate in the "experimental" act of founding a utopian black "Freeland" in order to inaugurate new possibilities of political, artistic, and erotic freedom.

As the libidinal aspect of the joke suggests, such alternative modes of being in common emerge not only from the shared struggle for freedom but also from the sensual pleasure of sharing common wit and talk. As Freud argues, we cannot laugh at the joke alone—the circulation of the joke requires the explicit or implicit witness of a third party. Thanks to their linguistic ingenuity, jokes lift internal or external inhibitions, and, vice versa, by lifting inhibitions, they liberate the collective, sensual character of linguistic play from the constraints of rational communication. By developing Freud's insights, we can say, therefore, that new modalities of community emerge not only from the triangular structure of the joke but also from its liberation of quasi-political, sexual, and aesthetic freedom. In Larsen's novel the collective performance of the utopian community of freedom through participation in laughter, pleasure, and linguistic play takes place in the "Finale" part of the novel, during the all-black party. This extremely fleeting occurrence of the common event of language precedes and disarticulates the binary oppositions of curse and oath. Inserted "in passing," such an event is bracketed by the presence of disaster: the bitter discussion of lynching at the beginning of the chapter and Clare's tragic death at the end. Yet, between the recurrence of murderous violence, Larsen includes a brief moment of aesthetic and libidinal pleasure in shared laughter, talk, and sensuous linguistic play. The participants gathered at the party experiment with different ways of being in common by throwing *"nonsensical shining things* into the pool of talk, which the others, even Clare, picked up and flung back with fresh adornment" (P, 237, emphasis added). What is most striking in this collective event, implied by the figure of the "pool of talk," is not only the subversion of mastery and the "dissolution" of oppositions between curse and blessing but a liberation of sexual pleasure in the materiality of language and collective nonsensical play. The "pool of talk" brackets the language of struggle and communication and transforms it into the festive event of sharing *"nonsensical shining things"* (P, 237). What each participant of this event adds is not a new meaning but a "fresh adornment" for the sensible—shall we say feminized?—body of language. The fresh adornment of language created in common repeats and resignifies the initial scene of the novel when, as a child, Clare is cursed by her drunken father for creating a new adornment—a red dress—for her own body.

This collective participation in the common event of language, sensibility, laughter, and improvisation performs a resignification of the most ambiguous and dangerous word in the novel—*things*. On the one hand, "things" belong to the world of commodities, which include both alluring and injured female bodies and desires, yet, on the other hand, "things" are associated with the violated black flesh, stripped of its social value and reduced to bare life. "Things" are also the material remainders of the destroyed African American female writing expelled from the American literary tradition. In all of these cases, things are synonymous with what I have called, in chapters 4 and 5, damaged materialities violently severed from collective forms of signification and subjected to violence. Already in the first paragraph of *Passing*, Clare's letter is indistinguishable from the "thin sly thing" (*P*, 143) provoking Irene's anxiety. Clare confesses in the most ambiguous manner that she wants "all the things" she "never had" (*P*, 159): things like kinship, love, and belonging that she assumes were freely available to Irene in the black community. Irene misinterprets this enigmatic desire for things as the desire for commodities and money because, for her, the accumulation of commodities provides a false protection against the dangerous "thing," the cause of nonnormative desires, which she repeatedly wants to kill ("But it [the thing] *would* die. Of that she was certain"; *P*, 188, emphasis added). Even more so, the glittering world of commodities becomes for Irene a defense against the most horrific things, the material traces of racist violence that petrify her tongue and her body.

In the last chapter of the novel, however, these damaged materialities stripped of value—brutalized bodies, torn letters, and destroyed things—are retrieved from the circuit of commodities and the cycle of violence and returned into the common "pool of talk." Steeped in language and laughter, damaged materialities receive a new form—"fresh adornment"—thanks to which they become "shining nonsensical things." What is the status of such "shining nonsensical things"? Though they circulate among the members of black community, they no longer function as commodities split into the naturalized use value and violent abstraction of exchange value masquerading as alluring immediacy. They are neither bare, paralyzing objects of dread—what Hortense Spillers calls lacerated black flesh, stripped of gender and collective identities—nor are they signifying objects, since, like jokes, they bring forth pleasure in linguistic nonsense. Rather, in the shortest imaginable parenthesis between recurring racist and gender violence, damaged materialities are transformed into collective objects of enjoyment freely drawn from the pool of talk. Although they bear traces of violence, such shining objects, like the sparkling wit of Dave Freeland or the vital glow of Clare's body, are characterized by the dynamic interconnection between form ("fresh adornment") and materiality ("things"), sensibility and expressivity, sense and nonsense. By contesting the violent abstraction and separation of form in politics and aesthetics, such a dynamic exchange between form and materiality restores the sensible and erotic dimension of collective language.

Participation in the shared event of talk and laughter requires nothing other than the most minimal utterance of a "yes" (*P*, 233). In a crucial turn of the narrative, Clare responds with such a repeated "yes" to Irene's warnings about the dangers of being "unmasked" as a black passer by her racist husband: "'Yes.' And having said it, Clare Kendry smiled quickly, a smile that came and went like a flash, leaving untouched the gravity of her face" (*P*, 233). The repeated "yes" in the novel surpasses any answer that can be given in response to Irene's questions and reenacts instead the affirmative power of the event of language. As the terminus of the traversal/transformation of the anomaly of social death and its spectral duration, the sheer semantic indeterminacy of a yes indicates a dimension of language beyond the oppositions of malediction and benediction, negation and affirmation, potentiality and actuality. As Derrida points out in a different literary context, *yes* indicates nothing in itself; it refers to nothing outside itself and yet is a preperformative condition of all performative acts.[43] As a counter to Noah's curse, Clare's yes precedes the very possibility of differentiating discursive acts into curse or blessing, inclusion or exclusion. Having no meaning in itself, yes merely modifies the movement of the trespass and the force of embodied, sensible talk. Clare's yes approaches, therefore, a modality of language that is neither referential (signification and meaning) nor performative (an act of curse or benediction), but manifests itself as the shared event that can subvert the historical and political determinations of the context in which it occurs. Nonetheless, it restores what the curse eliminates from language, namely, the address to the other. If yes is the condition of possibility of all performatives, it implies that even curse presupposes a response from the other who can counter its act of malediction with laughter and expose its violence as nonsense. Like the triangular structure of the joke, Clare's yes calls for a community.

On the edge of extreme danger, the traversal of language in *Passing* crosses—both in the sense of canceling out and trespassing—the violent oppositions between curse and blessing, social death and citizenship and transforms them into the subversive, affirmative possibilities of writing (Clare's letters, Dave Freeland's books), community (collective talk), and sensibility (laughter, play, desire). Although opposed to the more explicit political dimension of propaganda and romance, Larsen's choice of experimental literature transforms the petrification of bodies and language into a possibility of art, freedom, and nonoedipal female desires.[44] This traversal/transformation of language, from the romance of propaganda to the enigmatic script of black female modernism, from the destructive curse to jokes and laughter, from torn letters and the petrified tongue to the collective "pool of talk," constitutes the most subversive aesthetic and political dimension of *Passing*. Haunted by the spectrality of social death, signified in the novel by the figure of "walking on my grave," such a traversal leads toward the liminal experience of language that both the romance of propaganda and the violence of the curse obscure. The curse can indicate the liminality of language and being only through the ritualized exclusion that grounds the authority of law, religion, and power. Although the heterosexual romance of propaganda contests the authority of racist power, it fails to interrogate its own exclusions and presuppositions of linguistic clarity, heteronormativity, and the masculine ideal of self-creation. At the edge of danger and the edge of signification, *Passing* reaches a radically different dimension of liminality before it solidifies into racialized and gendered oppositions between inclusion and exclusion, male-diction and bene-diction. By suspending the reification of language into the paternal law and its juridical qualifications (inter-diction, male-diction, bene-diction), the threshold of signification in *Passing* is coterminus with "unfathomable" diction itself, which, as the Latin etymology of this word suggests, embraces both writing and orality, style and intonation, form and sensibility, sense and non-sense. As sensible eloquence without mastery, diction reveals the potentiality of the word as a creative event that no longer/not yet determines what is allowed to be (benediction) and what is foreclosed from being (malediction). Rather, such an event, to use Agamben's formulation again, manifests itself as a "common potentiality of saying, open to a free and gratuitous use of time and the world" (*TR*, 136). This affirmative, sensible dimension of language prior to negation and affirmation, inclusion and exclusion, benediction and malediction, opens up a collective, aesthetic, and political potentiality of freedom. Such freedom in Larsen's novels is at once frightening and exhilarating because it proclaims that "anything might happen. . . . Anything" (*P*, 236).

In the ending of Larsen's novel the affirmation of the radical possibility of feminist freedom and black community—yes, anything can happen—is negated as soon as it is proclaimed. Ironically, it is in the apartment of the Freelands, at the very moment when "Dave Freeland was at his best, brilliant. . . . and sparkling" (*P*, 237) that Clare finds her death. As the ambiguity of the novel suggests, perhaps the act of claiming freedom in all its manifestations is inseparable from the choice of death.[45] Despite Irene's wishes or actions, Clare could have chosen death for herself as the ultimate price and ultimate danger of freedom itself. The possible choice of death is implied in Clare's willingness to meet "the great conditions of conquest, sacrifice" (*P*, 236). Nonetheless, although Clare's letters are destroyed and her beautiful body broken into pieces, the affirmation of possibility and laughter remains inscribed on the pages of *Passing*. And they signify as yet unknown possibilities of writing, desire, and collective freedom that are yet to come from future generations of women writers. This is Larsen's tour de force, her transformation of impossible destruction into an aesthetic possibility, which affirms that "anything can happen," anything can come to pass.

Notes

Introduction

1. Virginia Wolf, *A Room of One's Own* (New York: Harcourt, 1981), 87. Subsequent references to this text will be cited parenthetically as *RO*.

2. Nella Larsen, *Quicksand* in *"Quicksand" and "Passing,"* ed. Deborah E. McDowell (New Brunswick: Rutgers University Press, 1986), 82. Subsequent references to this text will be cited parenthetically as *Q*.

3. See Gregg M. Horowitz, *Sustaining Loss: Art and Mournful Life* (Stanford: Stanford University Press, 2001); and David Marriott, *Haunted Life: Visual Culture and Black Modernity* (New Brunswick: Rutgers University Press, 2007).

4. See Judith Butler, *The Psychic Life of Power: Theories in Subjection* (Stanford: Stanford University Press, 1997); and Paul Gilroy, *Postcolonial Melancholia* (New York: Columbia University Press, 2006).

5. See Sigmund Freud, "Mourning and Melancholia." trans. Joan Riviere, in *Collected Papers*, vol. 4, ed. James Strachey (New York: Basic Books; 1959), 152–170; and Julia Kristeva, *Black Sun: Depression and Melancholia*, trans. Leon S. Roudiez (New York: Columbia University Press, 1989).

6. See Ian Baucom, *Specters of the Atlantic: Finance Capital, Slavery, and the Philosophy of History* (Durham: Duke University Press, 2005).

7. Nella Larsen, *Passing* in *"Quicksand" and "Passing,"* ed. Deborah E. McDowell (New Brunswick: Rutgers University Press, 1986), 176. Subsequent references to this text will be cited parenthetically as *P*.

8. bell hooks, *Art on My Mind: Visual Politics* (New York: New Press, 1995), xiv.

9. Sarah Worth, "Feminist Aesthetics" in Berys Gaunt and Dominic McIver Lopes, eds., *The Routledge Companion to Aesthetics* (London, Routledge, 2001), 437.

10. Lisa Ryan Musgrave, ed., *Feminist Aesthetics and Philosophy of Art: The Power of Critical Visions and Creative Engagement* (New York: Springer, 2011).

11. Hal Foster, "Postmodernism: A Preface" in Hal Foster, ed., *Postmodern Culture* (London: Pluto, 1985), xiii.

12. For a discussion of Bourdieu's critique of taste and the unacknowledged reliance of this critique on aesthetic categories, see Jonathan Loesberg, *A Return to Aesthetics: Autonomy, Indifference, and Postmodernism* (Stanford: Stanford University Press, 2005), 197–230. See also Raymond Williams, *Marxism and Literature* (Oxford: Oxford University Press, 1977), 154.

13. According to Winfried Fluck's astute assessment of the debates about aesthetics in cultural studies, without some reference to aesthetic specificity the significance of art is determined exclusively by external regimes of power. See "Aesthetics and Cultural Studies" in Emory Elliot, Louis Freitas Caton, and Jeffrey Rhyme, eds., *Aesthetics in a Multicultural Age* (Oxford: Oxford University Press, 2002), 79–103.

14. Drucilla Cornell begins her discussion of ethical feminism with a fable, with a feminist aesthetic response to Joyce, and concludes with a discussion of feminine writing. See Drucilla Cornell, *Beyond Accommodation: Ethical Feminism, Deconstruction, and the Law* (New York: Routledge, 1991), 1–20, 165–190; Hilde Hein, "Refining Feminist Theory: Lessons from Aesthetics" in Hilde Hein and Carolyn Korsmeyer, eds., *Aesthetics in Feminist Perspective* (Bloomington: Indiana University Press, 1993); Paul Gilroy, *The Black Atlantic: Modernity and Double Consciousness* (Cambridge: Harvard University Press, 1993), 35–40; Horowitz, *Sustaining Loss: Art and Mournful Life*; Marriott, *Haunted Life*.

"Death of art" is of course a Hegelian concept. For my detailed discussion of the political, rather than philosophical, death of art see chapter 2.

15. Lydia Goehr, *Elective Affinities: Musical Essays on the History of Aesthetic Theory* (New York: Columbia University Press, 2008), xv. See also 79–107.

16. John J. Joughin and Simon Malpas, eds., *The New Aestheticism* (Manchester: Manchester University Press, 2003), 3.

17. Thomas Docherty, *Aesthetic Democracy* (Stanford: Stanford University Press, 2006).

18. Elizabeth Grosz, *Chaos, Territory, Art: Deleuze and the Framing of the Earth* (New York: Columbia University Press, 2008), 7.

19. In addition to the particular authors I discuss in this book, I want stress the key role of Bonnie Kime Scott's two anthologies, *The Gender of Modernism: A Critical Anthology* (Bloomington: Indiana University Press, 1990) and *Gender in Modernism: New Geographies, Complex Intersections* (Champaign: University of Illinois Press, 2007). See also Scott's own *Refiguring Modernism*, vol. 1: *Women of 1928* (Bloomington: Indiana University Press, 1995) and *Refiguring Modernism*, vol. 2: *Postmodern Feminist Readings of Woolf, West, and Barnes* (Bloomington: Indiana University Press, 1995). Another monumental, now classic work from the late eighties and the nineties is the three-volume study of the position of

modern women writers by Sandra Gilbert and Susan Gubar, *No Man's Land: The Place of the Woman Writer in the Twentieth Century,* vol. 1: *The War of the Words.* (New Haven: Yale University Press, 1988); *No Man's Land: The Place of the Woman Writer in the Twentieth Century,* vol. 2: *Sexchanges.* (New Haven: Yale University Press, 1989); and *No Man's Land: The Place of the Woman Writer in the Twentieth Century,* vol. 3: *Letters from the Front* (New Haven: Yale University Press, 1994). For the important overview of the transformations in the field of modernist studies, see *The Oxford Handbook of Modernisms,* ed. Peter Brooker, Andrzej Gąsiorek, Deborah Longworth, Andrew Thacker (Oxford: Oxford University Press, 2010)

20. See Houston Baker, *Modernism and the Harlem Renaissance* (Chicago: University of Chicago Press, 1989); Mae Gwendolyn Henderson, "Speaking in Tongues" in Hein and Korsmeyer, *Aesthetics in Feminist Perspective,* 119–138; Hazel Carby, *Reconstructing Womanhood: The Emergence of the Afro-American Woman Novelist* (Oxford: Oxford University Press, 1989); Fred Moten, *In The Break: The Aesthetics of the Black Radical Tradition* (Minneapolis: University of Minnesota Press, 2003); and Marriott, *Haunted Life.* Working through Adorno's aesthetics, Bell proposes an aesthetic of blackness as an experimental shattering of nonreflective master values, including cultural classification of race, gender, sexual orientation, and nation (31). See Kevin Bell, *Ashes Taken for Fire: Aesthetic Modernism and the Critique of Identity* (Minneapolis: University of Minnesota Press, 2007).

21. Carolyn Korsmeyer, "Introduction: Philosophy, Aesthetics, and Feminist Scholarship," vii.

22. hooks, *Art on My Mind,* 9.

23. Rita Felski, *Beyond Feminist Aesthetics: Feminist Literature and Social Change* (Cambridge: Harvard University Press, 1989), 19. This view is modified but not challenged in her *The Gender of Modernity* (Cambridge: Harvard University Press, 1995) and *Doing Time: Feminist Theory and Postmodern Culture* (New York: New York University Press, 2000).

24. Felski, *Doing Time,* 175.

25. Theodor W. Adorno, *Aesthetic Theory,* trans. Robert Hullot-Kentor (Minneapolis: University of Minnesota Press, 1977), 228. Subsequent references to this work will be cited parenthetically as *AT.*

26. Theodor W. Adorno, *Notes to Literature,* vol. 1, trans. Shierry Weber Nicholson (New York: Columbia University Press, 1991), 39. Subsequent references to this text will be cited parenthetically as *NT.*

27. Jay Bernstein, *The Fate of Art: Aesthetic Alienation from Kant to Derrida and Adorno* (University Park: Pennsylvania State University Press, 1992), 188–223. For a discussion of Adorno's "paradoxical modernism," see also Lambert Zuidervaart, *Adorno's Aesthetics Theory: The Redemption of Illusion* (Cambridge: MIT Press, 1994), 150–176.

28. Bernstein offers a philosophical account of "the perpetual lateness" of modernism in *Against Voluptuous Bodies: Late Modernism and the Meaning of Painting* (Stanford: Stanford University Press, 2006), 1–3.

29. Frederic Jameson, "Presentation IV" in *Aesthetics and Politics* (London: Verso, 1980), 149.

30. See Sabine Wilke and Heidi Schlipphacke, "Construction of a Gendered Subject: A Feminist Reading of Adorno's *Aesthetic Theory*" in Tom Huhn and Lambert Zuidervaart, eds., *The Semblance of Subjectivity: Essays in Adorno's Aesthetic Theory* (Cambridge: MIT Press, 1999), 288–308. For feminist engagements with Adorno, see Maggie O'Neill, ed., *Adorno: Culture and Feminism* (London: Sage, 1999).

1. On Suffrage Militancy and Modernism

1. Elaine Showalter, *A Literature of Their Own: British Women Novelists from Brontë to Lessing* (Princeton: Princeton University Press, 1977), 236.

2. See Joan Wallach Scott, *Only Paradoxes to Offer: French Feminists and the Rights of Man* (Cambridge: Harvard University Press, 1996); and Denise Reily, *"Am I That Name?" Feminism and the Category of "Women" in History* (London: Macmillan, 1988), 80–81.

3. In addition to studies discussed later in this chapter, see also Rita Felski's analysis of feminist discourses of evolution and revolution in *The Gender of Modernity* (Cambridge: Harvard University Press, 1995), 145–173.

4. For a discussion of the conflicts and alliances between the WSPU and socialist and labor women, see Sheila Rowbotham, *Women in Movement: Feminism and Social Action* (New York: Routledge, 1992), 165–177.

5. In 1906 the conservative *Daily Mail* coined the term *suffragette* to refer to militant brand of suffrage movement.

6. Laura E. Nym Mayhall contests the exclusive association of militancy with the WSPU and points to militant tactics of other suffrage organizations. See "Defining Militancy: Radical Protest, the Constitutional Idiom, and Women's Suffrage in Britain, 1908–1909," *Journal of British Studies* 39 (2000): 340–371.

7. Sheila Rowbotham, *A Century of Women: The History of Women in Britain and the United States* (London: Viking, 1997), 11.

8. For my discussion of suffragettes' hunger strikes in the context of Agamben's *homo sacer*, see "Bare Life on Strike: Notes of the Biopolitics of Race and Gender," *South Atlantic Quarterly: The Agamben Effect* 107 (2008): 89–105.

9. For a discussion of the destruction of the selected works of art—mostly nude paintings, such as the Velázquez's *Venus* and portraits of famous men—altogether fourteen paintings—see Rowena Fowler, "Why Did Suffragettes Attack Works of Art?" *Journal of Women's History* 2 (1991): 109–125.

10. For the connections between militant suffrage and the tradition of British political radicalism, see Mayhall, "Defining Militancy."

11. The Women's Freedom League (WFL) emerged in September 1907 out of a split from the WSPU. One of the main causes of this split was a dissension over the governance—conspiracy or democracy—that militant action required. The conflict over the labor movement was another dividing issue.

12. Teresa Billington-Greig, *The Non-Violent Militant: Selected Writings of Teresa Billington-Greig*, ed. Carol McPhee and Ann Fitzgerald (London: Routledge, 1987), 148. Further references will be cited parenthetically as TBG.

13. Jane Marcus, ed., *Suffrage and the Pankhursts* (London: Routledge, 1987). Subsequent references to this text will be cited parenthetically as *SP*.

14. Julia Kristeva, "Women's Time" in *The Kristeva Reader*, ed. Toril Moi (New York: Columbia University Press, 1986), 193.

15. Hannah Arendt, *On Revolution* (London: Penguin, 1990), 28–29. Subsequent references to this text will be cited parenthetically as *OR*.

16. As Reily points out, socially engaged British women encountered significant difficulties translating their activism into political emancipation. See *"Am I That Name?"* 80–81.

17. Cheryl R. Jorgensen-Earp, ed., *Speeches and Trails of the Militant Suffragettes: The Women's Social and Political Union, 1903–1918* (London: Associated University Presses, 1999), 157.

18. Reily, *"Am I That Name?"* 94–95.

19. Anne Kenney, quoted in Mackenzie Midge, *Shoulder to Shoulder: A Documentary* (New York: Knopf, 1975), 23–24.

20. Emmeline Pankhurst, quoted ibid., 32.

21. Agamben credits Arendt with a critique of the confusion of constituting power with sovereignty in Giorgio Agamben, *Homo Sacer: Sovereign Power and Bare Life*, trans. Daniel Heller-Roazen (Stanford: Stanford University Press, 1998), 42. Subsequent references to this text will be cited as *HS*. For my critique of Agamben's inability to take gender and race into account, see "Bare Life on Strike," 89–105.

22. For a discussion of these divisions, see Rowbotham, *A Century of Women*, 7–26; and *Women in Movement*, 165–177. See also notes 4, 5, and 10.

23. Rowbotham, *A Century of Women*, 16.

24. Antoinette Burton, *Burdens of History: British Feminists, Indian Women, and the Imperial Culture, 1865–1915* (Chapel Hill: University of North Carolina Press, 1994), 13.

25. Ibid., 7.

26. Ibid., 14–17.

27. Ibid., 199. According to Burton, Gandhi visited London in 1906 and admired suffragettes' courage and willingness to serve time in prison. He also might have met some suffragettes. Ibid., 199–200.

28. Laura Mayhall, "The Rhetorics of Slavery and Citizenship: Suffragist Discourse and Canonical Texts in Britain, 1880–1914," *Gender and History* 13 (2001): 481–497.

29. Jorgensen-Earp, *Speeches and Trails*, 128.

30. Lady Constance Lytton in Midge, *Shoulder to Shoulder*, 133.

31. Jorgensen-Earp, *Speeches and Trails*, 226–227.

32. Julia Kristeva, *The Sense and Nonsense of Revolt: The Powers and Limits of Psychoanalysis*, trans. Jeanine Herman (New York: Columbia University Press, 2000), 1–19.

33. Walter Benjamin famously interprets constituting and constituted power as the law creating and the law preserving violence in his essay "Critique of Violence" in *Reflections*, ed. Peter Demetz, trans. Edmund Jephcott (New York: Schocken, 1978), 277–300.

34. For further discussion of the relation between suffrage and British political radicalism, see Mayhall, "Defining Militancy."

35. Although, as Arendt points out, the term *permanent revolution* was coined in the nineteenth century by Proudhon, women were excluded from being the agents of such revolution. See *OR*, 163.

36. See Kristeva, *The Sense and Nonsense*, 87.

37. Ibid., 106.

38. Glenda Norquay, "Introduction," in Glenda Norquay, ed., *Voices and Votes: A Literary Anthology of the Women's Suffrage Campaign* (Manchester: Manchester University Press, 1995), 2–8.

39. Wendy Mulford, "Socialist-Feminist criticism: A Case Study, Women's Suffrage and Literature, 1906–14" in Peter Widdowson, ed., *Re-Reading English* (London: Methuen, 1982), 179–192.

40. Tickner, *The Spectacle of Women*, 151–237.

41. Jane Marcus, "Introduction: Re-reading the Pankhursts and women's suffrage" in *Suffrage and the Pankhursts*, 9–17.

42. Marcus, "Introduction: Re-reading the Pankhursts," 10.

43. For an excellent discussion of Adorno's concept of autonomy, see Jay M. Bernstein, *The Fate of Art: Aesthetic Alienation from Kant to Derrida* (University Park: Pennsylvania State University Press, 1992), 188–196.

44. For my formulation of feminist democratic politics and ethics, see Ewa Płonowska Ziarek, *An Ethics of Dissensus: Postmodernity, Feminism, and the Politics of Radical Democracy* (Stanford: Stanford University Press, 2001).

45. Filippo Tommaso Marinetti, "Manifesto of Futurism" in Vassiliki Kolocotroni, Jane Goldman, Olga Taxidou, eds., *Modernism: An Anthology of Sources and Documents* (Chicago: University of Chicago Press, 1998), 251.

46. As an example of this approach, see, in particular, Gregg M. Horowitz, *Sustaining Loss: Art and Mournful Life* (Stanford: Stanford University Press, 2001).

47. Alain Locke, "The New Negro" in Alain Locke, ed., *The New Negro: Voices of the Harlem Renaissance* (New York: Touchstone, 1992), 12.

2. Melancholia, Death of Art, and Women's Writing

1. Gregg M. Horowitz, *Sustaining Loss: Art and Mournful Life* (Stanford: Stanford University Press, 2001), 5, 23.

2. Étienne Balibar, *The Philosophy of Marx*, trans. Chris Turner (London: Verso, 1995), 99. Further references to this text will be cited parenthetically as *PM*.

3. Juliana Schiesari, *The Gendering of Melancholia: Feminism, Psychoanalysis, and the Symbolics of Loss in Renaissance Literature* (Ithaca: Cornell University Press, 1992), 8–9.

4. Schiesari, *The Gendering of Melancholia*, 13.

5. Ranjana Khanna, *Dark Continents: Psychoanalysis and Colonialism* (Durham: Duke University Press, 2003), 150.

6. G. W. F. Hegel, *Aesthetics: Lectures on Fine Art*, vol. 1, trans. T. M. Knox (Oxford: Clarendon, 1975), 10. Subsequent references to this text will be cited parenthetically as *A*.

7. G. W. F. Hegel, *Introductory Lectures on Aesthetics*, trans. Bernard Bonsaquet (London: Penguin, 1993), 12. Subsequent references to this text will be cited parenthetically as *ILA*.

8. Eva Geulen, *The End of Art: Readings in a Rumor After Hegel*, trans. James McFarland (Stanford: Stanford University Press, 2006), 2.

9. Karl Marx, *The Marx-Engels Reader*, ed. Robert C. Tucker (New York: Norton, 1978), 145. Subsequent references to this text will be cited parenthetically as *MER*.

10. Theodor Adorno, "Commitment," trans. Francis McDonagh, in Ronald Taylor, ed., *Aesthetics and Politics: The Key Texts of the Classic Debate Within German Marxism* (London: Verso, 1977), 178. Subsequent references to this essay will be cited parenthetically as *C*.

11. Orlando Patterson, *Slavery and Social Death: A Comparative Study* (Cambridge: Harvard University Press, 1982), 26. Subsequent references to this text will be cited parenthetically as *SSD*.

12. W. E. B. Du Bois, "Criteria of Negro Art" in Sondra Kathryn Wilson, ed., *The Crisis Reader: Stories, Poetry, and Essays from the N.A.A.C.P.'s "Crisis Magazine"* (New York: Modern Library, 1999), 319. Subsequent references to this text will be cited parenthetically as *CNA*.

13. Judith Butler, *The Psychic Life of Power: Theories in Subjection* (Stanford: Stanford University Press, 1997), 179.

14. Julia Kristeva, *Black Sun: Depression and Melancholia*, trans. Leon S. Roudiez (New York: Columbia University Press, 1989), 234. Subsequent references to this text will be cited parenthetically as *BS*.

15. Sigmund Freud, "Mourning and Melancholia," trans. Joan Riviere in *Collected Papers*, vol 4, ed. James Strachey (New York: Basic Books, 1959), 152–170. Subsequent references to this text will be cited parenthetically as MM.

16. Sigmund Freud, *The Ego and the Id*, in *The Standard Edition of the Complete Psychological Works of Sigmund Freud*, trans. Joan Riviere (New York: Norton, 1960), 56. Subsequent references to this text will be cited parenthetically as *EI*.

17. Sigmund Freud, *Das Ich Und Das Es* (Frankfurt: Fischer Tachenbuch, 1993), 290.

18. Julia Kristeva, *Soleil noir: Dépression et mélancolie* (Paris: Gallimard, 1987), 54.

19. For transnational studies of modernism and modernity, see, for instance, Paul Gilroy, *The Black Atlantic: Modernity and Double Consciousness* (Cambridge: Harvard University Press, 1993); Laura Doyle, *Freedom's Empire: Race and the Rise of the Novel in Atlantic Modernity, 1640–1940* (Durham: Duke University Press, 2008); or Ian Baucom, *Specters of the Atlantic: Finance Capital, Slavery, and the Philosophy of History* (Durham: Duke University Press, 2005).

20. Jay Bernstein interprets melancholia as the interplay between social ideals and spleen in his "Melancholy as Form: Towards an Archaeology of Modernism" in John J. Joughin and Simon Malpas, eds., *The New Aestheticism* (Manchester: Manchester University Press, 2003), 167–189. For an analysis of mourning in relation to black humor, see Claudia Tate, *Psychoanalysis and Black Novels: Desire and the Protocols of Race* (Oxford: Oxford University Press, 1998), 158–161, 172–172.

21. Sabine Wilke and Heidi Schlipphacke, "Construction of a Gendered Subject: A Feminist Reading of Adorno's *Aesthetic Theory*" in Tom Huhn and Lambert Zuidervaart, eds., *The Semblance of Subjectivity: Essays in Adorno's Aesthetic Theory* (Cambridge: MIT Press, 1997), 288–308.

22. Virginia Wolf, *To the Lighthouse* (New York: Harcourt, 1981), 208. Subsequent references to this text will be cited parenthetically as *TTL*.

23. Fred Moten, "Black Mo'nin" in David L. Eng and David Kazanjian, eds., *Loss: The Politics of Mourning* (Berkeley: University of California Press, 2003), 59–76.

24. Alain Locke, "The New Negro" in Alain Locke, ed., *The New Negro: Voices of the Harlem Renaissance* (New York: Touchstone, 1992), 11–12.

25. Robert Hullot-Kentor, "The Philosophy of Dissonance" in Huhn and Zuidervaart, *The Semblance of Subjectivity*, 317–318.

26. Max Horkheimer and Theodor W. Adorno, *Dialectic of Enlightenment*, trans. John Cumming (New York: Continuum, 1993), 180. Adorno argues that modern reification is itself a mimesis of death. For an excellent discussion of the mimesis of death, see Jay Bernstein, "The Horror of Nonidentity: Cindy Sherman's Tragic Modernism" in Peter Osborne, ed., *From an Aesthetic Point of View: Philosophy, Art and the Senses* (London: Serpent's Tail, 2000), 126–127.

27. Bernstein, "The Horror of Nonidentity," 184.

3. Woolf's Aesthetics of Potentiality

1. Susan Gubar, "Introduction" in Virginia Woolf, *A Room of One's Own* (New York: Harcourt, 2005), xvii. Brenda R. Silver explores the function of Woolf as a cultural icon in relation to second-wave feminism in *Virginia Woolf Icon* (Chicago: University of Chicago Press, 1999), 3. For a discussion of the changing trends in feminist criticism of Woolf, see Jane Goldman, *The Cambridge Introduction to Virginia Woolf* (Cambridge: Cambridge University Press, 2006), 130–136.

2. Hermione Lee, "Virginia Woolf's Essays" in Sue Roe and Susan Sellers, eds., *The Cambridge Companion to Virginia Woolf* (Cambridge: Cambridge University Press, 2000), 97.

3. Diane Filby Gillespie, "Political Aesthetics: Virginia Woolf and Dorothy Richardson" in Jane Marcus, ed., *Virginia Woolf: A Feminist Slant* (Lincoln: University of Nebraska Press, 1983), 132.

4. Laura Marcus, "Woolf's Feminism and Feminism's Woolf" in *The Cambridge Companion to Virginia Woolf*, 230.

5. Toril Moi, *Sexual/Textual Politics: Feminist Literary Theory* (London: Methuen, 1985), 8–18. Moi foregrounds the importance of textual experimentation for a revision of sexual norms.

6. Naomi Black, *Virginia Woolf as Feminist* (Ithaca: Cornell University Press, 2004), 13. Black's discussion of Woolf as a political writer is in opposition to critics like Sue Roe, who sees feminist implications in Woolf's contestation of fictitious forms. Sue Roe, *Writing and Gender: Virginia Woolf's Writing Practice* (London: Harvester Wheatsheaf, 1990), 171.

7. Jane Goldman, *The Feminist Aesthetics of Virginia Woolf: Modernism, Post-Impressionism, and the Politics of the Visual* (Cambridge: Cambridge University Press, 1998), 1–10, 22, 207–208.

8. Virginia Woolf, "Modern Novels (Joyce)" in Bonnie Kime Scott, ed., *The Gender of Modernism: A Critical Anthology* (Bloomington: Indiana University Press, 1990), 644. Subsequent references to this text will be cited parenthetically as MN.

9. Jane Marcus, "Introduction: Re-reading the Pankhursts and Women's Suffrage" in Jane Marcus, ed., *Suffrage and the Pankhursts* (London: Routledge, 1987), 1–17.

10. At least since Kant the notion of genius has been associated with freedom of imagination and originality. For my discussion of Kant's genius in relation to gender, see "Impossible Inventions: On Genius and Sexual Difference" in *CR: The New Centennial Review* 8 (2009): 139–159.

11. Virginia Woolf, "Character in Fiction" in *The Essays of Virginia Woolf*, vol. 3: *1919–1924*, ed. Andrew McNeillie (New York: Harcourt, 1992), 422. Subsequent references to this text will be cited parenthetically as CF.

12. Marcus, "Introduction," 1–17.

13. Virginia Woolf, *Moments of Being* (New York: Harvest, 1985), 17.

14. For the classic analysis of the trope of the "madwoman in the attic" in relation to female authorship, see Sandra Gilbert and Susan Gubar, *The Madwoman in the Attic: The Woman Writer and the Nineteenth-Century Literary Imagination* (New Haven: Yale University Press, 1979).

15. As Laura Marcus notes, anger and androgyny are frequently discussed topics in *A Room of One's Own*. See her "Woolf's Feminism and Feminism's Woolf," 229–233. See also Jane Marcus, *Art and Anger: Reading Like a Woman* (Columbus: Ohio State University Press, 1988), 132.

16. For Nietzsche's critique of resentment, see Friedrich Nietzsche, *On the Genealogy of Morals*, trans. Walter Kaufmann (New York: Random House, 1969), 73–74. In her "Woolf's Feminism and Feminism's Woolf," Marcus suggests a more general Nietzschean "transvaluation of values" in *A Room of One's Own*. See page 229.

17. Friedrich Nietzsche, *Thus Spoke Zarathustra*, trans. Walter Kaufmann (London: Penguin, 1954), 139. For further discussion of this passage, see Giorgio

Agamben, *Potentialities: Collected Essays in Philosophy*, trans. Daniel Heller-Roazen (Stanford: Stanford University Press, 2000), 267. Subsequent references to this text will be cited as *PCE*.

18. Agamben, *PCE*, 267.

19. Virginia Woolf, "Professions for Women" in *The Death of Moth and Other Essays* (New York: Harcourt, 1974), 241.

20. Ibid., 241–242.

21. Julia Briggs, *Virginia Woolf: An Inner Life* (New York: Harcourt, 2005), 232–233.

22. Giorgio Agamben, *The Time That Remains: A Commentary on the Letter to the Romans*, trans. Patricia Daily (Stanford: Stanford University Press, 2005), 69. Subsequent references to this text will be cited parenthetically as *TR*.

23. As Woolf argues in "Professions for Women," "this freedom is only a beginning" (242).

24. Virginia Woolf, "Mr. Bennett and Mrs. Brown" in *The Essays of Virginia Woolf*, vol. 3: *1919–1924*, ed. Andrew McNeillie (New York: Harcourt, 1992), 384–389. Subsequent references to this work will be marked parenthetically as MBMB.

25. Arnold Bennett, "Is the Novel Decaying?" in Robin Majumdar and Allen McLaurin, eds., *Virginia Woolf: The Heritage* (New York: Routledge, 1975), 113. Bennett himself implies that there is a "feud" between himself and Woolf in his 1929 negative and condescending review of *A Room of One's Own*, entitled "Queen of the High-Brows." See page 259 of this same volume.

26. Woolf's letter to the *New Statesman*, quoted in Marcus, "Woolf's Feminism and Feminism's Woolf," 213.

27. Houston A. Baker Jr. challenges Woolf's "time line" of modernism and suggests that "a change in African-American nature occurred on or about September 18, 1895." Houston A. Baker Jr., *Modernism and the Harlem Renaissance* (Chicago: University of Chicago Press, 1987), 3–8.

28. Virginia Woolf, *Orlando: A Biography* (New York: Harcourt, 2006), 60. Subsequent references to this text will be cited parenthetically as *O*.

29. Gilles Deleuze is one of the few philosophers who has noted this ontological status of life as potentiality in Woolf's work. See his *A Thousand Plateaus* (London: Continuum, 1987), 232–309.

30. Woolf's brief engagement in suffrage activism has produced conflicting interpretations. In his *Virginia Woolf and the Real World* (Berkeley: University of California Press, 1986), 210–240, Alex Zwerdling stresses Woolf's "reluctant" participation in politics while Naomi Black in *Virginia Woolf as Feminist* (23–50) argues for its importance for the formation of Woolf's feminism. See also Barbara Green, *Spectacular Confessions: Autobiography, Performative Activism, the Sites of Suffrage, 1905–1938* (New York: St. Martin's, 1997), 143–144, 169.

31. Virginia Woolf, "Modern Fiction" in *The Gender of Modernism*, 633. Subsequent references to this text will be cited parenthetically as MF.

32. Kevin Bell, *Ashes Taken for Fire: Aesthetic Modernism and the Critique of Identity* (Minneapolis: University of Minnesota Press, 2007), 107.

33. Gayatri Chakravorty Spivak, "Unmaking and Making in *To the Light-house*" in *In Other Worlds: Essays in Cultural Politics* (New York: Routledge, 1988), 30–45; in contrast to fetishism, Spivak proposes the metaphor of the womb as a new linguistic/sexual allegory of artistic "production" (45).

34. At stake in fictional experiment is therefore a shift from what Agamben calls "decreation" to what he calls in passing *"Palingenesis"* (*PCE,* 271), which means another birth or rebirth.

35. Woolf, *Women and Fiction*, 170. Gubar, "Introduction," in *A Room of One's Own*, lv.

36. Minow-Pinkney follows the theory of Julia Kristeva's poetic language in order to address the question of jouissance of this split subject of female poetic practice. See Makiko Minow-Pinkney, *Virginia Woolf and the Problem of the Subject* (New Brunswick, NJ: Rutgers University Press, 1987), 16–23.

37. Briggs, *Virginia Woolf*, 231.

38. Sherron E. Knopp, in her "'If I Saw You Would You Kiss Me?': Sapphism and the Subversiveness of Virginia Woolf's *Orlando*," *PMLA* 103 (1988): 24–34, regards *Orlando* as "the first positive, and still unsurpassed, sapphic portrait in literature" (33). See also Jane Marcus, "Sapphistory: The Woolf and the Well" in Karla Jay and Joanne Glasgow, eds., *Lesbian Texts and Contexts: Radical Revisions* (New York: New York University Press, 1990), 164–179; and Eileen Barrett and Patricia Cramer, eds., *Virginia Woolf: Lesbian Readings* (New York: New York University Press, 1997). For more critical assessments of Woolf's "Sapphic" modernism, see Jaime Hovey, "'Kissing a Negress in the Dark': Englishness as a Masquerade in Woolf's *Orlando*," *PMLA* 112 (1997): 393–404; as well as D. A. Boxwell "'(Dis)Orienting Spectacle: The Politics of *Orlando*'s Sapphic Camp," *Twentieth Century Literature* 44 (1998): 306–322.

39. Elizabeth Meese, "When Virginia Looked at Vita, What Did She See; Or, Lesbian: Feminist: Woman—What's the Differ(e/a)nce?" *Feminist Studies* 18 (1992): 99–117, 112.

40. For Jane Marcus, who reads *The Well of Loneliness* as the subtext of *A Room of One's Own*, allusion and secrecy manifest both female conspiracy and seduction. See "Sapphistory," 164. For a critique of Woolf's relation to *The Well of Loneliness*, see Hovey, "'Kissing a Negress in the Dark.'"

Introduction: Rethinking

1. Judith Butler, *Bodies That Matter* (London: Routledge, 1993), 54.

2. Fredric Jameson, *Marxism and Form: Twentieth-Century Dialectical Theories of Literature* (Princeton: Princeton University Press, 1971), 328.

3. Ibid., 327.

4. Butler, *Bodies That Matter*, 54.

5. See, for instance, Raymond Williams, *Marxism and Literature* (Oxford: Oxford University Press, 1977), 186–187; or Derek Attridge, *The Singularity of Literature* (Oxford: Oxford University Press, 1977), 107–110.

6. For instance, Williams, in *Marxism and Literature*, argues that to understand form in material ways is to see it as active process, as "the activation" of the relations between subjects and things (187).

7. Attridge, *The Singularity of Literature*, 119.

8. Jameson, *Marxism and Form*, 4.

9. Ibid., 11.

10. Ibid., 39.

11. For the contestation of the divide in feminist political theory between the symbolic politics of recognition and the materialist politics of redistribution, see Nancy Fraser, *Justice Interruptus: Critical Reflections on the "Postsocialist Condition"* (New York: Routledge, 1997), 12.

4. Abstract Commodity Form and Bare Life

1. Agamben himself indirectly points to the link between commodity form and the destruction of bare life. However, that link is expressed in a stereotypical way through the commodified female bodies that, by bringing pleasure to male viewers, cover over the mangled corpses of the victims of violence. See Giorgio Agamben, *The Coming Community*, trans. Michael Hardt (Minneapolis: University of Minnesota Press, 1993), 46–50.

2. By focusing on the violence of abstraction, Irigaray's analysis goes beyond reification. For a discussion of reification, see, for instance, Sabine Wilke and Heidi Schlipphacke, "Construction of a Gendered Subject: A Feminist Reading of Adorno's *Aesthetic Theory*," in Tom Huhn and Lambert Zuidervaart, eds., *The Semblance of Subjectivity: Essays in Adorno's Aesthetic Theory* (Cambridge: MIT Press, 1997), 288–308.

3. For a fuller analysis of the debates on essentialism in Irigaray's writing, see my *An Ethics of Dissensus: Postmodernity, Feminism, and the Politics of Radical Democracy* (Stanford: Stanford University Press, 2001), 160–161, as well as my "The Abstract Soul of the Commodity and the Monstrous Body of the Sphinx: Commodification, Aesthetics, and the Impasses of Social Construction" in *differences* 16 (2005): 88–115. See also Naomi Schor, "This Essentialism Which is Not One" in Carolyn Burke, Naomi Schor, and Margaret Whitford, eds., *Engaging with Irigaray* (New York: Columbia University Press, 1994), 57–78; and Tina Chanter, *Ethics of Eros: Irigaray's Rewriting of the Philosophers* (New York: Routledge, 1995), 21–44.

4. Luce Irigaray, *This Sex Which Is Not One*, trans. Catherine Porter (Ithaca: Cornell University Press, 1985), 179. Subsequent references to this text will be cited parenthetically as *TS*.

5. Karl Marx, *Capital*, vol. 1, trans. Ben Fowkes (London: Penguin Classics, 1992), 126. Subsequent references to this text will be cited parenthetically as *CA*.

6. Luce Irigaray, *I Love to You: Sketch of a Possible Felicity in History*, trans. Alison Martin (New York: Routledge, 1996), 31. Subsequent references to this text will be cited parenthetically as *ILTY*.

7. As Derrida briefly points out, this abstraction and ideality of time is the condition of "any ideologization and any fetishization." See *Specters of Marx*, trans. Peggy Kamuf (New York: Routledge, 1994), 155.

8. Theodor W. Adorno, *Hegel: Three Studies*, trans. Shierry Weber Nicholsen (Cambridge: MIT Press, 1993), 23. Further references to this text will be cited parenthetically as *H*.

9. Such unacknowledged metaphysics of production is, for instance, at work in Gayle Rubin's classic essay, "The Traffic in Women." The definition of the sex/gender system as an economic system of production, evident for instance in the claim that kinship is "'production' in the most general sense of the term," never problematizes the autonomy of production as such. Gayle Rubin, "The Traffic in Women: Notes on the 'Political Economy' of Sex" in Laura Nicholson, ed., *The Second Waive: A Reader in Feminist Theory* (New York: Routledge, 1997), 38.

10. Judith Butler, *Bodies That Matter: On the Discursive Limits of "Sex"* (New York: Routledge, 1993), 1.

11. We should remark here that Irigaray fails to note the objectification of masculinity as well and, in so doing, inadvertently repeats this disavowal.

12. See Étienne Balibar, *The Philosophy of Marx*, trans. Chris Turner (London: Verso, 1995), 71–79.

13. Ibid., 72.

14. For further discussion of Irigaray's concept of sexual difference, see my *An Ethics of Dissensus*, 151–182.

15. Penelope Deutscher, *A Politics of Impossible Difference: The Later Work of Luce Irigaray* (Ithaca: Cornell University Press, 2002), 28–49 and 107–122.

16. Slavoj Žižek, *The Ticklish Subject: The Absent Centre of Political Ontology* (London: Verso, 1999), 273.

17. As Patricia Williams writes, "Blacks went from being owned by others to having everything around them owned by others. In a civilization that values private property above all else, this means a devaluation of person. . . . This limbo of disownedness keeps blacks beyond the pale of those who are entitled to receive the survival gifts of commerce, the life, liberty, and happiness whose fruits our culture locates in the marketplace. In this way blacks are analogically positioned exactly as they were during slavery or Jim Crow." Patricia Williams, *The Alchemy of Race and Rights: Diary of a Law Professor* (Cambridge: Harvard University Press, 1991), 71.

18. McDowell focuses on the impact of the ideology of primitivism and exoticism on the artistic production of the black women writers of the Harlem Renaissance. See her "Introduction" in Nella Larsen's *"Quicksand" and "Passing,"* ed. Deborah E. McDowell (New Brunswick: Rutgers University Press, 1986), ix–xxv.

19. As Gilroy argues, the enslavement represents a "deeper experience of reification than anything that can be mapped through the concept of the fetishism of commodities." Paul Gilroy, *The Black Atlantic: Modernity and Double Consciousness* (Cambridge: Harvard University Press, 1993), 124.

20. William Pietz, "The Problem of Fetish, IIIa: Bosman's Guinea and the Enlightenment Theory of Fetishism," *Res* 16 (1988): 87–88. For the cultural/economic history of fetishism, see also his "The Problem of Fetish, I," *Res* 9 (1985): 5–17 and "The Problem of Fetish, II: The Origin of Fetish," *Res* 13 (1987): 12–45.

21. G. W. F. Hegel, *The Philosophy of History*, trans. J. Sibree (New York: Dover Publications, 1956), 95.

22. Hortense J. Spillers, "Mama's Baby, Papa's Maybe: An American Grammar Book," *Diacritics* 17, no. 2 (1987): 68. Subsequent references to this essay will be marked parenthetically as MBPM.

23. I would like to thank Henry Sussman, who has pointed out to me this parallel between Spillers's discussion of black bodies and Hegel's characterization of Africa.

24. Hegel, *The Philosophy of History*, 99.

25. In *The Politics*, Aristotle makes a famous distinction between mere life and a good life in the context of the function of the *polis*: "while it comes into existence for the sake of mere life, it exists for the sake of a good life." Aristotle, *The Politics*, trans. Ernest Barker (Oxford: Oxford University Press, 1995), 1252^b27.

26. Arendt follows the Aristotelian distinction between *zoē* and *bios* in a number of her texts, most notably in *The Human Condition*, where she characterizes the political life not only with speech and action but with the condition of human plurality: "this plurality is specifically *the* condition . . . of all political life." Hannah Arendt, *The Human Condition* (Chicago: University of Chicago Press, 1958), 7.

27. As Agamben puts it in his critique of Hobbes, in the state of nature, mere life "is not simply natural reproductive life, the *zoē* of the Greeks, nor *bios*" but rather "a zone of indistinction and continuous transition between man and beast" (*HS*, 109).

28. Andrew Benjamin, "Spacing as the Shared: Heraclitus, Pindar, Agamben," in Andrew Norris, ed., *Politics, Metaphysics, and Death: Essays on Giorgio Agamben's "Homo Sacer"* (Durham: Duke University Press, 2005), 167.

29. Thomas Carl Wall, "Au Hasard," ibid., 38–39.

30. Michel Foucault, *The Order of Things: An Archaeology of the Human Sciences* (New York: Vintage, 1994), 318–321.

31. Catherine Mills is one of the very few of Agamben's interpreters to raise the question of sexuality and sexual embodiment. See her essay "Linguistic Survival and Ethicality: Biopolitics, Subjectivation, and Testimony in *Remnants of Auschwitz*" in Norris, *Politics, Metaphysics, and Death*, 215–218. For the most extensive discussion of sexuality and bare life in the context of slavery, see Alexander Weheliye, "Pornotropes," *Journal of Visual Culture* 7, no. 1 (2008): 65–81.

32. Ernesto Laclau, "Bare Life or Social Indeterminacy" in Matthew Calarco and Steven DeCaroli, eds., *Giorgio Agamben: Sovereignty and Life* (Stanford: Stanford University Press, 2007), 22. According to Laclau, the absence of the theory of resistance is intertwined with the lack of the theory of hegemony. For a differ-

ent critique of the lack of attention to resistance in the context of the body and the contingency of political struggles, see Andreas Kalyvas, "The Sovereign Weaver: Beyond the Camp" in Norris, *Politics, Metaphysics, and Death*, 112–113.

33. I am grateful to my colleague, Kalliopi Nikolopoulou, for discussing with me Aristotle's notion of slavery.

34. Aristotle, *The Politics*, 1254b2–b16.

35. See Weheliye, "Pornotropes," 65–81.

36. Saidiya V. Hartman, *Scenes of Subjection: Terror, Slavery, and Self-Making in Nineteenth-Century America* (Oxford: Oxford University Press, 1997), 51.

37. Weheliye, "Pornotropes," 66.

38. For a contestation of the divide in feminist political theory between the symbolic politics of recognition and the materialist politics of redistribution, see Nancy Fraser, *Justice Interruptus: Critical Reflections on the "Postsocialist" Condition* (New York: Routledge, 1997).

39. In his discussion of the survivors' testimonies in his *Remnants of Auschwitz: The Witness and the Archive*, trans. Daniel Heller Roazen (Brooklyn: Zone, 1995), Agamben defines such a link between the damaged life and the human as the aporetic task of witnessing to the inhuman. For my discussion of the ethical structure of the survivors' testimony in Agamben's *Remnants of Auschwitz*, see my "Evil and Testimony: Ethics 'After' Postmodernism," *Hypatia* 18 (2003): 197–204, especially pages 201–203.

5. Damaged Materialities in Political Struggles and Aesthetic Innovations

1. For the contestation of this divide, see Nancy Fraser, *Justice Interruptus: Critical Reflections on the "Postsocialist Condition"* (New York: Routledge, 1997), 12.

2. Falguni A. Sheth, *Toward the Political Philosophy of Race* (Albany: SUNY Press, 2009), 16, 38–39.

3. Jane Marcus, "Introduction" to Jane Marcus, ed., *Suffrage and the Pankhursts* (New York: Routledge, 1987), 2.

4. For a discussion of "bio-sovereignty," see Andreas Kalyvas, "The Sovereign Weaver: Beyond the Camp" in Andrew Norris, ed., *Politics, Metaphysics, and Death: Essays on Giorgio Agamben's "Homo Sacer"* (Durham: Duke University Press, 2005), 108–109.

5. Kyra Marie Landzelius, "Hunger Strikes: The Dramaturgy of Starvation Politics" in Diederik Aerts, Jan Broekaert, and Willy Weyns, eds., *Einstein Meets Magritte: An Interdisciplinary Reflection on Science, Nature, Art, Human Action, and Society*, vol. 5: *A World in Transition; Humankind, and Nature* (Dordecht: Kluwer Academic, 1999), 83.

6. For a brief discussion of the history of the hunger strike, see Gene Sharp, *The Politics of Nonviolent Action: Power and Struggle* (Boston: Porter Sargent, 1973), 363–367.

7. Maud Ellmann argues that the Irish nationalists might have been inspired by suffrage, yet in order to conceal this debt, they appealed to the medieval practice of fasting in order to compel debtors to repay a debt. A more recent and politically pertinent example would be, for instance, the 1912 hunger strike of the Irish Suffragette Hannah Seehey Skeffington. See Maud Ellmann, *The Hunger Artists: Starving, Writing, and Imprisonment* (Cambridge: Harvard University Press, 1993), 11–12.

8. Sharp, *The Politics of Nonviolent Action*, 637.

9. Midge Mackenzie, *Shoulder to Shoulder: A Documentary* (New York: Knopf, 1975), 110.

10. See Lisa Tickner, *The Spectacle of Women: Imagery of the Suffrage Campaign, 1907–1914* (Chicago: University of Chicago Press, 1988), 104.

11. Mackenzie, *Shoulder to Shoulder*, 135.

12. Cheryl R. Jorgensen-Earp, ed., *Speeches and Trails of the Militant Suffragettes: The Women's Social and Political Union, 1903–1918* (London: Associated University Presses, 1999), 105.

13. Lady Constance Lytton, "Speech Delivered at the Queen's Hall, January 31, 1910," ibid., 108–109.

14. Ibid., 107.

15. By stressing the sexual dimension of slavery, Weheliye argues that "violent political domination activates a surplus in excess of sexuality that simultaneously sustains and disfigures such brutality." Alexander Weheliye, "Pornotropes," *Journal of Visual Culture* 7, no. 1 (2008): 65–81, 67.

16. Houston A. Baker Jr., *Modernism and the Harlem Renaissance* (Chicago: University of Chicago Press, 1987), 76–81. For the discussion of resistance and embodied political practice as different modes of "redressing the pained body," see Saidiya V. Hartman, *Scenes of Subjection: Terror, Slavery, and Self-Making in Nineteenth-Century America* (Oxford: Oxford University Press, 1997), 49–78.

17. Ibid., 51.

18. Patterson develops the relation between slavery and freedom in his *Freedom in the Making of Western Culture*, vol. 1 (New York: Basic Books, 1992), in which he traces the evolution of three ideas of freedom: personal, civic, and sovereign from antiquity to the Middle Ages, followed by the second volume, entitled *Freedom in the Modern World*, vol. 2 (New York: Basic Books, 2009).

19. Robyn Wiegman, *American Anatomies: Theorizing Race and Gender* (Durham: Duke University Press, 1995), 11.

20. Fred Moten, *In the Break: The Aesthetics of the Black Radical Tradition* (Minneapolis: University of Minnesota Press, 2003), 16. Subsequent references to this text will be marked parenthetically as *ITB*.

21. Hortense Spillers, "'All the Things You Could Be by Now If Sigmund Freud's Wife Was Your Mother': Psychoanalysis and Race," in *Critical Inquiry* 22 (1996): 710–734, 725.

22. In particular, see Aristotle's theory of catharsis, or the purging of the passions, in Aristotle, *Poetics*, trans. Malcolm Heath (London: Penguin Classics, 1996), xxviii.

23. Hegel defines the sensuous aspect of art as between sensuous immediacy and "ideal thought" (*ILA*, 43).

24. Rancière defines the relation of aesthetics to the political in terms of the redistribution of sensible experience. See Jacques Rancière, *The Politics of Aesthetics*, trans. Gabriel Rockhill (London: Continuum, 2006).

25. See Luce Irigaray, *An Ethics of Sexual Difference*, trans. Carolyn Burke and Gillian C. Gill (Ithaca: Cornell University Press, 1993), 5; Julia Kristeva, *Revolution in Poetic Language*, trans. Margaret Waller (New York: Columbia University Press, 1984). For a discussion of the feminine invention of the new alphabet of the sensible, see Julia Kristeva, *Colette*, trans. Jane Marie Todd (New York: Columbia University Press, 2004), 1–16.

26. Claudia Tate, *Psychoanalysis and Black Novels: Desire and the Protocols of Race* (Oxford: Oxford University Press, 1998). For a theory of the dialogical, antagonistic, and sensible literary language, see Mae Gwendolyn Henderson, "Speaking in Tongues: Dialogics, Dialectics, and the Black Woman Writer's Literary Tradition" in Hilde Hein and Carolyn Korsmeyer, eds., *Aesthetics in Feminist Perspective* (Bloomington: Indiana University Press, 1993), 119–138.

27. For Grosz, the significance of art lies in the enhancement of the excessive forces of sexuality and sensations. Elizabeth Grosz, *Chaos, Territory, Art: Deleuze and the Framing of the Earth* (New York: Columbia University Press, 2008).

28. For an illuminating account of the gendering of aesthetic concepts, see Carolyn Korsmeyer, *Gender and Aesthetics: An Introduction* (New York: Routledge, 2004).

29. For my discussion of essentialism, see Ewa Płonowska Ziarek, "The Abstract Soul of the Commodity and the Monstrous Body of the Sphinx: Commodification, Aesthetics, and the Impasses of Social Construction" in *differences* 16 (2005): 88–115.

30. See Rita Felski, *Beyond Feminist Aesthetics: Feminist Literature and Social Change* (Cambridge: Harvard University Press, 1989), 10–19, 156, and 180. This view is modified but not fundamentally challenged in her subsequent works, *The Gender of Modernity* (Cambridge: Harvard University Press, 1995) and *Doing Time: Feminist Theory and Postmodern Culture* (New York: New York University Press, 2000).

31. See Fredric Jameson, *Marxism and Form: Twentieth-Century Dialectical Theories of Literature* (Princeton: Princeton University Press, 1971), 327.

32. See Irigaray's reading of Plato in Luce Irigaray, *Speculum of the Other Woman*, trans. Gillian C. Gill (Ithaca: Cornell University Press, 1985), especially pages 339–345, and her interpretation of Aristotle in *An Ethics of Sexual Difference*, 34–55. For Butler's interpretation of Irigaray, see Judith Butler, *Bodies That Matter: On the Discursive Limits of Sex* (New York: Routledge, 1993), 36–55.

33. Irigaray, *An Ethics of Sexual Difference*, 113.

34. Ibid., 115.

35. Paul de Man, *Aesthetic Ideology* (Minneapolis: University of Minnesota Press, 1996), 104. Subsequent references to this text will be cited parenthetically as *AI*.

36. G. W. F. Hegel, *Phenomenology of Spirit*, trans. A. V. Miller (Oxford: Oxford University Press, 1977), 421.

37. Adorno describes enigma as the constitutive feature of modernism: "Enigmaticalness peers out of every artwork with a different face but as if the answer it requires—like that of the sphinx—were always the same" (*AT*, 127).

38. Irigaray, *An Ethics of Sexual Difference*, 75.

39. For further interpretation of wonder, see my *An Ethics of Dissensus: Postmodernity, Feminism, and the Politics of Radical Democracy* (Stanford: Stanford University Press, 2001), 161–163.

40. G. W. F. Hegel, *The Philosophy of History*, trans. J. Sibree (New York: Dover, 1956), 91. It is precisely to contest this severing of Egypt from the rest of Africa that black scholars have often reappropriated Egypt as a symbol of Afrocentricity and black countermodernity. On this point, see Molefi Kete Asante, *Afrocentricity: The Theory of Social Change* (Trenton: African World Press, 1989). For a critical discussion of Afrocentricity, see Paul Gilroy, *The Black Atlantic: Modernity and Double Consciousness* (Cambridge: Harvard University Press), 188–196.

41. Hegel, *The Philosophy of History*, 94.

42. Ibid., 92.

6. The Enigma of Nella Larsen

1. For an overview of Larsen's reception, see Carla Kaplan's "Introduction: Nella Larsen's Erotics of Race" in Nella Larsen, *Passing*, ed. Carla Kaplan (New York: Norton, 2007), ix–xxix. This edition also includes a representative selection of secondary criticism on Larsen.

2. Linking negativity to otherness and textual absence, Pamela Caughie remarks that in Larsen's texts "are the many things that are *not* said, narrated, or verbalized" (780). Pamela L. Caughie, "Not Entirely Strange, . . . Not Entirely Friendly": *Passing* and Pedagogy," *College English* 54 (1992): 775–793.

3. Claudia Tate, "Nella Larsen's *Passing*: A Problem of Interpretation," *Black American Literature Forum* 14, no. 4 (1980): 142–146.

4. Similarly, Cheryl A. Wall considers the conventions of passing and the "tragic mulatto" to be a narrative "mask." Cheryl A. Wall, "Passing for What: Aspects of Identity in Nella Larsen's Novels," *Black American Literature Forum* 20 (1986): 97–111. See especially page 110.

5. Claudia Tate, *Psychoanalysis and Black Novels: Desire and the Protocols of Race* (Oxford: Oxford University Press, 1988), 5.

6. Ibid., 13. In turn, Henry Louis Gates Jr. argues that what "has been most repressed" in the tradition of Afro-American literary criticism is the "language

of the black text." Henry Louis Gates Jr., *Figures in Black: Words, Signs and the "Racial" Self* (Oxford: Oxford University Press, 1987), xix.

7. Wall, "Passing for What," 107. For instance, Davis sees Larsen's abrupt endings as more successful in her early stories than in her novels. Thadious M. Davis, *Nella Larsen, Novelist of the Harlem Renaissance: A Woman's Life Unveiled* (Baton Rouge: Louisiana State University Press, 1994), 176. For an alternative discussion of untimeliness and death, see Kate Baldwin, "Recurring Conditions of Nella Larsen's *Passing*," *Theory@Buffalo* 4 (1988): 50–90. See also Hazel Carby, *Reconstructing Womanhood: The Emergence of the Afro-American Woman Novelist* (Oxford: Oxford University Press, 1987), 166–175.

8. Davis, *Nella Larsen*, 245.

9. As Claude McKay writes to Walter White, "every work of art is in reality personal propaganda," quoted ibid., 240. For a discussion of this debate, see ibid., 240–247.

10. Alain Locke, "The Legacy of the Ancestral Arts," in Alain Locke, ed., *The New Negro: Voices of the Harlem Renaissance* (New York: Touchstone, 1992), 254–267, 267.

11. Carby, *Reconstructing Womanhood*, 168–169.

12. Tate, *Psychoanalysis and Black Novels*, 49.

13. Ibid., 49.

14. Carby, *Reconstructing Womanhood*, 173–174.

15. Kaplan, "Introduction," ix.

16. Ibid., xxi–xxv.

17. Thadious Davis, "Nella Larsen's Harlem Aesthetic," in Larsen, *Passing*, 384.

18. Walter White was an artist, civil rights leader, and a member and executive secretary of the NAACP. His novel *Flight* also explores the problematic of passing and return to the black community.

19. For an informative discussion of the historical and cultural background of Larsen's letter to *Opportunity* and Larsen's own aesthetics, see Davis, *Nella Larsen*, 200–207.

20. Nella Larsen, "Letter to Charles S. Johnson," reprinted in Larsen, *Passing*, 158–160, 159. Subsequent references to this letter will be cited parenthetically as LCJ.

21. For discussions of transatlantic modernism, see Paul Gilroy, *The Black Atlantic: Modernity and Double-Consciousness* (Cambridge: Harvard University Press, 1993); Laura Doyle, *Freedom's Empire: Race and the Rise of the Novel in Atlantic Modernity, 1640–1940* (Durham: Duke University Press, 2007); and Ian Baucom, *Specters of the Atlantic: Finance Capital, Slavery, and the Philosophy of History* (Durham: Duke University Press, 2005).

22. Davis, *Nella Larsen*, 173, 178.

23. Larsen, "The Wrong Man" in *An Intimation of Things Distant: The Collected Fiction of Nella Larsen*, ed. Charles R. Larson (New York: Anchor, 1992), 6. Subsequent references to this text will be marked parenthetically as WM.

24. Saidiya Hartman, *Scenes of Subjection: Terror, Slavery, and Self-Making in Nineteenth- Century America* (Oxford: Oxford University Press, 1997), 51. See also

Hortense J. Spillers, "Mama's Baby, Papa's Maybe: An American Grammar Book" *Diacritics* 17 (1987): 65–81; and Alexander G. Weheliye, "Pornotropes," *Journal of Visual Culture* 7 (2008): 65–81.

25. Weheliye, "Pornotropes," 66.

26. According to Moten, counterfactual sensual speech, interrupted by the scream of violated flesh, animates the radicalism of black artistic performance. See Fred Moten, *In The Break: The Aesthetics of the Black Radical Tradition* (Minneapolis: University of Minnesota Press, 2003).

27. For David Marriott, "haunted life" is a symptom of a failed mourning for the trauma of racial slavery. See his *Haunted Life: Visual Culture in Black Modernity* (New Brunswick: Rutgers University Press, 2007), xx–xxiii.

28. Houston A. Baker Jr., *Modernism and the Harlem Renaissance* (Chicago: The University of Chicago Press, 1987), 56.

29. David Brion Davis, *Inhuman Bondage: The Rise and Fall of Slavery in the New World* (Oxford: Oxford University Press, 2006), 64.

30. David M. Goldenberg, *The Curse of Ham: Race and Slavery in Early Judaism, Christianity, and Islam* (Princeton: Princeton University Press, 2003), 1.

31. Stephen R. Haynes, *Noah's Curse: The Biblical Justification of American Slavery* (Oxford: Oxford University Press, 2002), 8.

32. Goldenberg, *The Curse of Ham*, 176.

33. Haynes, *Noah's Curse*, 82.

34. Baker, *Modernism and the Harlem Renaissance*, 79.

35. For an excellent discussion of the imaginary father in *Quicksand*, see Tate, *Psychoanalysis and Black Novels*, 129–147.

36. Du Bois famously begins *The Souls of Black Folk* with the question: "How does it feel to be a problem?" W. E. B. Du Bois, *The Souls of Black Folk* (New York: Signet, 1995), 43.

37. Locke, *The New Negro*, xxv.

38. For a discussion of fetishism and queer desire in Larsen's novel, see Judith Butler, *Bodies That Matter: On the Discursive Limits of Sex* (New York: Routledge, 1993), 167–185.

39. Haynes, *Noah's Curse*, 101.

40. Sigmund Freud, *Jokes and Their Relation to the Unconscious*, in *The Standard Edition of the Psychological Works of Sigmund Freud*, trans. James Strachey (New York: Norton, 1989), 125. Subsequent references to this text will be cited parenthetically as *JTRU*.

41. In "Change the Joke and Slip the Yoke," Ralph Ellison discusses the political and racist aspects of jokes in America, especially the transformation of "grotesque" racist stereotypes into black jokes about these stereotypes, which not only contest the racist images behind the mask of the joke but also express the sheer pleasure of joking itself. Ralph Ellison, "Change the Joke and Slip the Yoke," *Shadow and Act* (New York: Quality Paperback Book Club, 1994), 45–59.

42. Ibid., 54. I am grateful to Professor Devonya N. Havis for this reference to Ellison and for her careful reading of this chapter.

43. See Jacques Derrida, *Acts of Literature*, ed. Derek Attridge (New York: Routledge, 1992), 294–308.

44. Referring to Hortense Spillers's notion of the pornotropic, Weheliye stresses the sexual dimension of slavery. The main question he raises is how the history of "violent political domination activate[s] a surplus and excess of sexuality that simultaneously sustains and disfigures such brutality" ("Pornotropes," 67). As he points out, the surplus of pleasure "moves in excess of the sovereign subject's *jouissance*; pleasure . . . and violence . . . deviate from and toward each other, setting into motion the historical happening of the slave thing" (72).

45. For an excellent discussion of "the choice of death" as an act of freedom not limited to the Hegelian master, see Gilroy, *The Black Atlantic*, 63.

Index

Feminist aesthetics: Adorno and, 12–13, 175, 180; on body and sensibility, 171, 245n27; destruction, women's literature and exclusion from politics, and, 5; diverse literary practices and, 15; feminist analyses of philosophical aesthetics and, 1–2; feminist debates about impossibility of, 10–11; form, materiality and body in, 170, 179–80, 187, 188; freedom/ domination contradiction and, 49; heteronomous autonomy of art and, 84; literary modernism and, 1; loss, invention and dilemmas of, 1–15; melancholic forms and, 63–65; modernism and, 7, 181, 184, 185; modern women writers and, 1; paucity of theories of, 8; possibilities and impossibilities of, 3; racial and gender politics of modernism, and, 15; racial and sexual differences, and, 180; of renaissance, 191; spirit in, 178; suffrage militancy and, 40, 43
Feminist aesthetics and politics, 14; form/matter divide in, 123–27, 172–73, 187–88; in modernism, 4; of Woolf, 87–88
Feminist aesthetics of potentiality, 3, 5; modernism and, 123; of Woolf, 106
Feminist analyses: of female body commodification, 135–36; of philosophical aesthetics and feminist aesthetics, 1–2; of racial and gender politics, 13
Feminist debates: about art and politics in modernism, 7–8; about feminist aesthetics impossibility, 10–11
Feminist historians, on British suffrage militancy, 21
Feminist politics: of sexual differences, and experimental aesthetics, 87; suffrage militancy in philosophy of, 20–21; see also Feminist aesthetics and politics

Feminist theory: British suffrage militancy and, 20, 23; on essentialism, 136; of heteronomous autonomy of art, 39–50; sensibility in, 11, 80; see also Feminist aesthetics; Race and gender
Fetishism: commodity, 131, 134, 136, 137, 138; terminology of, 139; time and, 131, 241n7
Forcible feedings: hunger strike and, 159–63; as rape, 161, 162
Form: aesthetic innovation, materiality and, 170–89; dialectic of content and, 124–26; feminist aesthetics and materiality, body and, 170, 179–80, 187, 188; feminist aesthetics and melancholia, 63–65; materiality, violence and, 123, 127; materiality and, 123, 124, 126, 127, 157–58, 170, 240n6; matter, body, and, 127, 157, 170; value and, 129, 130–31, 135, 137, 138; see also Abstract forms; Aesthetic forms; Commodity form; Literary forms; Political forms
Formalism, 9, 11, 43, 56; materialism and, 72, 188–89; new, 8, 125–26, 188; see also Abstract formalism; Literary forms; Political formalism
Form/matter divide: in feminist aesthetics and politics, 123–27, 172–73, 187–88; political struggles and, 182, 187–88; race and gender, and, 173, 180, 188, 189; violence and, 124
Freedom: aesthetic novelty and, 45–46; in art, 42–47, 49; art as propaganda and, 197; British suffrage militancy and, 35–37, 42, 47–48; jokes and, 220; melancholia relation to loss of, 63; right to vote as right to revolt, and, 26; see also Aesthetic freedom; Political freedom
Freedom/domination contradiction: art and politics, and, 49; feminist

GPSR Authorized Representative: Easy Access System Europe, Mustamäe tee
50, 10621 Tallinn, Estonia, gpsr.requests@easproject.com

www.ingramcontent.com/pod-product-compliance
Lightning Source LLC
Chambersburg PA
CBHW072058020426
42334CB00017B/1550